Cass

Cass

Cass Pennant

JOHN BLAKE

Published by John Blake Publishing Ltd,
3 Bramber Court, 2 Bramber Road,
London W14 9PB, England

First published in paperback 2002

ISBN 978 1 90340 290 0

British Library Cataloguing-in-Publication Data:

A catalogue record for this book is
available from the British Library.

Typeset by t2

Printed in the UK by CPI Bookmarque, Croydon, CR0 4TD

10

Papers used by John Blake Publishing Limited are natural,
recyclable products made from wood grown in sustainable
forests. The manufacturing processes conform to the envi-
ronmental regulations of the country of origin.

Acknowledgements

Writing this book has brought back a lot of memories of names and faces. If there are names I have for the minute forgotten, rest assured your memories are not forgotten.

For inspiration, encouragement and faith that I had a book in me, it is with great thanks I acknowledge my wife, Elaine, and the following professionals: Peter Faulkner, Cathy Gale, Ian 'Butch' Stuttard, Al Hunter, Liz Comstock-Smith, Dennis Lewis, Robin McGibbon, Dave Courtney, Richard Burletson, Ranald Graham, George Marshall and finally a genuine lady who knew the right path to take, best-selling author Kate Kray.

Special thanks to Sue Preston who stuck with the task of transcribing my ramblings, not forgetting the girls who voluntarily deciphered my handwritten accounts: Linzi, Liz, Lisa, Niomi plus my collection of Van Morrison tracks that allowed me to delve back into my past. The majority of photos in this book are from Cass Pennant's private album, save for the footie photos of the boys, thanks Brett, Tim & Ted.

Thanks to my publisher John Blake, Rosie Ries and their enthusiastic and sincere team. I hope John's right when he says my story reads like a movie. Personal thanks also go to co-author Mike Ridley for helping rekindle my memories and writing it like I told it, straight from the heart.

Cass Pennant

West Ham

In the days we stood on the terraces, I heard someone in the crowd turn round and ask, 'What the fuck's going on?' Someone else said, 'West Ham's Firm is in here,' all heads turned round:

John Sikora, Pamph, Morse, Rob and Peter King, John Bowers, Indian Charlie, Thompson Bros, Chris Boakes, Roger Q, Kieron Oliver, Greengrocer Paul, Steve Head, The Bagnells, Charlie, Mark Young, Freddie Davis, Tommy Mann, Ernie, Mole, Terry Fagg, Little Tony, Carlton Leach, Paul & Timmy Dorsett, Danny Cassidy, Lol Pearman, Keith Lewis, Keith Geisha, Vic Dark, Vince Riordan, Vic, Johnny King, Matthew Thomas, Tim McCarthy, Ray Goff, Rolo, Bugsy, Vic Harding, Paul Williams, Tiderman Bros, Hampton, Steve Morgan, Felix, Hodges, Binsey, Grimsby, Bromley, Irish Sean, Dickie, Billy Gall, Dean Haggerty, Timmy Reed, Len & Gary Aylen, Orient Jess, Wheeler, Paul Hammond, Big Fred, Dave, Defratis, Mickey Crighton, Mouthy Bill, Alfie Barker, Martin, Stavros, Bill Gardner, Big Ted, Bunter, Simo, Foley, Del, Lol & Scoeby, Carlos, Alex & James Anderson, Andy Swallow, Grant Fleming, Mickey Ramsgate, Brett Tidman, Shane Hagger, Johnny Turner, Dave Fraser, Dave Stimpson, Wagsy, Bimbo, Bubbles, John Butler, Mickey & Terry Liddy, Wayne Harris, Jimmy Smith, Chris & Joe Harris, Gus, Danny Harrison, Mick & Terry Downes, Wayne Sutton, Ronnie Pole, Neil, Lawrence Wilkinson, Silly

Acknowledgements

Billy, Seamus, Scully, Bruce, Mickey & Andy Bowers, David & Terry Sherrin, Steve Clark, Billy Jacobs, Spike, Joscelyn, Lewisham, Woolwich, Stamford, Frank, Bullit, Graham, Johnny Andrews, Ratford, Whitehouse, Jela, Natalie Leslie, Richard Wildman, Armeedi, Animal, Musky, Roger Francis, Crawford, Cheddar, Danny Brown, Slug, Tallman, Square, Jed, Dermont, Churchy, Stevie Hunt, Robbo, Parker, Bacon, BJ, Jono O'Brien, Taffy, Vaughny, Avis, Fellman, Tony Barker, Andy Smith, Bigsby, Newbury, Barry, Big Kenny, Big Pat, Paul Wells, Terry, Pat & Kevin Oates, Mickey, Woody, Lugford, Lol Prior, Tony Gold, Bob Street, Shakesy and Little Jeff.

These were just some of the lads who shaped my football days when we were getting bricked at Middlesboro '75; dodging petrol bombs at Newcastle '80; smashing the Red Army at Upton Park in '75; scousers in the snow-covered streets, Liverpool League Cup fifth round; on the pitch at Birmingham, FA Cup '84; The End is Nigh, Old Trafford day out FA Cup sixth round '85; Bristol City in that park '77; They're coming across the graveyard, Stoke '76; Shed End mounted horse year; Jenkins North Bank Arsenal years; Millwall every time; Castilla scum tours.

You knew, I know, they knew Sheffield was a bad injustice. United we could never be defeated so thanks to everyone that supported that campaign, in particular those I haven't mentioned. Your support will always live with me.

Cass Pennant

Bouncers

'You're not a member, you're not coming in unless you're on my door ...' — Saxon Tavern, Kisses, Breeze Inn, Squire, Dutch House, The Castle, Heaton Arms, Scottish Stores, Dr Crippen's, Red Lion, White Hart, Albany, Bruno: Big Nick, Big Steve, Keith Price, Stilks, Jaffa, Big Lenny, Tony Bowers, Bobby Ford, John & Chris Long, Floyd, Leon Shakes, Harry M, Danny Byles, Noah & Kenny Charlery, John Fortune, Owen & Owen, Jeff Mitchell, Steve, Dave, Vince, Nick, The Cornwall brothers, John Waters, Black Peter, Mac, Dee, Little Dave, Fraser, Bob & Troy, Dave O'Connell, Alwyn, Richard Kelly, Calvin, Bill 'Mr T' Kelly, Felix Ntumazah, Adam Waldron, Natalie Leslie, Shaun Fray, Chris 'Demo' Powell, Paul Green, Max Burrell, David Jones, White Mick, Des, Guy, Carlton, Butler, Craig and Little Danny.

Enough respect to the guys who worked on the doors with me, you had your work cut out.

Old Friends and Relations

The Bowers clan: Tony & Mandy, Neil, Martin, Paul, Diane, Mickey & Andrew, Jack, Wally, Charlie & Ruth; Vic & Sue King, The Sherrins: Terry & Lisa, Maureen, Debbie & David and Bombhead; Wraithy, Gary & Lorraine McKenzie, Phil the Mec, Rex & Jane, John Garatty, Frank & Laura Bruno, Al & Sue

Acknowledgements

Hunter, Roy Hilder, Lou, Bill the Bomb, John & Angie Andrews, Ron Wakefield, Fred Buckland, Frank Burke, Mick & Bob, Daddy Len, Diane & Gary Aylen, Steve & Tony Ward, Alan & Heather Jones, Ali Forbes, Terry Lawless, Ambrose Mendy, Gunter Roomes, Mark Kaylor, Jane Medhurst, Marie Basitel, Ann Betell, Julie Reading, Barbara Brennan, Pearl Agana, Karen Park, Judith, Trevor Harding, Del Clements, Rusty Broadbent, Cribby, Paul, Peter Trainer, Vas; the Famous Card School — The Grey Fox, Gravesend, Wilko, Tallman, Churchy, The Ashmans, Joe the Furrier, Fat Cat, Leslie Turner, Will, Noel, Bill the Carpet, Dave Tree, Adrian & Peter, Mouthy Bill, Larry Lamb, Mickey Franks, Matthew, Big Ted, Jumbo — Barry Cooper, Jeff, Roger, Younghead, Ishmeil, Errol, Steve Wells, Tommy White, Martin Lee and John Kinlough of Attridge & Co, Peter and Nick Gould, Johnny and Andy Morris, Bert the Tyreman, Darren and Sally Barret and Bill Malley.

My family: Doll & Cecil Chambers; Beverley, Leon, Josh & Joe Anderson; Lily; Pat & Joyce; Steven and Clare Coles; Pat, Dena, Darren, Dale, Richard Chambers, Cecil Powell, Celeste, Steve & Diana, Sharon, Linda, Colin and Robert.

Finally, I would like to thank the most special people in the world to me for giving me a value and purpose in life, Elaine, Marcus and Georgina.

My motto is: 'Never give up in life, as you never know what's around the next corner.'

Personally, I could have given up when the bullets slammed into me, or when I was arrested in Operation Own Goal or the time I was staring at a possible murder charge.

From the moment my mother placed me in a Dr Barnardo's home at just six months old, it's never been in me to give up. Along the road I've made many good friends, dear friends. There's a lot to be said for that saying, 'You can't choose your family, but you can choose your friends.' One friend I can never give up on is Big Lenny of Wanstead.

Dedicated in memory of Len Aylen.

As friends we ran with you,
As friends we drank with you,
As friends we fought right with you,
As friends we loved you,
As friends we tried to protect you,
As friends we weep in memory of you,
As friends we can never replace you.

Glossary of Slang

blagging	armed robbery
burn	cigarettes/tobacco
caff	café
Clint Eastwood	movie
civvies	civilian
compo	compensation
cons	prisoners
coronation street	northern
cozzers	police
dosh	money
dossed	slept
dough	money
gaff	building, home, place
geezer	bloke
giving large	mouthing off
grass	inform on
jip	to be fobbed off
knocked	out of pocket
knock-off	stolen goods
leak	to urinate
low life city	typical inner city town with more losers than winners
Mancs	Manchester lads
meat wagon	prison transport van
Methers alley	where down and outs, often meths drinkers, rough it

Mickey Mousers	Scousers from Liverpool
nuts	testicles
obbos	louts
Old Bill	police
pikey	gypsy, traveller
posh fart	upper class snob
row	fight
ruck	fight
screwing	eyeballing, staring
screws	prison officers
scribbler	reporter
shell suit folk	council tenants
Sid	CID
sovs	sovereigns
snouts	police informers
squirt	ammonia
steaming in	fighting
stress bucket	fast life in a city
stripe	knife slash
swartzer	black prisoner/ black person
tache	moustache
tear up	fight
Tom & Dick	sick
tools	weapons
twat	wally or pratt
Uncle Stan	Stanley knife
up west	London's West End

Introduction

If you've never heard of Cass Pennant, I ain't a gangster nor a boxer but I've been involved in more violence than most people will experience in a hundred lifetimes.

I've been shot, I've been stabbed and I've dished it out. My favourite weapons are my fists, the axe and Uncle Stan, my trusty Stanley knife. Twice I've experienced death, that moment when your spirit leaves your body. When you've stared death in the face, you fear no one on earth.

I'm a street fighter. I once ran the tastiest team of doormen in London; trouble was our trade. Before that I was one of Britain's most notorious soccer hooligans. As one of the leaders of West Ham's infamous InterCity Firm I probably brought brutality and bloodshed to the streets of your town. I paid a heavy price when an Old Bailey judge made an example of me in an attempt to rid football of the cancer that was destroying the game. If you remember ox-blooding your DMs — even painting them silver — monkey boots, desert boots, Squire shoes, Gola and Adidas trainers, then you lived through those times when football violence was a way of life.

Perhaps *you* wore the cloth, chanted the songs, steamed in, kicked off and revelled in the headlines. Maybe you are reading this book because you were sickened by those headlines in the seventies and eighties and want to know why, why, why? I can't defend the savage thuggery that went on, except to say that for thousands and thousands of young men aged 15 to 30 violence was a way of life on Saturdays. To many of us it was inexplicable. The ICF were no different to other soccer gangs all over the country in our thirst for violence. During the week most of us were law-abiding citizens. Soccer violence was a buzz to us. A buzz so great it took you through every emotion: terror, fear, dread, excitement, elation, a sense of belonging, pride and above all a feeling of sheer power. It was a buzz that gripped you just like a drug.

We were young men in peacetime with money and no responsibilities or commitments except to ourselves who found a high in violence that could not be found anywhere else in our lives. We didn't mug old ladies or innocent by-standers. The soccer gangs fought amongst themselves, deciding when and where to kick it off and how far they wanted to take it.

My days as a football thug ended as I watched the sickening scenes unfold in the Heysel Stadium in Brussels as 39 fans lost their lives. That wasn't how it was meant to be. No one was supposed to lose their lives. Football has changed so much since then and although not without some problems, as we witnessed during Euro 2000, I don't believe the bad old days will ever return.

Perhaps when you've read my story you'll understand.

Chapter One

BOOM!

'What the fuck?'

Revellers milling around in the nightclub foyer scream and start stampeding. The bullet entering my chest registers no pain. Instead, my brain is screaming 'attack!' I lunge forward towards the threat.

A hazy figure stands behind the smoke, two hands on silver metal. He fires again. A flash of flame then, BOOM! I can smell the cordite. I'm flying backwards in slow motion, just like a Clint Eastwood. I must be wounded but I'm still on my feet. Everyone around me has hit the floor. I am the bouncer, so instinct is still telling me to attack, go forward. Where's my friend Mr T? He must be the target. He's had a real problem with troublemakers tonight. Can't see him in the dark, but I sense he's there. Where's Leon? There's

1

confusion everywhere. We've got to group together and go on the attack.

You stupid prick, Cass. You're offering him a target. He's taking aim again, so why are you fronting him? You're the target — the only target — get yourself out, you big fool.

My only instinct now is survival. Going forward is suicide; that's where the assassin is.

Got to get back. The blue double doors behind me lead to the dance floor. Big man, get yourself through those doors for dear life.

A blue flash. BANG! A third shot rings out. I'm no longer on my feet. I'm six feet four, seventeen stones and I'm flying through the air. I crash through the doors, carried by the force of the blast. Bullet number three is in my back. I'm on my feet again, stumbling, staggering, trying to put some distance between me and the assassin. A sea of terrified faces rushes towards me. More screams. The faces part. I lurch forward. One more set of doors to go and I'm safe inside the club. Screaming people are running all over the dance floor. They're trying to get out of my way.

My only chance of safety is to get out through the back fire escape where my driver is waiting outside. If the gunman follows me now he can finish me off. He's probably thinking I'm dead already and if he's got a brain he'll get out before he's nicked. His sidekicks were shitting bricks when the second shot went off. Fearing for themselves, because they'd be done as accessories, they tugged at the gunman to leave: 'C'mon, you've done the black cunt. C'mon, we've gotta slip.' Coked out of his brain, the gunman ignored their pleas and fired off the third shot.

Lurching like a drunk, I climb the stairs. Everyone else is coming down, screaming. I push them out of the way. It's pitch black and I don't know if there's blood pouring out of me or not. For the first time I feel real, raw terror. I'm losing the battle to live. I know my way blindfold. Clawing at the banister, I pull myself hand over hand up the thirteen steps. My strength ebbing with every second that passes, sheer willpower takes over. I reach the gallery that leads to the celebrity bar where the wannabe gangsters hang out. Turn left. I clatter down the last flight of stairs to the emergency exit. Safety is just yards away now.

I find the fire escape doors I've been blindly searching for. I'm alone. I'm dying for sure but, spurred on by the thought of safety on the other side of these doors, from somewhere I summon up the last ounce of strength to lift the bars. Jesus Christ, I can't open them. Am I so weak? Oh, no ... chains. The emergency doors have been chained shut.

You fucking fool, Cass. Fire escapes don't exist in

this building. For weeks I'd been arguing with the club promoters not to chain the exits shut. I wanted to put a doorman on each entrance but the club was losing money and they couldn't afford it. They kept the chains on to keep out gatecrashers and make more money. I'm full of holes but my mind travels back to a Monday meeting in the office here in the club arguing about these fire doors. The bosses are shouting at me, telling me to shut up. You fool, Cass, you're the head of security — you, more than anyone else, know these doors are never going to open. I curse myself for not thinking clearly enough.

As I rattle the chains in despair, anger wells up inside. I'm close to tears. You fool, Cass, you fool. I've made it this far and used up all my energy. It had taken an eternity to get this far. It was like being at the bottom of a well. I'm a dead man now. My only escape is back through the minefield, back into the club. I can feel my life draining away. I've got to find the strength to climb those stairs again ...

Next thing I know I'm lying on my back on the desk in the club office. There are people on top of me. It's hazy; I can't see properly. I can hear Leon speaking to me. Panic makes his voice breathless, urgent. 'Keep talking, Cass, keep talking.'

Somebody's pressing down on my chest. I want to fight them off but I feel my spirit lift out of my body.

One

I'm in no pain, floating on the ceiling looking down on my body sprawled on the table, claret everywhere. There's a crowd around the table, their faces ashen. In the middle of them is Mr T, my mate Bill who really does look like that guy out of *The A Team*. He's jammed a credit card over the bullet hole nearest my heart and his powerful arms are pressing the piece of plastic to my chest to keep the blood from spewing out. Somehow, I know I'm dead but the strange feeling of peace lasts only a moment. I'm back down on the table lashing out at the crowd around me. I've remembered that the last place I saw a silver gun was in this office.

My mind's telling me everyone in this club is a wrong 'un. They're all enemy; any one of them could have been in on this conspiracy. I've got to get away from here 'cos everyone's bad. I keep thinking, the gun came from this office; who are all these people in front of me? No one's allowed in the office except for the people I'm working for and they've set me up. I'm fighting them all. I can't understand it.

T's trying to keep me down. I'm dead ... I'm dying. I shout out for my wife: 'Elaine! Tell Elaine I love her.'

There's Leon again: '... Ambulance is on the way, Cass ... Keep talking ... Stop wasting energy ... Keep talking ...'

I try to get up off the table and grab him. 'Ambulance? Ambulance? They haven't called a fucking ambulance. It won't come; get me out of here.' T's fighting to keep me on the table. Blood is still gushing out from under the makeshift plug over the hole in my chest.

My mind had flashed back a year to the first night we ever worked at this club. A running street battle erupted in the street outside and a kid was stabbed. That night the management ignored our requests to call an ambulance.

I might be dying but I'm still Cass, the leader. 'Oi, get me out of here. They haven't called no fucking ambulance. It's a scam.' I can see the promoter and co-promoter: in my tormented mind they're the enemy. I'm trying to claw at them, but they're actually trying to help save my life.

I'm in and out of consciousness. As I come round I'm on a stretcher going out through the very doorway where the gunman had stood. A feeling of utter relief washed over me. For the first time since the gun went off I feel safe. I sense Leon is next to the stretcher, speaking to me all the time: 'Keep talking, Cass, keep talking.'

My life was over. I gasp, 'Tell Elaine, tell her I love her. My kids ... tell them I love them.'

My spirit leaves my body again. I'm floating,

One

watching two ambulancemen wheel the stretcher out to the waiting vehicle. Then, what seems like only a second later, I'm back on the stretcher. I can hear the ambulance engine throbbing. We stop. They must be about to lift me into the back of the ambulance.

I hear their voices. They're talking calmly, matter of fact. To them, I'm probably just another piece of meat on a busy Friday night. I'm trapped, strapped on the stretcher and I can hear the pair of them debating. 'Lewisham's nearest.'

'No, Greenwich,' says the other.

'They're about the same,' comes the reply.

'No, Greenwich.'

They're talking about hospitals. I must still be alive.

I cut them short and gasp, 'Don't matter what hospital. Just get me out of here. Don't let me die in Low Life City.'

Chapter Two

'Carol Pennant?'

'Yes.'

'Carol Pennant?'

'Yes.'

'Carol Pennant?'

'Yes! Here!' I said loudly, but through gritted teeth trying to contain tears of temper as the frustration of being a boy called Carol gets to me again. The classroom sniggers grow louder and louder. This new teacher can't understand a boy's voice replying as he calls out from the register. He thinks the class is playing a joke. His patience frays. 'Will the real Carol stand up, please?' As I rise to my feet my emotions reach boiling point and I tip the desk up and over, sending books and ink flying everywhere. It was more than I could do to stop myself throwing it at the dopey new teacher.

'Carol Pennant is *me*, sir,' I say in a snarling whisper, fixing the whole class with a stare that warned, I just dare ya to say Carol's a girl's name. We've been down that road so many times before that the class decide they ain't going to push it. The teacher straightens the desk, picks up the mess and marks the register. After the lesson he pulls me up: 'Sorry, I thought Carol was ...' I'm thinking, go on say it, pal, Carol's a girl's name. I'm eleven years old and about to lose it big time. Realising an apology is making things worse, he says, 'Err ...' changes tack and just says, 'I understand everyone calls you Cass, pleased to meet you, Cass.'

I'm big and I'm hard but now you know my one weak heel — my name. I was born Carol Lindo Powell Pennant on March 3rd 1958. For most of my life I didn't know where I was born or who my parents were. At six months old a social worker handed me over to the Dr Barnardo's home in Barkingside, Essex. Within weeks a gentle couple had fostered me. Cecil and Doll Chambers were getting on in years and their own children had grown up. They were white, happily settled in their lives and they didn't have to take on a black boy. It was an act of pure love.

Home was a massive Victorian council house with

geese and goats running round the large garden. The house was in Slade Green, a village near Erith on the border of London and Kent. Everybody who lived there — man, woman or child — was white. There weren't even Asians there in those days.

Cecil worked as a precision instrument toolmaker at the nearby Woolwich Arsenal weapons factory. Doll didn't work and in the 17 years I lived at her home I can only remember her being away just one night. I knew almost instantly I was her favourite. She doted on me and treated me like one of her own. Her daughter Pat had married and left home but she only lived round the corner, so I looked on her like an auntie. Doll's son Richard was still there but he was a teenager by then.

My earliest memory is Doll pushing me around in my pram and seeing strangers peering in under the hood, putting out their hands to touch my black fuzzy hair. I was an oddity even then. As I grew older we'd walk down the street, me clinging to Mrs Chambers' hand, and kids would shout out 'Blackie!' 'Nigger!' 'Golliwog!' Even adults passing in cars would hurl insults. But Doll Chambers came from blitz stock. She'd survived the worst Adolf Hitler could throw at the East End, so a few names were never going to bother her. She just ignored them and held her head up high as if to say, Yeah, he's black, he's my son and I love him.

Then I started school. The other kids in the class had never seen a black boy before, let alone one who was called Carol. The name-calling and the taunts started from day one. I was four years old and had come from a home where I was protected, so this was new and terrifying. There was none of this political correctness or trying to understand different cultures in those days. Why should there be? You couldn't have all that set up for just one boy. So like all the rest I played with golliwogs and read golliwog books. At the end of the first day, I cried my eyes out to Doll. She told me, 'Sticks and stones may break my bones, but names will never hurt me.'

Next day the torment started all over again so, just like my foster mum told me, I started singing, 'Sticks and stones may break my bones ...' It stopped the insults all right — just long enough for the kids to pick up a load of stones and hurl them at me.

In those days your mum didn't take you to school — you went on your own. Without a brother or sister to protect me, I ran the gauntlet of hate every single day. I'd arrive at North End school covered in bruises and lumps from bricks and cobbles that had been thrown at me. I'd have spit all over my nice clothes. School should have been my safe haven but I was trapped with nowhere to run. Finally, after weeks of taking all this torment I snapped. I can still see this boy, his face pressed right up against mine, screaming, 'Wog!' Anger and humiliation welled up inside like a mini volcano; my right hand formed a fist and bash! I smashed him in the face. He recoiled in horror.

The teacher told us off but it didn't matter. Forget 'names won't hurt me', I had something that really worked ... my fists. Every time any child said anything I thought was an insult, or flicked something at me, bosh! I'd become a windmill of flailing fists.

The playground became my battlefield. The only way to escape my abusers was to stand up and fight. I fought tooth and nail, no matter what the size of the persecutor. It didn't take long for me to go from being the poor pathetic victim to being branded a bully. I bashed everyone in my class. Some of the girls were the worst because they thought they would never be hit — they were wrong. Once I'd hit them, tormentors never came near me again. I never hit anybody, boy or girl, who didn't start on me first.

A procession of parents would bang on Doll's door wanting to know what she was going to do about her 'black bully boy'. Doll spent most evenings at the huge Mecca bingo hall in the middle of Erith. Even there, mums would complain about me and I'd get a clip round the ear when she got home.

There'd be kids from the other street calling me

names, new kids in the road calling me names, kids ganging up and, just for a laugh, throwing stones at me. It was non-stop but she never stood up for me. She always used to turn on me. One day I rebelled against her for not taking my side and to her credit she marched up to school, knocked on a few doors and gave 'em what for. But it was too late: I'd learned to love fighting.

I didn't realise the reason Mrs Chambers didn't defend me was that she was scared stiff Dr Barnardo's would think she wasn't up to controlling me and take her little boy away. Mrs Chambers was an honest, decent woman and though I never, ever lied to her I didn't tell her what I was going through. I'd absorbed so much punishment from my tormentors I'd become inward and deep. I didn't talk to my foster parents about my feelings like someone who's been brought up by their real parents can. I'm always shocked at how my kids and my wife are so open with each other.

Social workers from Dr Barnardo's would visit me four or five times a year, including Easter, Christmas and on my birthday. Mrs Chambers used to dress me in my best clothes and I'd never get a clip round the ear that week. One day the social workers suggested getting someone for me to play with and shortly afterwards Beverley Grant became my foster sister.

Beverley is three years younger than me and her real parents lived only as far away as Peckham in south London. Because they were so close, Barnardo's encouraged her to stay in touch with them. So every Christmas, Easter and birthday she went over to see her mum, dad, brothers and sisters. Partly because she saw her folks so rarely and partly because of their guilt, she'd come back with her arms full of presents.

These presents would cause competition between her real mum and Mrs Chambers. It cut me up seeing my foster mum and dad spending money on presents like a black and white portable telly for Beverley. I knew Mrs C didn't have to prove her love to Beverley, and I also knew she couldn't afford it.

Someone may have sensed the effect in staying behind while Beverley went off to see her real folks was having on me, because next Dr Barnardo's asked if I wanted to contact my own mother. 'No thanks,' I said, hesitantly at first, then again more firmly when I realised it pleased my foster mum, who seemed to hang on every word. The truth was I was nearly three years older than my sister — well as far I was concerned she was my sister, the only one I was ever likely to have — and I could see the trauma all this was putting on poor old Mrs C. As far as I could see, I only needed the love of one mum. I couldn't betray that love, so the answer was always 'no' every time

Barnado's asked. To be honest, they were really pissing me off. Because I'd bottle up everything inside, I couldn't express my feelings to them properly. And besides, every time I did ask them a question about my mum they couldn't answer it. The fact is they knew bugger-all about my real family. The only time they did help was when I asked for a photo of her; I'd started to get a kid's curiosity about what she looked like.

Months later a photo arrived and even then they seemed to get it all wrong. Barnardo's people passed the picture over right in front of Mr and Mrs Chambers. Watching my foster mum's face, I felt guilty of betraying her so I refused to take it. They left it on the side like I was rude and ungrateful. Later that night, I grabbed the picture and rushed up to my bedroom to study the pretty face staring out at me. I slept with it by my pillow. Early in the morning I moved it to pride of place on the windowsill next to all my Airfix soldiers and climbed back into bed.

Later Mrs Chambers came in to open my curtains and saw the photo. I watched her look at it then carry on pulling back the curtains. 'Time to get up,' she said. Her eyes were red and I swear she was holding back tears. As she left the room I shouted after her, 'Don't worry, Mum, I wouldn't betray you for another mum who obviously doesn't want me.' I climbed out of bed and took the photo off the sill. I looked at it again and then threw it in the bottom of a box of old Corgi and Dinky cars I never played with. I don't remember ever seeing that photo again, and Barnardo's never again brought up the subject of contacting my real mum.

I was eight years old when Cassius Clay fought 'Enry Cooper for the second time and all of a sudden as I was walking with my mother down to the shops in Erith the insults stopped. Instead of shouting 'nigger', people going past in cars would wind their windows down and call out, 'Hey, Cassius Clay!' He'd captured the hearts of the nation and become a real hero. Because I was the best fighter at North End Primary everybody started calling me Cassius and I liked it. I decided never again to be called Carol — from now on I was Cass Pennant.

By the time I was eleven I was quite a popular kid. I was already huge and strong. I had size ten feet and could kick the old leather lace-up footballs from one end of the pitch to the other. While the other kids on the football team had hand-me-down woollen socks and boots with wooden studs I had the PE teacher's smart new kit to wear.

Slade Green is next to a huge marshalling yard and the town is split down the middle by the railway line. Big school, Slade Green Secondary Modern, was across the railway. Working class kids from the council estates all went there. From Slade Green Secondary the world wasn't exactly your oyster. If you were tall you could be a fireman or a copper; otherwise you'd get work on the railway or a job in a factory. There were only two options for girls — to nurse or be a secretary.

On my first day there I was still the only black kid and all the fancy fighters in the school were queuing up to take me on. I'd fight kids who were years older than me. My past had made me tough inside. They rained punches down on me but I'd never back off, never flinch. Big opponents would punch themselves out and I'd still be standing — I earned their respect and soon I was being invited into their gangs.

The late sixties saw the skinhead explosion — shaved head, Ben Sherman shirts, braces and Dr Marten bovver boots. SGB, Slade Green Boot Boys, was born and they needed everyone they could get to defend the town's reputation. So, for once I wasn't the target of the bigger lads. But being the only black face around I was a target for our rivals, and I loved it.

The fairground came to town three times a year and it was a big event. School would be buzzing with what had happened at the fair the previous night. It would be gossip about how the fairground workers with their swarthy looks, checked short-sleeve shirts, tight jeans and well-worn Doc Marten Air Soles, were pulling our birds. These fairground kids never went to school and they looked and acted like James Dean. Sometimes we'd try and pick fights with these wannabe gypsies but they always had plenty of real hard fairground workers who'd rally round pretty sharpish to back them up. Some of them had flick knives and they didn't care about using them because they were always moving from town to town and no one ever knew who they were. We'd scarper, leaving them to take our girls ... the slags. Then we'd talk about going back next night for a row with them fairground pikeys, only this time we'd have our own reinforcements.

There was trouble every night at the fairground, though it wasn't always the fairground workers who gave us the most aggro, because all they really wanted from you was money for going on their rides. No, the real trouble came from rival boot boy gangs. Skinheads from North Heath, Crayford, Dartford and Belvedere would arrive at Slade Green fairground to scrap with us. Because Slade Green was a popular site with fairground people, we had some tasty travelling families fighting on our side in a row.

In a short space of time I became leader of Slade Green Boot Boys. I was 15 and could take on guys who were a lot older than me. I also discovered I had another skill — at three-card brag. I'd play merchant seamen who came in off the river and take their wage packets. One Irish bloke I took to the cleaners said, 'That's the only nigger I know with golden bollocks.'

My teachers certainly didn't think I had golden nuts. They kept telling me I was a born loser who'd end up as a binman. Now that was bollocks because even when I was still at school, I made more money than most of my teachers. At nights I was knocking doors, selling stuff like ironing board covers and pens for charities like the Spastics Society.

Only a penny in the pound went to the charity, leaving the sellers a carve-up of the 99p and 'cos I had more front than Del Boy I could easily make twenty-five pounds a night. That wasn't bad dough in 1973 and I spent it all on clothes like leather coats and sheepskins. The old teachers were getting jealous and started digging me out about where the money came from. I sat at the back of the class in my smart clothes and told 'em, 'Don't keep tellin' me I'm gonna be a dustbinman, right. I earn more money than you even now. It's in the paper that teachers only earn £20 a week, so don't keep picking on me. I ain't a loser.'

My mum was proper old school working class, with principles. You pay your bills, keep a roof over your head and always turn up on time for a doctor's appointment. She also lived through the Depression and always drummed it into me that I had to have a trade. Plumber, painter, bricklayer, mechanic; anything, it didn't matter. She'd tell me again and again, 'If you go into a factory and it closes you could be on the dole for the rest of your life. If you have a trade somebody will always give you work.'

I'm a natural artist and I was always the best drawer in my year. Although I took CSEs in everything else, I went for O-level art and passed blindfold. Art was the only thing I didn't rebel at. I turned down art school because I didn't fancy having no money for five years, only to become a teacher on their poxy wages.

So I went to Erith College and tried my hand at all the trades. Bricklaying was out: by now I was six feet four tall and bending down all day gave me a bad back. Carpentry was no good. In woodwork class at school the teacher always said I made firewood. I couldn't handle plumbing because it was too much like maths. Painting was great: being an artist, I had a steady hand. At six feet four, I didn't need step ladders to hang wallpaper and I could lie down to do skirting boards, giving my back a rest. Painting and decorating was the nearest I could get to art and be paid for it. I was an apprentice with the local council in Abbey Wood and thanks to Mrs Chambers I've never been out of work for long in my life.

Cass Pennant

I was 16 and to most of my mates I looked seven feet tall. I weighed well over 14 stone. I was becoming a man quicker than my own age group and with a lifetime's fighting I was as strong as an ox. Word of the big black fella with the girl's name spread to towns all around. I started going around with guys from North Heath and Belvedere. We'd go to discos and have fights with soldiers from Woolwich barracks.

At a disco in the Lord Kitchener pub at Welling I met up with the King twins. They were 24-year-olds who fought for Great Britain at judo. They were also right fearsome skinheads. One night at a party, we took a bit of a hiding from a gang of greasers. We were out of our depth because these blokes were about 30 and they chased us through gardens flailing bike chains. That hammering sealed a bond of friendship with the King twins. We travelled around with them in a Mark One Cortina and began to see the world.

More important, they were into West Ham.

As a kid I used to like Tottenham because they had Jimmy Greaves. The family next door to us fostered children and their son was a West Ham supporter. They used to ask me to go along with them to Upton Park. Mrs C would give me extra pocket money, so for a couple of years I used to go to every home game. It was the old days of Bobby Moore and Martin

Peters. I was a big lump, but the old men used to pick me up and pass me down to the front of the terraces.

Every Saturday I'd travel with the King twins to Woolwich — the gateway to the East End. From Woolwich you could cross by ferry or foot tunnel to North Woolwich, which is in East London. We'd sit all morning in Greasy Joe's cafe in Woolwich, showing off our Doc Martens and braces, waiting for all the gang members to arrive. Then we'd go to the game.

My first brush with football violence came at Wolves away. Three of us went from school to our first away game. We were walking back to the station through a shopping street and there was a rumpus behind us. We carried on walking, then all of a sudden I saw somebody put through a shop window. Suddenly this group of badly dressed local lads came towards us. They looked startled. One of 'em shouted, 'Cockneys!' We looked behind us. There was no one, just people doing their shopping. Next thing they're running towards us. It's the same lot that put this fella through a shop window. So it must have been a Cockney they put through a shop window ... We run up the street. They're chasing us and we're running hell for leather. The other two disappear up ahead. Blind panic. I'm on my own in a strange town when I run into a human wall — right across the road, thirty horrible, hard-looking blokes in leather trench coats, steel toe-capped Doctor Martens. Stop. Jesus Christ, my number's up. One of them speaks up — bloody hell he's a cockney. They're Londoners, I don't know 'em but West Ham's the only London team in this neck of the woods today. I pulled out my West Ham scarf that I'd hidden inside my jacket.

'I'm West Ham,' I said.

They're giving it all the nigger stuff: 'Where ya goin', nigger? What ya running from?'

I gasped, 'Jesus, they've put a fella through a shop window down there. I've lost me mates. I'm tryin' to find 'em.'

I'm trying to tell them the story but they're just looking through me. I'd said the magic words. They're not interested in me, but the leader came forward and growled, 'Where?'

By now I'm gibbering and pointing: 'Back there.'

'Shaddap, mug. West Ham's here now. You're gonna show us where.'

Now I knew for certain, it was the South Bank mob — the hardest gang at West Ham. No one but nutters went into the South Bank. That was the end where the visitors stood.

They set off marching past me and I was left on my own again. I didn't know where I was. The only Londoners I could stick with were walking off to find the geezers who'd thrown the kid through a plate glass window, so I joined them. We went down the hill and there were fifty Wolves thugs just hanging around in the high street.

West Ham were fanned out across the road and I was in the middle of them, right next to the leader. It just went. I saw the leader go into action. He put one down and stuck the boot in good style. He'd gone in first and was right in the thick of 'em. My gang instincts came back in an instant. I just steamed in behind him. Another geezer was on the leader's back. I pulled him off, decked him and put the boot in. Lashing out. Didn't know who's who. Next thing the fight broke up a bit. We walked down one side, they walked the other. Bang! We came in again, all kicking and punching each other. I was getting kicked and punched but I loved it. I was back where I belonged. We backed 'em off and it broke up. We formed together and walked in an orderly manner towards the station where the police pushed us into a line to get on the train. We were laughing and joking about our adventure. I looked round: here were West Ham's hardest guys; they'd done Wolves good and proper and I was with 'em.

On the train, I went from carriage to carriage looking for my mates. They were relieved to see I was OK. They were worried I'd been put through a shop window. From up front came the noise of a rumpus, people getting a bit of a beating. All of a sudden these scruffy guys got into our carriage. They were smaller than me, but older, the sort I could take out with one punch. They were smashing up the carriage as they bowled through, having a go at the normal supporters. I thought we were gonna be next. They stopped at our table and some of them started: 'What you lookin' at, nigger?' But one jumped in, 'Nah, he's awright. He was with us.'

Then the leader came through, looked at me and said, 'You fought well today, mate. Who are ya?'

I told him my name and that I was with the Woolwich mob.

'Nah you're not,' he said. 'From now on you're wiv us.'

Soon I was hanging out all weekend with West Ham gangs. First with the Swan boys from Stratford in East London and later I met Big Lenny Aylen who introduced me to his firm who hung out in The George pub in Wanstead. This was the strongest gang I'd ever encountered, some of the most notorious faces around that area — Jaffa, Dean Haggerty and Mickey Scully were on the firm.

I was taller than most of them but I towered over Jesse Jacobs who once took me round his house to meet the family. I smashed my head going through the living room door and when I stood up again I knocked the chandelier flying. Jesse's mum, dad and sister were all sat there on the sofa in stitches. Jesse's old man was Philly Jacobs, otherwise known as the Little Caesar. He'd had a massive house built, but the ceilings and doors were below British standard height so his diddy family would feel at home.

Giant or not, they always made me welcome when I called around with Lenny Aylen. In fact, it was Lenny's family who helped me discover that East End folk are special people who will never question your colour or what you do as long as you can take a joke.

After a night of partying and fighting with the Wanstead lads, Lenny said I could stay at his place. It was three o'clock in the morning and I was too tired to say anything, other than to ask, 'Won't your folks mind?

'Nah, course not. You'll love 'em, they're good as gold.'

So lagging drunk and still buzzing from one almighty dance floor row, I ended up back at Lenny's place. It was a huge house and from what I could remember wandering through the streets most of the gaffs were big. I was puzzled. From the look of these homes the boys round here didn't have to fight every night just to survive. They'd obviously *chosen* violence as a way of life. Still their roots were in the East End and those folk love a row.

I dossed on the sofa, while Lenny went up to bed. In the black of night I desperately needed a leak. A fucking big house like this must have a downstairs toilet, so I stumbled about, head still banging from the booze. I couldn't find it so, not wanting to wake the household, I crept upstairs. I was half cut but I saw a 'ghost'. I shit myself there and then. Suddenly the ghost starts waving it arms and screaming, 'Wake up, Len! We're being burgled by a big black man!' It was Lenny's mother, Diane, in her white nightie. She'd got up to go to the loo and she bumped into me. Her old man, who's also called Lenny, ran straight into his sons' bedrooms. Fucking hell! I flew downstairs and dived on to the sofa, making out I was sound asleep.

Upstairs, Lenny was shouting, 'C'mon boys! Gary, Lenny, wake up; we're being robbed by a black man.' Gary's up in a flash while big brother Lenny was trying to get his head straight ... black man? ... black man? His head was still fogged ... *black man!* 'Dad, go back to bed; it's only Cass, the fella I've been tellin' ya about.'

I could hear the dad's voice. 'You sure, son? Your mother's in a right state!'

'Course I'm sure, he's downstairs on the sofa.'

I waited for the lynch mob but it never came. In the morning, Diane apologised for scaring me and insisted I had breakfast with the whole family. In fact, she put more food on my plate than she did for her own sons.

I ended up staying so many weekends that I became part of the family. So much so that years later in my wedding speech, after thanking Mrs Chambers I also thanked Diane for being my part-time mother! Sadly, Diane died suddenly and the pain hit the two Lens and Gary very hard. It was a pain I shared because of the way that family accepted me without question. To my friends there's no colour — I'm just Cass. And when people — black or white — cross my friends I'll show them no mercy and have no problem with it.

I held my eighteenth birthday party up West, at Global Village, a club down the side of Charing Cross station. It was the punk era — the Sex Pistols and Johnny Rotten. Steve Strange had the club at the time. Sixty of us piled in to celebrate my birthday and we hadn't been there too long when Billy Gall an ex-soldier and fighting legend over West Ham screamed out that the bar had done him out of a tenner. So we all went over, poked our noses in and started having a go at the bar staff. Then a bouncer came over and watched as the head barman went through all the tills. The money added up with the till receipts — no tenner. The bouncer growled, 'You heard, move off.'

'You bastard,' someone shouted and a split second later all hell broke loose. The heaviest firm I've ever run with are getting stuck in to the bouncers. There were already about three or four hundred people in the club and most of them joined in as well. The place looked like a saloon fight in a John Wayne film. Bouncers were piling in from other clubs. Our firm had split up and were scrapping all over the club. The DJ cut the music, the dancers got the hump and they ploughed in hell for leather, too. There was even a battle going on in the toilets.

In among all this mayhem was a big, fat, brick shithouse of a bouncer standing in the middle of the dance floor headbutting a pillar and grunting like a dangerous deaf mute.

'Excuse me, mate,' I said as I tiptoed past this growling lunatic sticking the nut on a lump of concrete. It was his club and he'd lost control of it ... bang! bang! bang!

We piled downstairs where a load of Chelsea fans had arrived and stuck the boot into them. The Old Bill turned up, hundreds of them. We'd done some right damage and had to get out before we were nicked. As we surged for the door, the bouncer was still there smashing his nut against that pillar, blood pouring down his face.

Everybody was trying to get out as the Old Bill

were trying to storm in. Outside is a very narrow street that runs from Charing Cross station to Embankment tube station. It was wall-to-wall with coppers. These were the days of the IRA's first London bombings and the cops were on full alert, patrolling the streets in green military buses. That night two hundred police were sent to our ruck. We're out in the street now, still rowing and battling the cops. In the middle of it all Patsy Rice gets bitten in the bollocks by a police dog! As a policewoman nicked him, we slipped away down the side street. We were always having rows in discos so we never parked close by in case somebody clocked our number plates. We sprinted to the motors parked a few streets away and drove like lunatics to Epping Forest where there was an all-night burger van. Three or four cars were already there and more were pulling up. As Lenny, Jaffa and me got out of the car, Billy Gall was at the van buying a burger. We wandered over. 'How'd you get on back there, lads?' asked Billy, still waiting for his hamburger to arrive. A few moments later he handed over a ten quid note. We all looked at each other and thought the same thing.

Lenny said, 'Bill, you were skint at that club. They done you out of yer last tenner. We've come straight from the club to here, so where d'you get that ten pound note from?'

Jaffa jumped in: 'You cunt. Two hundred Old Bill, Patsy Rice has had his balls bitten off by an alsatian, the disco's smashed to pieces, the club's shut down and you've still got yer tenner for bloody hot dogs!'

On Sunday lunchtime we met in The George in Wanstead to have a count up of who'd been nicked. The place was buzzing: everybody telling their stories again and again — the grunting, nutcase bouncer, battering the Chelsea mob, who we found was their top firm out of Stockwell, and Patsy with a policewoman tending his bitten bollocks. It turned out that Patsy was still in hospital, so after a few beers we wandered over to see him. He was lying there with four stitches in his balls and a smile all over his face. Just thinking about it made me wince, so what had he got to be happy about? He chirped, 'Well, look at it this way, Cass, two weeks off work with full pay can't be bad.'

Chapter Three

The atmosphere was electric as we poured out of Sheffield United's Bramall Lane ground. It was gonna go off in the streets. Pockets of fans from United's deadly rivals Sheffield Wednesday were showing us where we could get ambushed. There was a hundred of us and no escort. The police just placed beat bobbies at strategic points along the route. Their attitude was to let us make our own way back to the station: with a bit of luck the locals would give it to us flash Londoners and then they could nick what was left to justify their overtime.

Scotty's mob joined up with us. Scotty was a two-team Jock and he wore a Celtic scarf. It didn't matter, because the East End lot didn't understand or care about the politics of Celtic or Rangers. The only important thing to them was that Jocks always carried a blade. All the ones I ever met were a good laugh and dangerous bastards. Scotty's posse had just come from a small skirmish where they'd cut up a couple of Sheffield yobs.

As we approached Sheffield Midland train station the group split, one lot heading towards the platform while a group of faces wandered on past. I caught up with them in some sort of bus station. Hundreds of Sheffield fans were milling around; some of them were the mob we'd fought against behind their goal in the first half. There were only about forty of us West Ham in this shelter, and nothing had been organised, so we just went mental, with everyone lashing out. I fought alongside a big black guy called Natalie — another one of us with a girl's name who could pack a punch. Northern sods were going down all around him and when the Sheffield lot saw me as well there was terror in their eyes. It was brilliant: every yell, every thump, every scream echoed in this bloody great hangar of a building. The fuckers were coming at us from everywhere, from side entrances, from behind. Punches flew in all directions as we cleared the whole bus terminus. As we surfaced into daylight again, the Old Bill were waiting to frog-march us back to the railway station. I'd gone up by car with a couple of the Stratford boys so the three of us slipped away down the hill to where our car was parked.

Three

A brick whistled through the air and smashed to the ground nearby. We looked round to see a huge mob of a hundred Sheffield lads following us down Pond Hill, desperate for revenge. I'm the giveaway: they want the big black Cockney. The car park is close and if we leg it we can get some tools from the motor to take this lot on. We're in shit, but we're laughing as we run, taking the piss out of each other. The car park is in sight. Our cars are at the far end and the mob are catching up fast. The drivers are nowhere to be seen: we're done for. There was just one chance … Sat in a car over in the far corner were five West Ham lads. A fella called Jimmy climbed out of the motor as bricks rained down all around us. The main entrance was now a sea of red and white scarves. Looking to the left, there was another entrance — and another mob. To the right another group were closing in. With the sound of a bomb going off, a red half brick landed on the bonnet of our Cortina.

Jimmy yells, 'Cass, the train station's just up over this bank. It's the only way out!'

It looked like the north face of the Eiger, too steep to get a good footing. Slipping and scrambling up the first few feet we clawed at the earth with our hands. If that wasn't bad enough, we were also being bricked to fuck. We'd never make it. As rocks and building site debris clattered around me I remembered the terrorised look that came over the face of the Sheffield lads in the bus depot. It was Natalie and me they were afraid of, like they'd never seen a black man before.

Jimmy had already given up trying to scale the bank and ran back to his car. I raced after him and gasped, 'I'll get us out of here but I need a tool. For fuck's sake ain't yer got nothin' in the motor?' Jimmy shoved a small knife into my hand. It was a poxy fruit peeler, useless in reality — but it was a knife. There was no time to weigh up the odds. I just leapt into action. When I was a kid we used to act out the film *Zulu* on the school field. Being the only black, I was always the Zulu with all the divs on my side to make up the numbers against the jack-the-lads. Everybody tried to get a piece of me, but I'd just go mental, like I was the whole Zulu nation on my own.

Now I was Zulu again. With stones, bottles and bricks bouncing off me, I ran straight at the enemy. Eyes bulging with hatred, I screamed, 'I'll stab ya. The black man's gonna stab ya!' Those terrorised faces were back again. They must have thought I was mental. I could feel the West Ham lads running at my heels, screaming war. I wasn't mental at all; I knew exactly what I was doing. I chose the side entrance with the smallest mob opposing me. They turned on their toes, scrambling out of the gate, falling over one another to escape being stabbed. It was crazy: I had

Three

seven West Ham lads chasing my arse, and about fifty Sheffield bovver boys running away from me out of the car park and into Sheaf Street. Then there were about another four hundred Sheffield chasing us. A lone copper stood on a bridge in the road, hand held up, shouting, 'HALT!' He'd have had more chance stopping a train. I didn't see him until the Sheffield mob I was chasing had run past him. I near knocked him over, knife still in my hand. As I raced past him, a police van screamed to a halt. Cozzers bombed out of the van and grabbed the West Ham guys behind me. I chucked the knife and kept on running to the railway station where I tried to mingle with West Ham fans waiting for the football special. No chance, I was spotted instantly, nicked and bailed.

Two weeks later I was up before Sheffield magistrates. I hadn't stabbed anyone so I was done for having an offensive weapon. The guy in front of me got one month in jail for the same offence. I'm next: 'Not guilty. Self defence, your honour.' I told the story of how we were trapped like rats in the car park. The magistrates listened in disbelief. *Eight* against *five hundred* and a hail of bricks and boulders? They questioned the officer who'd been on the bridge about my version of this incredible story.

He half laughed. 'They weren't boulders, sir, just stones. Five hundred Sheffield fans? More like two

37

hundred.'

The magistrate asked, 'How many West Ham fans was the defendant with?'

The copper replied, 'Not eight, more like twenty.'

This was a magistrates' court so it was no surprise the beaks found me guilty, but they added that, even allowing for exaggeration on the defendant's part, they were still pretty heavy odds. Fined £100, to pay at a fiver a week.

Just another crazy weekend in the life of Cass of West Ham. The black man with no fear had become a legend among football hooligans all over the country. West Ham had the most notorious gang of thugs in the history of British football. Fighting was a way of life. It was the mid-seventies when every weekend raw violence turned the terraced streets outside soccer grounds all over the country into battlefields. It was the days when your dad turned on the telly to watch Brian Moore's *Big Match* and had to turn the volume down sharpish to avoid hearing the crowd chanting 'You're gonna get yer fuckin' head kicked in ... dud ... dud ... dudda ... dudda ... dud ...!' Harold Wilson was Prime Minister; flower power had wilted and died to be replaced by skinheads, proud of being working class. A life of dead-end factory jobs and manual work stretched ahead, so all your hopes and dreams were invested in your local team. There was something

Three

extremely disloyal, bordering on betrayal, if you stayed on the manor but supported Man United. It was like looking down on the area you came from and branding your local team as a bunch of losers. We hated Man U as they chanted, 'There's only one united!' because there really was no reply to that. Everybody supporting another team called United felt the same.

In the mid-seventies, Man United's Red Army wreaked havoc everywhere, smashing up soccer specials and laying waste to every town they went to ... until they reached West Ham. The old dockers, the hard guys of the East End, were not prepared to allow the upstart northerners to take those liberties at Upton Park. The Red Army rolled into town like the Russians driving west. Inside the ground were evil-looking East End faces I've never seen at a match before or since. In those days there were no fences and you could move all around the ground. Most of Man United's thousands of travelling fans were behind the South Bank goal. They started their chant that normally put the fear of God up home fans, 'You're going home in a fucking ambulance ... dud ... dud ... dudda ... dudda ... dud ...'

The East End weren't intimidated. We just got our revenge taunting them about the terrible Munich air disaster which wiped out eight of Man U's finest players, chanting back, 'Who's that lying on the runway!!!'

Among the Man U hordes were the hated Cockney Reds, traitor Londoners who supported a team nearly two hundred miles away. Furious fights broke out all over the South Bank. A half-pint Cockney Red put the boot in on me, so I cracked him with a right-hander in the face and he went down. Within minutes the great Red Army were driven out of the South Bank and on to the pitch. They tried to take refuge in the Chicken Run in front of the east stand. Hooligans never stood in the Chicken Run: that was home to the old guard, the men who'd worked in the docks. Any Man U fan trying to climb in their territory was given a clump and thrown back on to the pitch. The North End boys behind the home goal began to feel left out so they piled on to the pitch and steamed into the Reds as well. The only hope of safety was the West Side but Man U stood no chance as Hammers from the North and South Banks poured through to attack from two ends. Fighting was so fierce the game was held up.

West Ham won 2–1 and after the game police horses charged up and down the streets. The Old Bill were there in their hundreds, but that still didn't stop us waging running battles, bashing the Mancs all the way to Euston station. Hardly a fan went home unmarked, and the Cockney Reds were singled out for the roughest treatment. A West Ham regular nicknamed Bubbles penned a rebel song that's still a classic today. A quarter of a century on you'll hear it in pubs or on away trains. When the booze is all drunk someone will start singing it while the others listen and remember that day:

'Some talk of Man City and Bury as well,
Oldham Athletic I've often been told
But the team to remember, the team to recall
Was the great Man United, the best of them all.
They came down to West Ham in '75
They came in the south bank, they came in the
  sides,
But the Cockneys were many and ready to ruck
And those poor Man United got battered to fuck.'

I fought on the terraces and in the streets every single weekend for well over ten years. I was hooked on an adrenalin so great you knew you could never walk away from it no matter how great the danger. The buzz was far better than any drug. Fear and anticipation would knot up in my stomach as we walked the enemy streets expecting to be ambushed. Your tingling senses could almost smell danger in the air. Sooner or later people wearing the same Dr

Martens and crombie coats would appear as if from nowhere. Only their scarves would be different. Your mind's on red alert: How many? Will they be tooled up? Will I be up against grown men who want to kick my head in? Will we get split up? What then?

It was all done in the name of West Ham — we really believed that. You were defending the territory and defending the club's honour, proving we were true supporters. You couldn't take part on the field as a player, but you could be a warrior and battle for the club. Part of the attraction of football violence was anyone could play. You didn't need to be a big lump with muscles of steel. Bottle and front was all you needed. Even seven-stone weaklings could become little legends.

Critics and the rent-a-quote pundits reckoned we weren't interested in football, just scrapping. Here's why they were talking bollocks. Fighting broke out at Coventry away, forcing the home fans into the far corner. Police formed a segregation line, but aggro continued from both sides of the divide. Half a house brick lobbed from the Coventry side hit Gravesend Terry on the head. The crowd around him backed away in horror. His eyeball was hanging out of its socket, blood squirting everywhere. St John's Ambulance shipped him off to hospital, where doctors popped his eyeball back in and stitched up the ripped skin around his eye. Ignoring doctors who wanted him to stay while they checked for the effects of concussion, Tel checked out of casualty. With a huge patch over his left eye, his white Fred Perry shirt and brushed denims soaked in claret and a huge envelope with his X-rays in, he thumbed a lift back to the ground. When Terry was carted off to the ambulance, Coventry had been leading one–nil but he was back on the terraces in time to use his good eye to see Bobby Gould equalise in the dying minutes.

West Ham's travelling army was a collection of tasty gangs under the general command of Bill Gardner and Teddy Bunter's firms. The Canning Town mob were shifty-looking bleeders, who for some reason weren't as tall as the average beer-gut Hammer. They didn't mix well with the main West Ham support but hung around on the fringes, sniping at the enemy. Hampton and Stevie Morgan ran the South Bank crew. That left all the pests, wannabes and young up-coming fighters to tag along where they could. Most of this lot were under 16 years old. The beard and beer-gut brigade who'd established West Ham's fearsome reputation didn't need the excess baggage of these kids following them around enemy towns and cities, attracting the Old Bill.

Much to our annoyance, loads of these youngsters were travelling to away matches. They'd collected

those tokens from boxes of Kellogg's cornflakes and
Persil soap powder. If you were under 16 you could
trade in the tokens for cheap rail fares on the InterCity
network. The older guys doubted whether the
youngsters had the bottle to stand their ground against
rival opposition. Those doubts evaporated on Boxing
Day 1975.

The Holte End at Aston Villa was imposing and
impregnable. It was so big it scared you more than any
threat from Villa's fans. Stood at the other end of the
ground with Ted and Gardner's mob, I witnessed the
astonishing sight of a gap opening up at the very back
of the Holte End as West Ham guys laid into Villa
fans, sending them scattering for safety. Had West
Ham taken the Holte End for the first time ever? But
how and who? Every firm and known face were
standing here in the away supporters' end.
Nevertheless, somebody was doing the business. Villa
went mental at the liberty of it. The gap closed again.
Chants of, 'We're proud of you! We're proud of you!'
erupted from our end as the police led the
perpetrators down the side of the pitch to our end.
There were just a hundred of them grinning, smiling,
still sporting the claret-and-blue French berets and
balaclava helmets they'd pulled on to confuse Villa
fans as they attacked the Holte End. Like West Ham,
Villa also play in claret and blue. Led by a young black

guy, Matthew Thomas, there they were, all the under 16s we'd slagged off so often: Swallow, Ramsgate, Brett, Tiderman, Fellman, Liddy, Ameidi, Sherrin, Hagger, Grant and Turner.

As the youngsters strolled into our block they gave it to us, in particular a guy called Bromley who'd goaded them badly: 'Bromley, Bromley, where's your boys? You like makin' all the noise!' they chanted. In shamed admiration, we took the point. By using their Persil discounts on InterCity, this little firm was back in London a good hour before we got back on the football special which gave them enough time to attack hated Millwall fans as they returned to St Pancras station. Sixteen-year-old Andy Swallow made a real name for himself that day. The youngsters had earned the respect they deserved. All they lacked was a name. By the next big game Swallow and Grant Flemming arrived with badges sporting the British Rail logo, cut from the back of Persil boxes.

The InterCity Firm was born.

More daring incidents followed the Holte End attack to mark the arrival of the legendary ICF. A Cockney Red with the absurd name of Banana Bob had taken liberties by bashing ordinary West Ham supporters around Euston as he travelled up and down to Man United. He milked it for all it was worth and even sent out challenges to Bill Gardner and other

West Ham faces. Every time we travelled up north rumours reached us that Banana Bob would be waiting when we returned. Each week we looked, waited, then hunted but he never showed up. We realised the Cockney Reds were deliberately avoiding us by travelling InterCity rather than risk getting on football specials carrying London teams. The day came when both Man U and West Ham were playing in the Midlands. On the way home we jumped off the West Ham football special and boarded the same InterCity as the Cockney Reds. We'd planned for two hundred to come on board but only 50 managed to slip the Old Bill on the soccer special. Skirmishes broke out as we dug out Cockey Reds from each carriage. When we reached Banana Bob's carriage we sent back for Gardner.

'Banana Bob, meet Banana Bill,' I said.

Banana Bob quaked as we all laughed in his face. His reputation was in tatters. Not one for taking liberties, King Billy let Banana go with a warning: any more mouth and we'd be back.

The day wasn't done yet. Arriving back at Euston well before the football special, the Old Bill weren't out in force. As the Cockney Reds scattered home, we clashed with Arsenal travelling back from out of town. With the Old Bill hot on our trail we bumped into Man City boys heading back up north. It had

Three

been a hooligan's dream day. From then on the West Ham hierarchy always travelled InterCity. The trains were free of police and we'd arrive in our rivals' towns while the enemy were still eating breakfast. A sinister legend was born — ICF meant West Ham and violence. But the letters were still a mystery.

Northerners would call out to us, 'Hey, Cockney, what does ICF mean?'

'Whaddya think?'

'Ice Cream Firm,' replied the soppy northern bastards. And that became our alias.

Critics and rent-a-quote pundits always branded us as mindless morons, but most of us had decent jobs. Organising several hundred fans travelling on one train took special skills. As well as being good fighters, the hierarchy were born organisers. They ran the ICF like a well-oiled business and everybody had their part to play. Railway workers stole tickets for us; Persil upped the age limit on their scheme to eighteen or so; printers started forging student cards for us. By now the Ben Shermans and Doc Martens had disappeared and the ICF were casual, so shoplifters on the team stole Lacoste shirts, American air force jackets, jeans and trainers. We had T-shirts printed with Andy and Grant's British Rail logo and before long young Timmy produced the infamous ICF calling cards and we really did stick them to our victims' backs.

The ICF even had their own songwriter, a kid who spent all week thinking of nothing else but new chants for the following Saturday's game. Chanting was vital to the whole atmosphere. You travelled on the same stinking trains to grounds where the toilets overflowed and sewage ran down the terraces. You'd eaten shit food and been herded like cattle, so when you sang you were bonded together. Hardened men and boys singing for all they were worth to unite around their team, or just to stir up hatred in their rivals, driving them to anger so they'll climb over the barriers to get at them. Most teams were jealous of West Ham's cockney wit. The Spinners had a hit with a song called 'In My Liverpool Home', which we twisted to taunt the Mickey Mousers: 'In your Liverpool slums, you look in the dustbin for something to eat ... you find a dead cat and think it's a treat ... in yer Liverpool slums!'

From Aberdeen to Plymouth Argyll the whole of British football had heard of the ICF. But West Ham didn't even have to be playing for us to be involved in violence. Arsenal played Celtic in a testimonial. Thirty of the young ICF went along and jumped in with a load of Glasgow Rangers fans to attack the Celtic mob in the North Bank at Highbury, Arsenal's north London ground. Our lads sprayed ICF on the back of the stand and stuck calling cards all over the ground. The Gooners tumbled what was happening and followed the small West Ham team out into the road. By chance one of the lads spotted a van with a pile of reproduction barley twist legs in the back. They quickly broke into the van, armed themselves with chair legs and laid into their pursuers, smashing them all the way down the road. The ICF's reputation spread far and wide. Even holiday reps warned holidaymakers arriving in Playa Las Americas on Tenerife to avoid certain discos because the ICF were on the island!

For over ten years I fought battles all over the country. In the north, Newcastle, Sunderland, 'Boro, Manchester, Liverpool. In the Midlands against Birmingham City, Villa, Coventry, Leicester. In London, Spurs, Chelsea and Arsenal were deadly rivals. But our sworn enemy were Millwall. Whenever guys from those days meet, conversation inevitably gets around to one question: who was the best fighting team — West Ham or Millwall?

Who could ever forget that *Panorama* documentary featuring Millwall's notorious F Troop, the guys who stood at the halfway line wearing surgical masks? Millions of ordinary viewers watched horrified as a character called 'Arry the Dog steamed in good and proper at Bristol. It didn't take a documentary to tell me that Millwall were mad and their ground, The

Den, was a home for the criminally insane. To get to the ground you had to make a terrifying walk along Cold Blow Lane — a hundred yards of hate that takes you under two bleak, black railway arches daubed with spine-chilling graffiti. The atmosphere inside The Den was pure evil.

I don't think anybody's ever bothered to look into why West Ham and Millwall hate each other so much. To me they seemed to have so much in common. Dare I say it, they were the same kind of people with just a river to separate them. I reckon it boils down to simple jealousy over who had the right to be dockers in the Port of London — Millwall men from the south bank or the West Ham on the north bank. No derby could be as potentially life-threatening as Millwall v West Ham. I'm sure the football authorities knew it too because the cup draw both sets of fans prayed for was never called. But the football authorities couldn't stop testimonial games between the two.

It was the time of Shaft movies and Barry White sounds; we still had proper summers and girls looked pretty horny in cheese cloth. Millwall held two testimonial games against us, for Harry Cripps and Bobby Neil. At one of these games two hundred of us followed Bill Gardner down Cold Blow Lane and into the Millwall end. Everybody knew what they'd come

for and it wasn't to watch a poxy testimonial. Millwall
were chanting, 'Chim chimaney, chim chimaney,
chim-chim, cheroo … we hate those bastards in claret
and blue … chim chimaney, chim chimaney, chim-
chim, cheroo …' But something wasn't quite right.
Millwall's top firm weren't in sight. Gardner calls me
and a mob of about fifty chosen ones to follow him
down to the halfway line. Suddenly a black man of
about my height sprints through the gangway with
three or four others following, sticks a full-blooded
punch on my nose and keeps on running. Everything
had happened in a split second, I think out loud,
'What the fuck? A black man has just singled me out.'
Gardner moved down behind me and said, all matter-
of-fact like, 'That's Millwall's Tiny'. I went mad. Tiny
was older than me and had a long-standing reputation
as leader at Millwall. There'd been whispers for a
couple of seasons about a clash between him and me,
London's two best-known black hooligans. If I had
my way, that clash was gonna happen right now. I
dropped down into the gangway. It was the signal for
the others to follow me. Tiny and his crew had
stopped by the entrance to the Cold Blow end. Seeing
me charging towards him, he pulled a screwdriver out
of his coat and waved it about like a knife. A quick
grin and he'd gone, vanished into the safety of the
Millwall end. A large West Ham mob gathered just

outside the Cold Blow. There's that anxious moment-of-truth feeling again. That tense, scary buzz. The knot in my stomach gets a hold. The buzz is uncontrollable. This is my chance to make a mark on fearsome Millwall. I'd come up fast through the terrace ranks, so fast I was now considered an up-and-coming face. Gardener and Co were already an institution. Could I take over Tiny's title as London's black top boy?

In my greaser's studded leather jacket, I moved in with the serious faces, pushing and shoving to get up there with the top boys. We were so psyched up we felt mental. We moved into the Cold Blow chanting, 'We hate Millwall! We hate Millwall! We hate Millwall!' When the noise reaches a crescendo that's the moment the two mobs come together. It's an unbelievable male experience. It's one on one with all your mates behind you. Those of us directly in front of the enemy have got seconds to star and maybe become a legend if just for that one match. This is steaming, and we're doing it to Millwall. We hate Millwall; fuck the reasons why. I'm kicking, punching, yelling at everything in front of me. All the Hammers doing the same around you keeps the momentum going. Stay on your feet at all costs: the thought of falling down in front of the Millwall mob is too dodgy to even contemplate. Odd fists and boots

Three

clashing against you. No noise; you can hear your own voice. We've done it, we've taken the Cold Blow Lane end. The boys all chant, 'West Ham aggro! West Ham aggro!' The match has kicked off and we didn't even know when it started. It's official: West Ham are the guv'nors and all of London knows it.

Top faces took up positions around Gardner, Big Ted, Simmo, Hampton, Bunter and me. Millwall were all around us, from time to time mobbing up to try and find our weak spot. We were like Roman centurians among the barbarians as we all try and stick together.

'MILL...WA...LL! MI...LL...WALL!' Their eerie, echoing chant is pure evil to intimidate before the kill. By half time we were surrounded on three sides, two hundred of us against eight hundred of them. One of the Millwall lot moved to the front line and called out, 'Oi, Cass!' It was one of the Foy brothers. I knew him through drinking in the Black Boy pub with my mate Carlos the Greek. Foy shouted over, 'Cass, you've nothing to prove. We're gonna do your boys but I can give you safe passage out. No sweat, our old man's doing a 12 stretch: his word goes around 'ere.' I grinned back, thanks but no thanks and he melted back into the Millwall mob. In the middle of all that hatred, it was a fine gesture and I've never forgotten it.

We kept moving back up the steps so they couldn't

get behind. We knew what was coming but as a face you can't just slip away. I felt pride for the guys I was with; they were the gamest I'd ever seen. There was no fear, just a grudging regret that we didn't have a big enough firm to hold the end we'd taken. The Old Bill was there, but they might as well not have been. One almighty steam and a roar and, just as Foy had predicted, we were well and truly ousted. All chance of having a go back was lost when the invisible Old Bill started making their presence felt. It was only just after half time but the cops had opened the doors and they slung us out into the street. I was the last to be left at the top of the stairs and some arsehole whacked me on the head with a lump of wood. I went mental, 'You cowardly bastards! You're producing it now the odds have changed. You weren't so full of it when we were firm on firm.' I couldn't believe it when they told the Old Bill I was carrying a blade.

A copper rushed me, and his colleagues pinned me against the back of the shelter. They went straight down the lining of my tatty old leather biker's jacket until they felt something. My heart raced. Was there something there I'd forgotten about? They ordered me to take out the knife they could feel through the lining. I put my hand down and pulled out my six-inch college ruler! Not this time, gentlemen!

Jealousy over who was the hardest firm in London

would lead to dozens more clashes over the years between West Ham and Millwall, each looking to prove it once and for all. The mighty Mile End mob, who fought for West Ham but were a law unto themselves, decided to ambush the cream of Millwall on a train. Millwall were travelling to a game at Orient which would decide whether Millwall or Birmingham were promoted that year. Tooled right up, the Mile End mob struck at Whitechapel in East London. It was mayhem with fire extinguishers going off all over the place. Fighting spilt on to the tracks and railway officials had to cut the power to the line to prevent deaths. Still the battle was bloody; both sides were carrying blades and many of the fighters were cut.

To the media, West Ham were the most racist bunch of supporters on earth. The reality is that the National Front lot were a tiny minority and they never had much influence.

Claret and blue were the only colours most of the West Ham fans saw and they just used the Front for their own purpose ... for violence.

Here's how crazy it was. There was another well-known black geezer at West Ham who was a little bit tasty. Well *he* went on the marches with the National Front. One day the NF were lined up at Stratford ready to march on Brick Lane. Their ranks were swelled with hooligans. The NF leader Martin Webster walked along the line inspecting his 'troops'. He walked back again and again. He couldn't believe his eyes: 'We've got a nigger in the crew.'

'Who?' asked the West Ham mob. 'That's our mate, he ain't no nigger. He's with us.'

It was a bit awkward for Webster. He didn't want to upset the boys because they were a tidy firm, so he said, 'Nothing personal against him. It isn't me; it's the others. We can't have him in.'

The West Ham blokes were outraged! 'Fuck off, yer little runt. This is our party. If you take him out, you take us out.'

I never went on the marches because I've got a conscience. But I had the right hump because I was missing out on the violence. Then I got my chance, I discovered the Socialist Workers' Party, the sworn enemies of the National Front. They were a tasty mob in battle and suddenly the ICF joined them. Webster's NF mob couldn't believe it: 'You've been on Front marches every Sunday for weeks; you can't just change sides.'

'Oh yes we can, just watch us. This lot don't look a bad firm!'

I've told you how I fought week in, week out to become a legend on the terraces at West Ham. Well, there was a spell when I wasn't there because I was inside. I'll tell you more about that later.

The first game I came out to was the London derby, Spurs v West Ham at White Hart Lane. The ICF boys were up and out early. With them were West Ham's new youngsters, the Under Fives. They were like the ICF had been in our early days but this mob carried blades and although many were still at school they weren't afraid to use their tools. The previous Monday a pack of Under Fives had been up at Euston to do the Gooners coming back from Wolves, and had found a leaflet dropped by Tottenham fans who had been through the station that day. Season after season, West Ham's fighters had taken every Spurs end. This leaflet was a call to arms, urging Spurs fans to restore years of lost pride. It told them to be at the Corner Pin pub near the ground early on derby Saturday: 'West Ham think we're soft. Our reputation depends on it.' Well thanks for the invitation, lads. We travelled up in two mobs, one by tube, the rest in a fleet of vans, so if the Old Bill stopped one firm, the other would get through.

Luck was on our side and both teams arrived within minutes of each other at opposite ends of Tottenham High Street. We were so early Old Bill hadn't even thought about leaving his cosy canteen. We charged the unprepared Spurs mob as they gathered at the Corner Pin. In a charge you don't hang about; you get stuck in because the bleeders behind will get in front and you'll miss out on the real action. This was gang warfare football style. It wasn't pretty stuff but we only ever targeted those who wanted to hurt us. The Corner Pin mob scattered, leaving their Pride Of Tottenham leaflets blowing in the wind. A wall of noise to our right was the signal for another ruck. Spurs had re-grouped outside the Bell and Hare. Hurled beer glasses smashed all around our feet as we charged again. Panicked by the sight of the West Ham mob who'd been on the tube bearing down on them as well, they fled into the pub and locked themselves in. 'Smash the fuckin' pub up!' cried one voice.

'That's not our way, we're not fuckin' Chelsea,' said a senior. We were jeering and taunting them from outside when the Old Bill were on top of us. Now we were like Tottenham, scattering in all directions as cops with horses and dogs attacked us from side streets, herding us back to the High Street. There were too many of us for them to nick everyone and the ICF were marshalled into the ground earlier than planned.

Me and my bouncer mate Danny Byles, who the lads thought was a relation of mine, gave the Old Bill the slip by making out we were locals from the nearby Broadwater Farm estate. We made our way to the neutral Paxton Road End, opposite the spot where West Ham were penned in. Now the Paxton was next to The Shelf, the spot where Tottenham's thug army gathered. As well as fighting there was lots of humour at football. Because of Tottenham's Jewish connections, we called their yobs the Yids, though I never saw one of them that looked Jewish. At first they had the hump and thought it was an insult, but in the end they even started calling themselves the Yids.

Over the next hour about sixty West Ham thugs slipped their way into the Paxton to stand beside us. Swallow introduced me to this huge black bloke who looked like a super heavyweight. He was just 17 years old, weighed 19 stone and was in command of the Under Fives. His name was Richard Wildman.

'He's the new Cass,' said Swallow.

I'd heard a lot about him when I was inside. I shook his hand, genuinely pleased another black man was making it big to take the heat off me. I took him to one side and said, 'I've got respect for you, but you've gotta make your own name. I told the same thing to Matthew Thomas when they started calling him Little Cass. Now they all know him as Maffy. You do the same.'

Then one by one they all slipped off in the direction of The Shelf. No one had said a word, and there was no plan; everyone just moved off. Danny, who was standing beside me, wasn't a hooligan, though he was a tasty fighter, and he hadn't a clue what was happening. We watched as they snaked along the pitchside gangway. Wildman turned and looked up: 'Cass, you coming or what?'

'You don't need me, big fella. You're the new Cass, so why are you waiting for me?'

We watched the sixty of them slip along the lower half of The Shelf and steam into about two hundred Spurs fans. Fists and boots flew all over the lower Shelf. As usual, Swallow was in the thick of it and Wildman really was wild. He whacked six of 'em good and proper before the Old Bill piled in mob-handed and pushed the West Ham boys, five at a time, backwards on to the pitch. The last 15 realised there just weren't enough of them left for any more heroics and got out of it.

The massed ranks at the top of The Shelf united with the shell-shocked battlers on the bottom rows. To salvage their dented pride they were giving it the big 'un chanting, 'We are the YIDS! We are the YIDS!'

I said to Danny, 'They're mugs. They ain't done West Ham; the Old Bill did their work for 'em. You and me can do this lot. C'mon, let's show 'em.'

Danny replied, 'Err ... I'm with ya, what do you do?'

Three

So I told him, 'Just steam in, mate. Just have it, have a mental.'

And that's what we did. We marched into The Shelf heading for the corner where a group of about 150 were giving our boys wanker arm signals. I clocked the activity, bodies tracking us, closing in, while others set off to tip off the mob at the top of The Shelf. An uncontrollable rage is building up inside. A Yid closed in, shouting his head off that West Ham are still on The Shelf. I decked him with a big right to the chin. As he buckled I let out a blood-curdling scream: 'C'mon, you mugs! We're West Ham!'

Then I kicked the geezer beside him. I charged forwards, kicking and punching, changing direction, still steaming towards the mob. Bodies were going down all around me. Danny was getting on well. By the looks of things he's a one-punch specialist. He'd whacked as many as me, if not more. As the Yids fell a big gap opened up around us. The space filled with voices of hate: 'Kill the black bastards! It's that cunt Cass — kill 'im!' The whole end erupted. Adrenalin surged around my body. I loved it; it was like old times again. The main faces on the Top Shelf, at the back of the stand, surged forward, trampling on the ones below, gobbing their venomous spit. The ones we'd battered were trying to get in behind us. No matter how good you are, if you let 'em round the back you're finished. You've got to keep on high ground. They've got to climb up the stairs to you. Danny was going further and further down the stairs. They were forming behind him and in a moment he'd be overwhelmed. I shouted to him, 'Dan! It's me, Cass. Grab my arm!'

Two black men, towering almost six feet six, and linked by our right arms, so we were facing in opposite directions. Lashing and booting it was unbelievable: when you're in a crowd you can't miss. The shitters in front of us were trying to dodge but they were stopping the real hard bastards from reaching us.

The teams weren't even out on the field yet. We were the entertainment, and the whole stadium had their eyes on us. My reputation shot up another ten notches. We stood our ground as they came at us. The enemy couldn't do us. We were just too much for them. The West Ham mob crammed in the Park Lane roared us on. Finally, sheer weight of numbers broke the link. Now we were in trouble, both fighting individually for our lives. The Yids were going mental. This was the biggest insult ever. First being done by the Under Fives, now just two madmen were doing as much damage as a mob of sixty. They'd never live it down. The real Tottenham faces burst through.

Three

I could no longer see Danny — it was nearly over for us. A blow to my mouth, another to the nose, the boots were going in but I wouldn't keel over. To survive I needed higher ground. There was a wall where the gangway met the upper shelf. Now I was in the gangway, safety barriers to the right, a wall to the left. In this narrow canyon they could only come at me one or two at a time. I'd been hit all over and I was covered in blood, but I was still fighting them off. I pressed my back against the wall. I could no longer focus on the blows coming in and the weight of numbers crowding down pushed me back along the gangway. There was still no sign of the Old Bill. They couldn't get through. Bang. I fell into blackness. Retreating with my back against the wall, I'd been so busy fighting I hadn't noticed a gaping hole in the wall where the stairs came up. I'd crashed backwards into the stairwell. I broke my fall halfway down. By now I'd really lost it. Charged up on high-octane anger, I raced back up the stairs to get out on the terraces. I still wanted those mugs. It was nothing personal: I was high on an adrenalin rush. A mass of jeans and trainers was waiting as I neared the top of the stairs. Whooping and yelling, they jumped and kicked me all the way back down the flight of steps. As I landed in a heap I knew I had to get up. There was no baying mob around me as I staggered to my feet. As I focused in the semi-dark, I could see why. I was in the refreshment area under the stand, with Old Bill stood all around. They looked at me as if I'd dropped in from Hell. As my eyes adjusted to the poor light, there was Danny still lashing out, this time at the coppers. I was thinking, the job's over, mate. Don't fight the Old Bill, you'll just get yerself nicked. In my mind I rehearsed my lines: 'Self defence, Officer. There was only two of us against a mob of two hundred, attacked 'cos we were black.'

I rushed over to where Dan was grappling with a group of sweaty coppers. I said to the one with the stripes, 'Listen, he's me mate. I can call him off but you'd better not nick us. We was jumped on for being black, that's why my pal's so angry.'

I got the assurances I wanted, and yelled to Dan, 'Rest easy, pal. They ain't gonna nick us.'

Rucking with the cops, Dan hadn't noticed me. Relief showed all over his face and he stopped throwing his long arms around. The cops ushered us out though another entrance and escorted us back in front of The Shelf. The Yids just looked on with grudging respect. I was half tempted to have a go at them again, but I just grinned at them through the fencing and gave a two-fingered victory salute. As we stepped out on to the side of the pitch the roar of applause was deafening. I looked on the field and

Three

realised there were still no players out. 'Fuckin' hell, Danny, that's all for us.' Danny's great big chops grinned from ear to ear. 'You're a West Ham hero, Dan, mate. You're on the firm for life,' I said. As we walked through the perimeter fence into the enclosure the whole West Ham following rose as one to cheer us home: 'West Ham run from no one! West Ham run from no one!' they chanted. The sixty who'd been in The Shelf, guys like Swallow, Wildman, Brett, Sherrin Harris gathered around us. I looked at Wildman, who'd never seen me in action before and said, 'Now you know why there can only be one Cass.'

That day went down in football folklore. Alastair Campell, now Prime Minister Tony Blair's press spokesman, was then a reporter on the *Daily Mirror*. He went undercover to witness the whole day's events. On Monday morning his article took up a page full of the usual bollocks: ICF; Under Fives; calling cards; blades; mounted police. But what left him flabbergasted was the way supporters not involved in the fighting cheered us on instead of condemning us. It was a horrible fact, but the majority of fans actually had a sneaking admiration for the 'mindless minority'.

Maybe that's why the headline above his article read 'Soccer's sickness'.

Chapter Four

We were like locusts, a plague swarming through the country trashing everything in our path. Vandalising the British Rail system, spreading violence to the high streets of our cities. We were scum, making headlines faster than newspapers could print them. Front page, sports pages — a complete industry was feeding off our exploits. Wherever the notorious hooligans of the West Ham InterCity Firm went, controversy followed. You couldn't turn on a radio talk show without someone bleating, 'They've behaved like animals. They're destroying our national sport. What are the government doing about it?'

The government blamed the courts for only handing out fines to football thugs. Joe Public wanted us birched. The country needed a court case where someone could hand out a stiff sentence to show these hooligans the error of their ways.

Your honour, I think we have just the case. It's as bad as it can get. Two football matches within two miles of each other on the same night, riots, two fans in a coma and West Ham supporters were involved in both incidents. The defendant, m'lud, is Cass Pennant.

Shoved in a metal box prison van like a battery hen, I was whisked away from the Old Bailey, the judge's speech still ringing in my ears: 'The time has come to make an example ... this scourge on society must stop ... I sentence you to three years. Take him down.'

Like a steel toecap to the head, I felt my lights go out. Three years, no more West Ham, no more laughs with the gang. What about my job? I was halfway through my college exams. It couldn't be happening. As the verdict was announced, I gave my brief a look that said, 'You hear what that bastard's saying? He's twisted this jury.' Sensing I was rearing up for an outburst, my barrister shuffled over offering to discuss it downstairs in the cells. Four big jailers were already on me. This is their buzz, pouncing on behalf of society to take away a man's freedom. As they took me down, cursing and swearing, I tried to look at the jury. I needed to see from their faces why they did me. Not one of them would look at me. Doors slammed, keys jangled and I was down for the Scrubs.

I had been briefed to expect the worst. I'd been on bail for two years, that's sentence enough. I was 18, I had a home, an apprenticeship and I even wore a suit for the trial — no sign of a Doc Marten boot. All these pointers count when they reckon your sentence. Everything taken into account, the worst I could expect was borstal. Prison was unheard of for football thugs unless you'd done the Old Bill and then you could count on three to six weeks. But this was *three years*. The jury's verdict was not guilty with the hard bit, GBH, but affray was just the slip-in charge, a last-minute move by the Old Bill to close all routes and make sure I was nicked on something.

I had to ask my solicitor what affray was. Threatening behaviour, abusive language, assault on the police — they were all occupational hazards when you took up life on the terraces. But affray was an new one. My lawyer James McGoldrick said it was a very diverse charge which could cover anything from IRA bombers to more than two people having a punch-up in a pub. I was fuming: 'So I'm a one-man riot, am I? You'll have to speak to my mum for me, I can't face her.'

He said, 'We'll certainly contact Mrs Chambers and assure her we're putting in the strongest of appeals.' Three years for a poxy football match. We were football thugs, not hardened criminals. Take out Saturday afternoons and most of us had clean records — law-abiding citizens.

Wormwood Scrubs loomed over the meat wagon. It looked as imposing and impregnable as the Tower of London. As I passed through the gates, the judge's words began to sink in: 'To make an example ... three years ...' I felt totally and utterly defeated.

Now the processing routine: 'Spread your legs and bend over.' A pervert posing as a doctor, but dressed as a screw, went under my balls and gazed into my arse. After that was the ultimate humiliation — I became a prison number. A trusty issued my clothes and on the way back to the cell another black prisoner pointed out that I'd been stitched up on the clothing they'd given me. There was no slip-over jumper, the worst style of plastic shoes and ill-fitting jeans you wouldn't be seen dead in. My old self came roaring back. I was going to kick up a fuss and sort out that trusty but the screws told me I'd got what I was entitled to. They led me on to the wing where everybody was on 23-hour bang-up. A card on the cell door listed surname, number and what bird I was doing. I was lucky and there was only one prisoner greeting me but there were three beds in this ten feet by six feet cell. I longed for a good night's sleep because it had been a long day, and I didn't care if it was on a sponge mattress with itchy blankets. My feet hung a good twelve inches over the iron bed end, a light glowed permanently in the ceiling. I couldn't sleep for the sound of the spy hole flap in the door being pushed aside ... again and again and again. My cell mate said, 'It's just the screws checking and counting. The sad bastards do nothing else all day, counting and turning keys.' The flap went again but this screw wasn't moving on. More footsteps outside the cell. I leapt up and went to the door. The flap dropped shut. I put my ear to the door and could hear a screw saying, 'Did you see him? That's our first hooligan.'

Next day my downfall was all over the papers. The whole country was rejoicing that at last somebody had got tough on football violence. Radio stations held phone-in debates all day. I was now infamous, but these people having their say on hooligans knew nothing. They didn't know us and didn't understand us. That night the flap started again. There were more voices. Mad as hell, I rushed the door, crashing against the metal.

'Anything the matter, Pennant?' asked a voice from the other side.

'Yeah, what's your problem? What you keep looking at me for?' I screamed.

'We just want to look at the Scrubs' first hooligan. You're all over the news, you know.'

Cass Pennant

Compared to the usual crowd of burglars, thieves, robbers and life's losers, I was a novelty to the screws. The inmates thought I was different, too. Whenever I appeared on the landing to collect my food or during the half-hour exercise, a cry of HOO ... LEE ... GUN would go up. I'd turn instinctively to face my foe but it would just be the sing-song call of the Jamaican prisoners, walking off laughing. 'Hoo ... lee ... gun. Yo! Alright, man.' To break the bang-up, prisoners would follow the news and then, because the Scrubs was an allocation prison where everyone came from the London courts, they'd look out for celebrity prisoners.

Inside prison I was a leper, not because I was a convicted football hooligan but because of my background. I began to question just where I belonged. On the outside, I was just Cass, an alright geezer to my friends, an absolute bastard to my enemies. Outside there were no colours, your mates were your mates and though I was black I was English through and through. Inside nick was a different world. It was the most racist place I'd ever been in my life. The whole wing was segregated black against white. Racist taunts I hadn't heard since my childhood were spat out with real venom. The walls rang with the sound of white prisoners calling black inmates 'nigger', 'coon' and a new one to me, 'swartzer'. This was the favourite, so I assumed it was borstal slang. The ever-watching screws just seemed to tut in approval.

The screws ruled with sheer oppression. Blacks never got the best jobs. Put a few in the Muppet shop, but get the balance right: be careful of pairing too many up in the cells; end their visits at the allocated time; if it kicks off, use full force because they're violent by birth. Finally, get shot of them to Camp Hill prison — that'll wreck their visits.

Oh, well, I could always turn to my poor oppressed black brothers for friendship. No one can say I ain't black, can they? Don't you believe it. When you came out of the cells all you could hear on the landings was black guys shouting out 'bomber clart', 'ras clart'. Everything was clart this and clart that. If they wanted your attention it was 'Yo!' It was nothing I hadn't heard before going around London but the intensity was scary. I'd never known what it was like to be brought up in a black neighbourhood, so when they gave me a friendly greeting, like, 'Yo, ras,' I'd come back with 'Awright, mate'. The black guys would give me a wide berth because I talked like a Cockney. To them I was choc-ice: black on the outside, white in the middle.

Choc-ice, my arse! I'd fought more battles for being black than those lot had ever done. They could never understand that if they'd had my background they'd talk like me, too. I couldn't change the colour of my skin and I wasn't about to change my principles. I was black, British and proud of it. I hadn't survived white society to take this shit from my own colour. I would fight someone for supporting the wrong team but never for being the wrong race.

I was locked up with a black guy who the white prisoners nicknamed Zulu. The card on the door said eight years and everyone knew it was for chopping a man's hand off with a kebab knife. My man Zulu flipped his lid when a caller to a late-night radio phone-in started bad-mouthing Idi Amin, Uganda's tyrant dictator. I agreed and said, 'The man's a bastard; he's killing his own people.'

Zulu went berserk. In a split second, he was off the top bunk, pummelling me on the bed underneath. This unprovoked attack made me blazing mad. I steamed out of bed in my underpants. We crashed and slammed against the iron bunk. The other cellmate just sat on his bed speechless as we smashed the sparse furniture and catapulted off the walls. All the pent-up frustration I'd been holding in ever since I arrived at the Scrubs came flooding out as I fought for my life. Zulu was six feet one, his skin the deep black of Dominica. He was strong as a lion and wild as Idi Amin himself.

Four

Battered, bruised and exhausted I stood like a lion tamer facing him with the chair he'd slung at me. I'd taken his best and fought him to a stop. He looked as exhausted as I was. I taunted him over his bullshit about the black man going back to Africa. I shouted at him, 'If you wanna live in a mud hut in a country where blacks are killing each other, then go. But don't take your sound system, the gold rings and the BMW you got while you were living here, you fucking hypocrite!'

I'd got him so mad he picked up a razor from the corner cupboard, the only bit of furniture left unscathed. He came forward, slashing at me with the blade. I whacked him back with the chair. He hacked the air again, trying to slice open my bare chest. I thought, Jesus, this arsehole's got nothing to lose; his sentence has decided that. The alarm buzzer is at the other end of the smashed-up cell. It wouldn't have mattered if I had rung it. It was the middle of the night, one solitary screw was on duty and he wouldn't give a shit — one less black to worry about. I called Zulu's bluff: 'I know what you're in for. You've nothing to lose, but I'm not backing down. You'll have to kill me first.' As suddenly as it started, it was over. Zulu climbed into bed cursing under his breath, muttering something about me not being a real black man. I spent the rest of the night on my bunk with one eye open. In the morning the screws moved us to different cells.

I ended up sharing with a hard man white prisoner. His name was Frank Burke from the Slough–Newbury manor. He had jet black hair, eyebrows that met in the middle and a fighter's physique. He'd already done more than one borstal and a few lots of porridge and now he had a four-year sentence. He wouldn't take any shit from the screws, They had it in for him, but he knew his rights and they couldn't do much. He was a real survivor and we struck up a friendship straight away. After last roll call and bang-up, he pulled out a small lump of puff and passed it over with a Rizla. I declined, but he said, 'Take it. It's the only escape you'll get from here.'

I hesitated, then asked him to roll it. He fell about laughing. 'That's a first, a swartzer who can't roll!'

I took a drag. 'I'll tell you another first. I'm a black man who can't dance, either.' Then the four walls started moving. I had to lie down. We laughed, joked and swapped stories. A good cell mate can make a real difference. When you're banged up with somebody 24 hours a day you find out a lot about yourself and the blokes sharing your peter. In all the time I was banged up with Burkey I never saw a weakness.

By now, I was used to the sights and sounds of prison: the constant screaming from the bars all night;

prisoners yelling from wing to wing; hardened cons going to pieces over a Dear John letter; insane inmates tapping the pipes all night. The pipes were the worst. Tap! Tap! Tap! The sound travelled all along the cells. You saw weak souls taken out of their cells, their wrists slashed and dripping blood. Most of it was a cry for help, but some never returned to their cells.

In the middle of the night a screw who always called me Hooligan slung open the cell door and shoved in some rockabilly kid. 'What?'

'Don't worry, Pennant. We'll have him moved first thing in the morning. Just look after him.' The door slammed shut. The kid was shaking like a leaf and tried to tell me his problems. I didn't want to know. 'Look, kid, we've all got problems in 'ere, so shut up and get some kip.' I was woken by a terrible stench. He was only having a shit in the corner of the cell. I had a golden rule — nobody shits in my cell, ever. I wanted to kill him. I leapt out of bed, ranting and raving. The kid had shit himself and pissed everywhere. He cowered in the corner, apologising for the trouble he'd caused. I backed off because something wasn't quite right with this kid. The shit parcel went out of the window for one of the cons to clean up in the morning.

The rockabilly kid began to tell me the most horrendous tale. He was a car thief who was only inside for breaking his probation, but the screws had paired him with a killer who was detained at Her Majesty's pleasure with no release date. The killer warned the screws that he wouldn't share a cell with anybody and when they ignored him, he buggered the kid. I accused rockabilly of not acting like a man. He cried out in pain and told me this big bastard had beaten him to a pulp with a lump of wood and an iron bed leg. The kid whimpered, 'He was gonna kill me if I didn't let him. He's killed once already, I knew he meant it.'

I'd heard enough and told the kid to sleep. First thing in the morning I told the screw that the kid needed hospital treatment. As the screws went down to see him, I nipped along the landing to the cells of two people I needed to talk to and gave them the SP. All the landing doors were opening for breakfast and I got a few cons to crowd the duty screws as the two blokes I'd spoken to, with two more in tow, moved across the landing to the killer's cell. We all looked the other way to avoid attention. Moments later, the alarm went off — the boys had done the job. When the screws got to the bastard's cell he was only fit for the hospital wing and ship out.

The long, hot summer of '78 was no time to be shut away from the sunlight. You could feel the tension simmering, just waiting to explode. The black population inside the Scrubs was growing daily. Nobody had seen so many black faces in one nick. The whites had always had the numbers to keep control. Now they were under threat. Twenty-three-hour bang-ups in the sweltering heat, the endless pipe-tapping and constant hollering of the West Indians. White prisoners believed in doing their bird quietly. Attract no attention and you can go about your business, smuggling drugs, flogging burn, changing currency, without attracting attention. The only time prisoners could wheel and deal was on the exercise yard. There you could see everybody who was on your wing. C-Wing at the Scrubs was the biggest in the country with six hundred inmates. As the whites walked round the yard they felt intimidated by the black explosion. They seethed at how the blacks had taken over football in the yard. The problem between Zulu and me had been sorted since that turnout in the cell and I knew I had his respect because he would pick me for his team. We would often play against the best team in the yard — the one run by Ambrose Mendy. He was a smallish, slim-built black guy out of Mile End and spoke like an East Ender. He was never fazed when he heard me speaking in the best East End voice you're likely to hear from a dark man. Ambrose was so passionate about his football he not only pissed off the players but the cons who were watching, too. Because of the game and Ambrose's arguments the guys who weren't playing lost out on exercise time. One or two of them took on Ambrose over it, and more often than not he'd talk his way out of it. He was one of the greatest talkers I'd ever seen. When it came to charisma he was on a par with Muhammad Ali or Jesse Jackson. Many of the cons I came across were total bullshitters, but whatever Ambrose said he'd done on the out, he could prove. He showed me photos of himself in a white top hat and tails as the MC on the unlicensed fight at the Rainbow between The Guv'nor, Lenny McLean, and Pretty Boy Roy Shaw. Ambrose would keep us captivated in the Muppet Shop with his stories. Some of his scams seemed so unbelievable. I was in the Scrubs three times between 1978 and 1985 and every time Ambrose would be inside serving a fresh sentence. You guessed it: for one of the scams he'd told us about!

Later, I met Ambrose at a club where I worked on the door. Millwall's star player John Fashanu was having a private party there and many of his guests were affluent blacks, most of them sports personalities. With his smooth tongue and love of the good life, Ambrose had got into this circle. Black players had just made a major breakthrough in establishing themselves in pro football. Guys like Cyril Regis,

Four

Laurie Cunningham, Fash, Bright and Wrighty.

Looking round the room Ambrose said to me, 'You're a football man, Cass, see how the black players from different London clubs stick together like an elite unit. But I bet you haven't noticed that none of them have agents.' Ambrose was sharp as a razor and he was hustling to be their manager. I thought to myself, how are you going to hide your past, Ambrose? All these players were high profile. It would only take a screw or Old Bill to reveal that the agent was a fraud specialist. But I'd forgotten about Ambrose's silver tongue. Within days of that conversation, he'd signed up West Ham's Paul Ince. Hammers fans loved Incey because he was hard and could stick it up the opposition. But before Ambrose could say 'I told you I'd do it', the whole thing went pear-shaped. Ince was being sold to Man United but while he was still officially a West Ham player he appeared in the *Sun* wearing a hated red United shirt. The fans were so outraged West Ham had to stop playing him until the deal went through. Even the club who were selling him couldn't believe how Ince could insult the supporters who'd idolised him. Today, more than ten years later, Hammers fans still cry 'Judas' and boo every time Ince gets the ball at Upton Park. A long while afterwards, Ambrose admitted to me that the Ince picture fiasco had been a cock-up. No insult had ever been intended. Ambrose was going to be abroad on business when the Ince deal went through. So it made good business sense to have a photo session done in advance. But a misunderstanding led one of the girls in Ambrose's office to wrongly hand over the photos to a reporter and the journalist knew he had gold dust in his hands. So there you have it, that photo of Ince in the Man U shirt should never have come out when it did. For some unknown reason Ince remained silent until two years ago when he offered some half-hearted words of regret in the Hammers News. But he has never explained to the fans what really happened.

Back in the prison yard on a hot summer afternoon two black teams were playing each other. It was too warm for walking around and hundreds of white cons sat on the edge of the makeshift pitch. One of them was East End legend George Davis, a minicab driver who ended up doing 20 years after the Old Bill claimed he'd taken part in an armed robbery on an electricity board office in Ilford, Essex. The evidence against him was iffy, to say the least. You couldn't go anywhere in London in those days without seeing 'GEORGE DAVIS IS INNOCENT, OK' daubed on walls. Somehow a Free George Davis banner ended up wrapped around the top of the Post Office tower. Even police snouts were so outraged they held a silent mutiny and stopped giving info to the Old Bill. Two years after being sent down, George walked free from Albany jail. But a year later he was banged up again for robbing a security firm delivering fifty grand to a bank in Holloway. The masked gang had a shoot-out in the street with cops before taking an 84-year-old passer-by hostage. This time George was fingered by a grass. White cons in the yard all looked up to George and his Cat A mates, but a lot of the blacks just thought he was a mug for doing another armed robbery. Well, when the ball went into George's group they didn't throw the ball back. One of them shouted, 'We ain't no swartzer's joey.' One of the black guys trampled in among the white guys to get the ball. George Davis reared up and Zulu flipped his lid. That was the spark that ignited the tinder box. I was in the shower block at the time and as I came round the corner five white cons I didn't know rushed me. But they didn't attack. Instead, they formed a protective ring around me. Everywhere I looked black was fighting white. The first real race riot in modern prison history had erupted. It was my worst nightmare — the day when the colour of a man's skin prevailed over who he must fight. There was none of the adrenalin buzz normally associated with a fight. This was bewildering, confusing, shocking. It was a fight gripped by fear — fear of your fellow man, fear of your own brother. Every man was ready, willing and able to fight the nearest man of a different colour with nothing even said.

The screws did nothing to stop it until the dog section arrived. Then they bundled us back on to the wing. As my cell door closed I could hear fighting still going on along the landings. The whole prison was on 24-hour lock-up. We were allowed out only one at a time, frog-marched to meals and back again. I thought about those white cons who had formed a protective ring around me. They were just normal blokes who thought I was an alright guy. Eventually life returned to normal, and much to my relief the black guys I got along with in the Muppet Shop were all OK, even though they had been in the exercise yard at the time. The white cons had steamed into the rastas, the militant guys with the dreadlocks. The rastas had given plenty back but as usual had been outnumbered. In the weeks after the riot a lot of blacks were shipped out to other nicks. Zulu remained down in the punishment block, firmly established as top man.

A card game called Kooluki was the national sport in prison. It's a kind of two-deck rummy where you score points. Now I like a game of cards — three-card brag was my main vice in life — and I really got into this Kooluki. To play it well you need a photographic

Four

memory and it really hooked up the brain and made the day pass quickly. I played in a little circle with Delroy and the guys in the workshop. As long as the work for the day had been done, the Muppet Shop screws, who were really civvies, didn't bother too much. Playing cards here wasn't like being on the out with a few bob. The maximum wage inside at the time was £1.50 a week, so life's little luxuries, like Mars bars, biscuits and burn were used as stakes. Come pay day I'd pay up or collect debts owing. I've always considered myself a gambler and a true gambler always pays his debts but one week I was in debt by more than I could pay back. It was all right; nobody was going anywhere, so you could carry your debt on or maybe even win it back.

I didn't know I had a problem until bang-up when the daylight through the spyhole blacked out and a deep, angry voice growled, 'Hooligan, you fucking owe me two packets of biscuits.' I was playing cards with Burkey and I couldn't believe this con was coming down on my door for two poxy packets of biscuits. I looked at my cellmate in total disbelief. What is this shit? My word has always been my bond. I was mad as hell inside, but I got up to the door to see reason. The guy on the other side was one of the little circle from the Muppet Shop. Bramble was his name; a big bloke, six feet six tall who looked even bigger because he had a high forehead. He just carried on giving it large. Inside I exploded. 'You're fucking knocked. You hear me, Bramble, you're fucking knocked!' I raged, smashing the door with my fists.

Bramble fucked off down the landing but a little while later he was back at the door. 'Hoo ... lee ... gun, you think you're tough behind that door. Wait 'til tomorrow. You owe me.'

Now I had a problem.

'You either pay him, or do him,' said Burkey matter-of-factly.

'Well, I ain't paying him. He's knocked.'

I didn't sleep much that night. I knew what I was going to do and I just wanted that door to open. I downed my breakfast quick, slipped on my prison boots and stepped lively to the workshop. Good, Bramble wasn't there yet. I deliberately took a seat nearest the gangway opposite the spot where Bramble would sit. He came in laughing and grinning his way up the gangway. I was out of my seat like a panther — BANG! — I caught him with the sweetest uppercut I'd ever thrown. He collapsed like a giraffe, lying totally bemused in the gangway. No one in prison had seen me perform before and the other cons looked on in disbelief. 'Blood clart,' exclaimed one prisoner. They all knew Bramble from the out and he had a reputation as a hard bastard. I stood over him, but he didn't wanna know. A screw walked in. I hissed, 'Geddup, ya mug, unless you want us both nicked.'

Rubbing his chin, Bramble climbed gingerly to his feet. For the rest of the week he left well alone, but come pay day Bramble was still muttering that I owed him two lots of biscuits. I was unfazed. In fact I was looking forward to giving him the same again. Soon after another, more confident voice started outside the cell door, 'Hoo ... lee ... gun. You think you're tough behind that door 'cos you dealt with my brother. But now you owe me. I've taken on his debt and you'll not knock me.' The spyhole flap dropped and he was gone. I knew who it was ... Zulu.

Burkey looked at me across the cell. 'Tough one to call,' he said, thinking back to the race riot.

'I know,' I replied, but I was thinking back to our fight in the cell.

'What are you going to do?'

'Dunno, but I ain't paying him. As far as I'm concerned the debt's paid.'

Burkey's bushy black eyebrows formed a frown. 'Taking on Zulu is like taking them all on.'

'All who?' I asked.

'Swartzers,' he said quietly.

I lay back on the bed staring up at the ceiling light. Burkey sensed I was troubled. 'I'm with you all the way if anyone else jumps in, Cass.' He meant it too.

The screws thought he was a psycho loner and I'd never seen a con even attempt to bother him. I would have to attack Zulu during the morning but he didn't work, so the only time to get him would be in the exercise yard, where he held court with all the black cons. That was my problem, I was ready to take on Zulu but not the whole Zulu nation.

Burkey must have read my thoughts. 'It's going to have to be breakfast. He's on his own then, you and him,' he said.

The boots came on; I quickly grabbed my breakfast but instead of going back to the cell, I hid in the recess. The other landing was out. Zulu carried his breakfast on a tray as he climbed the stairs to where I was waiting for him. I could see my size 12s would be in line with his head. I heard his feet pounding up the steps. It would just be like running up and taking a corner kick. Remembering the fury of that night he slashed me with a razor, I started to run, my feet crashing on the metal landing — Whack, I took that corner kick. Clang! The metal tray went flying up in the air as Zulu somersaulted backwards down the stairs. I'd got him good, even if the tray had protected his head a bit. I'd done him so good I was battling to stay mad inside; I just really wanted to burst out laughing. Who's sorry now? But I hadn't reckoned with Zulu's madness. He didn't fall all the way to the bottom of the stairwell but managed to check himself on the other cons following up the steps. He groaned and grunted like a wounded animal — and charged to the top of the stairs. I didn't think anyone could come back at me after that boot I'd got in on him. Still, I held the top of the stairs and screamed, 'C'mon Zulu! C'mon!' He steamed in to me — my height advantage counted for nothing as again I was fighting for my life. It was like trading punches in a submarine. He battled me back along the cramped landing, his fists crashing on my head and upper body. But I could soak up the punishment. I was loving it. This was my kind of fight. I was back on the terraces again, throwing crazy swinging punches and high kicks, trying to take his head off with my heavy prison boots. None of the cons would go back into their cells: they were witnessing a classic. It came to an abrupt end. Zulu wasn't in front of me any longer. Seven screws jumped on me. I looked through the mass of uniforms to see Zulu trussed up and on his way down to the punishment block.

The following day I appeared before the Governor's kangaroo court.

'Anything to say, Pennant?'

'Nothing, sir.'

Fighting was a serious offence. The Governor could add days or weeks to your sentence, leave you segregated down in the punishment block or at best you'd lose privileges with no recreation for a fortnight. Stood in front of the Governor's desk, jammed between two screws, I thought that anything he doled out would have been worth it — I'd fought Zulu to a standstill. Go on, just give me the worst ... but not Camphill, that hellhole in the back of beyond where they sent all the troublemakers nobody wanted.

Instead, he gave me two weeks loss of privileges — nothing at all. As they frog-marched me back to my cell one of the screws said, 'Hey, Pennant, you won't have to worry about your mate. He's being shipped out to Camphill.'

Two weeks loss of privileges was not equal punishment, so how did their apparently racist system work in my favour? It seems the prison system has ratings — bad blacks, not-so-bad blacks. They'd never forgotten the race riots.

Zulu was their most hated.

Chapter Five

Sheffield Wednesday away. It was the last game of the 1981 season and West Ham had already clinched the championship and promotion to Division One. I hadn't been to many matches that year because there were only a handful of teams in the second division to have a battle with: Newcastle, Cardiff, Chelsea and, of course, Sheffield Wednesday. Clubs like Orient, Notts County and Shewsbury hardly had proper teams, never mind real hooligans as supporters. The ICF was at its peak — we were the toughest, meanest firm of football hooligans Britain had ever seen. We were also the best dressed. Poor Northern sods were still wearing jean jackets from the seventies but the ICF uniform was now shiny green American air force MA jackets, Lois jeans and designer trainers.

Any hopes of a pitched battle that night were

dashed the minute we pulled in at Sheffield station. As the sea of green spilled off the InterCity, the police were waiting for us in force. All seven hundred of us filed out of the station like cattle, hemmed in by coppers. A copper fell in behind me, hassling all the time, 'Move faster! Stay on the pavement.' I assumed it was all part of a risky game. Perhaps this Old Bill was hoping he could nick me before I'd even seen the match. I shot him an evil stare that said, 'What's your problem?' He just harassed me more. I blanked him and kept telling myself, 'Keep walking, Cass, ignore him.'

Soccer grounds always seem to be miles from the railway station and after half an hour we reached Hillsborough stadium. One of the officers started pointing me out to other coppers on ground duty. One of the lads whispered, 'Watch yerself, Cass, they've got it in for ya.'

A copper walking with them had said, 'I thought all you West Ham ICF boys were National Front. What you doing with a black guy? He looks like your leader; what are you lot doing following a black fella?' The boys didn't like that and a couple of them jumped down the copper's throat. 'That's Cass. He's our mate, we don't wanna hear it, OK.' The copper walked off.

West Ham won one–nil but the game was boring and there was no trouble, not even verbals. On the way back to the station the police were bang on us again and even the Artful Dodger couldn't have given them the slip. We were herded on the non-stop express back to London. As soon as we were onboard the card school started. Ted, Simo, Kingy and Gravesend Terry were up for a game, so deal me in. They didn't call me The Legend for nothing. In those two hours on the train I could win a load of dough at three-card brag. The train hung around for half an hour and the lads were getting impatient. We wanted to be out of this boring Northern town and back to the Smoke in time to have a scrap on the Underground with mobs from other London teams making their way home from away matches.

Soon word came down the train that three or four of our lads had managed to skip the escort and been toe to toe with a bunch of Wednesday supporters in town. One of our mob had stabbed a Sheffield fan, so at least the ICF had left a calling card. A little while later, when the train was under way and there was no chance of the cops catching him, the guy who'd done the stabbing wandered up and down bragging how he'd carved up this geezer. He went a bit sheepish when he came into our carriage because everyone with me was a right heavy. To us, this incident he was boasting about was nothing.

Suddenly, the train squealed to a halt in the middle

of nowhere. It was pitch dark. It moved on again at a snail's pace and eventually stopped at Chesterfield. The station was deserted. Uniformed police started appearing on the platform. We just thought some of the underlings must have got bored and trashed the buffet or pulled the emergency cord. We sent word down the train to get the young 'uns to start behaving themselves or at this rate we'd never get to London. Some of the lads leaned out of the windows, chatting to the Old Bill, and one of the coppers let slip there'd been a stabbing in Sheffield and they were looking for the culprit on our train. The news spread like wildfire. Without moving from their chairs, the hierarchy sent word out, 'No one talks to the Old Bill. Tell the bragger to lose himself and if he still has the knife — lose it, too. That goes for anyone else with tools on 'em.'

Coppers swarmed all over the train, pulling off anyone who was wearing green air force jackets, to be searched on the platform. Everyone stayed stum. A decent copper came into our carriage. We had nothing to hide. He told us, 'A lad's been stabbed, bad they reckon.' So now we knew it was serious. They wanted to speak to everyone in a green bomber jacket. Always the showman, I was wearing a green leather safari jacket, worth four hundred quid. I'd won it from my mate Lenny Aylen in a game of cards. The

Five

copper searched us in the carriage then went off down the train. I thought no more about it.

All of a sudden, a face peered through the carriage window from the platform and he was staring directly at me. I knew I was clean, and the other ICF top men who were sat with me weren't worried either; they were cool customers. How's this for ice cool? Earlier in the season at Newcastle the soppy Geordie bastards spotted me and started chanting, 'Chicken George! Chicken George!' So West Ham shouted back, 'Cass is our leader! Cass is our leader!' The next thing a petrol bomb whizzed over the top of my Afro and hit two of our lads stood behind me, setting light to their trousers. As the petrol bomb lay on the terrace, spewing flames and smoke, the ICF leaders stood round it ... warming their hands!

That face was still at the window and I sensed his eyes were on me and nobody else. I couldn't believe it. It was one of the coppers from Sheffield. What was he doing here in Chesterfield? I gave him a fearful glare and he moved away. Next thing he's in the carriage. 'You! Off! Out!' On the platform I expected the usual: take everything out of your pockets; search; pick it all up again; get on the train; be a good boy.

Instead, two CID men took me away to a waiting room on the end of the platform.

They ordered me inside. I was sitting on a bench,

all cool. This big fat bloke pulled round a table and plonked himself behind it. His mate, who looked like Dennis Waterman from *The Sweeney*, leaned against the wall. Sid the Lard thumped his fist on the table and snarled: 'A kid's gonna die in hospital tonight. One of your fucking bastard ICF mates stabbed him and put him there.' I felt for the kid, I really did, but I thought what's this got to do with me?

They said they'd checked the files on me. Sid the Lard started going on about my criminal record, how I'd run at five hundred Sheffield United supporters, how I'd done three years for football violence. They knew I was notorious.

The big lump shoved his face so close to mine I could taste his dirty breath. 'If that kid dies tonight, that's murder. Now, think about this one Mr Tough Guy.' He told me he thought I'd done it.

I jumped up and raged, 'What the fuck's going on here? You cunts have been bugging me all fucking day. What the fuck's your problem?'

At last I was taken to a police station. I wasn't alone; the cops had dragged in four of the West Ham Under Fives. Some of them couldn't have been much older than 14. One of them was Juggy, a skinny kid with ears as big as the FA Cup, another was a lad called Joscelyn. The bragger wasn't among them. They were all laughing and joking. Obviously they

Five

didn't realise we were in serious shit. Cops were all around, so I ran my finger across my throat, warning them what would happen if they talked. Stripped to my underpants so my clothes could be sent for forensic tests, I was slung in a cell where the CID men started questioning me. He said, 'We've got kids of 13 in here who won't say a bloody word because of you. What is it with you Cockneys? You think you're so hard.'

I took it without fighting back. I wasn't going to give them an excuse to charge me with police assault. I didn't think it would go any further because I knew I was innocent.

They went out. A bit later the kids started banging on my cell door. The police were letting them go. 'Don't worry, Cass, you'll be out of here soon,' they chirped.

Some hope. The door flew open and the cops came in again four-handed. The CID man laid into me: 'You? Fucking innocent? That's shit. Do you know what we found?' The lump of a detective had a crumpled fiver in his fat hand. He slowly opened the bank note to reveal a bright red stain. My heart sank. My whole body went to jelly. He rammed the fiver right in front of my eyes. 'What's that look like?' My mind was screaming, 'It's blood!' But I couldn't say a word. The copper said it for me, 'It's blood. This stain's blood!' I knew I was innocent, so where had it come from? He was there again, 'Guess where it's from? Your pocket, that's where!'

They left me looking at four walls. My world had collapsed. I was looking at life for a blood-stained fiver I won on the card table. I kept thinking back to that card school on the train. The losers would get up and sit somewhere else and a new player would step in. A couple of the new players were members of the little posse involved in the stabbing. Now I was the biggest loser of the lot.

They took me out of the cells and threw some rags at me. The jeans were miles too short for a man of six feet four. The shirt had hardly any buttons. It wouldn't have mattered if they'd all been there — it was far too small to stretch over my barrel chest. My street cred in showing these northerners how to dress was no more. I looked like a scarecrow. They shoved me into a waiting police car. I thought we were going to HQ so they could break me.

Instead we pulled up at the hospital where the kid was dying. Wearing rags, handcuffed and sandwiched between four CID heavies, I looked like a convict. Nurses watched on open-mouthed as the cops jammed me into a lift, then took me on to a ward. The injured guy, Alan Butler, lay propped up on a bed in front of me, wired up to loads of machines. I

Top: Crazy, but great times: the West Ham Barmy Army.

Below: The Warriors! That's me in the middle with Tony Ward, Big Steve and Cousin Darren. We got dressed up for a fancy dress contest at our local, but later stayed in our gear to lead 400 fans to Tottenham v. Liverpool, after the Sunderland match was called off. Everyone thought I was nuts!

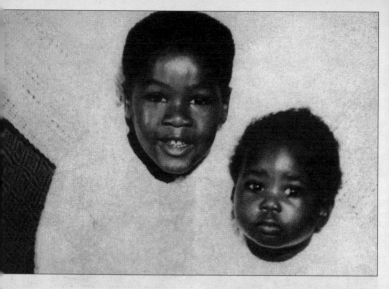

Top: Me and my foster sister Beverley, who was also a Barnado's kid: we owe a lot to that great organisation.

Below left: Mr and Mrs Chambers, my foster Mum and Dad. It means a lot to me that they lived just long enough to know that I finally settled down.

Below right: Bev and me with our foster parents.

Top left: My mates, Neil Bowers and Terry Sherrin, who led the campaign to No 10 Downing Street after my arrest for the Sheffield stabbing.

Top right: With Mark Kaylor, West Ham hero and boxing legend. He is thanking me for sorting things out when the threat of violence nearly ruined his boxing career.

Bottom left: Me with the treasured FA Cup.

Bottom right: The Hammers fans in Germany in 1976.

Top: May 1982. When news got out that I had been arrested for the Sheffield stabbing, the West Ham fans defied a march ban, clashing with a CND march en route, to campaign outside 10 Downing Street and protest my innocence.

Below: More recently, the old firm turn out for West Ham's first trip back to Europe since 1980/81. As Cass's son, my boy was the only kid allowed on this coach trip. (He hates Milwall as well, though he's too young to know why!)

Top: West Ham's south bank in the 1970s: it became a no-go area for away fans.

Below: Leaders of the terraces mind a real leader: me and Natalie Leslie were appointed as Harold Wilson's bodyguards for the day.

Back in the nightclub security days. *Top*: Danny Byles and me at Kisses nightclub and, *below*, Lenny Aylen and me running security for a Showaddywaddy gig.

Top left: With my good mate Bill Kelly: a dead ringer for Mr T!! Any security bookings I get, he's the first name I pencil in.

Top right: The man who puts the Red in Redhill, Big QPR fan Johnny Wraith.

Below: Tony, Wally and Martin Bowers. I've had many adventures with them, and can count on them all.

looked hard — not fierce — at his ghostly white face. Had we ever had a battle before? Had we given him verbals somewhere? No. I was looking at a total stranger. Butler mumbled to the cops, 'That's him.' With that the cops dragged me out and put me into the car.

Back at the cop shop, they refused to let me make a phone call. I was thrown in front of a court and then banged up in Armley Prison, 35 miles away in Leeds. It was worse than the Scrubs. On the outside Armley looks like a castle; inside it's a dungeon. The stabbing was all over the local papers, and the kid was still hanging on to life by a thread. I was the only Cockney on remand, so everybody in Armley knew all about me but they all kept out of my way. Seven days later I was back in court with a duty solicitor batting for me. I'd told him my story, but past experience told me that in these situations you want your own brief batting for you. The court heard how Butler was stabbed in the stomach. He was still alive, just about. But he was still in a bad way: his spleen had been taken out. And they'd got a suspect with a blood-stained fiver on him. The magistrate looked at me down his nose: 'You're not going back to London. No bail.'

I was banging the walls with frustration. Eventually, I managed to get word to my foster parents to get me my own lawyer. I'd been on remand for nearly two months when one day a barrister arrived in my cell at court. I really cheered up when he said, 'I've come from London and I'm not going back without you.' I told him everything, the whole story including how I came by the blood-stained fiver, and he promised to challenge it. In court my brief asked for the forensic results on the fiver. They wouldn't be ready for two weeks.

A fortnight later I was back in court. The prosecution came up with the same old thing, 'Man been stabbed ... lucky to be alive ... West Ham supporter, he's the man ... blood-stained fiver.' The magistrate said, 'We've had all this. What does the forensic say?' I think the beak thought I was guilty as hell and he was just going through the procedure.

Reluctantly, the prosecutor started reading out the forensic report. I was half-asleep, feeling sorry for myself with not a hope of seeing daylight, when I heard him say 'hamburger sauce'.

Hamburger sauce! The magistrates couldn't believe it. The 'blood stain' on my £5 note had been hamburger sauce. I'd been banged up in Armley for two months for a splodge of hamburger sauce. That was it. I was going home.

I arrived at King's Cross station in the rags the cops had given me with my possessions in a cardboard box. Before I was nicked, I'd been sharing a three-bedroom

Five

house with Lenny Aylen and Laurence Wilkinson in Stratford, East London. I got there to find the landlord had snatched it back. I was out on the street with nowhere to go.

I went out with my West Ham mates to Epping Country Club to celebrate my first night on bail. At the end of the evening a young Hammers fan called Terry Sherrin took pity on me and said I could stay at his house in Forest Gate. I hardly knew him, but that's East End people, hearts of gold — so different from the miserable, vindictive sods I'd grown up with in Slade Green. I kipped on Terry's sofa but at four in the morning I woke up to find a torch shining in my face. There was a policewoman standing over me. I thought I was dreaming. But no, there she was ordering me to get up and stand against the wall. Another copper started rifling through cupboards and drawers.

Terry stumbled down the stairs. 'You alright, Cass?' They made Tel stand next to me and then Terry's dad appeared. I'd never seen his old man before in my life. His nickname was Bombhead and there was no mistaking why. He was short, strong as an ox, with a huge barrel chest and bald head that really did look like the business end of a nuclear missile. Dressed only in his boxer shorts, Bombhead was telling the Old Bill, 'You'll find nothing here,' when suddenly bundles of knock-off cigarettes started flying out of the cupboards. I hadn't a clue what was happening but fags were coming out of hiding places all over the house. Mountains of them piled up on the living room floor.

Bombhead put up his hands. 'Fair cop, Guv.' He was old school and they'd got him bang to rights. It turns out the cigs had been nicked in a lorry heist.

The copper pointed at Terry and asked, 'Who's this?'

'That's my son Terry. Leave him out of it. He's nothing to do with this.'

Then the cop looked at me. 'So, who's the black fella? Your accomplice, no doubt.'

Bombhead stared at me — a hulking great black bloke he'd never clapped eyes on before — turned back to the cop and said, 'He's my other son!'

Chapter Six

Stratford station in East London was deserted. It was a hot summer Sunday afternoon; most people were at home tucking into a Sunday roast. I was an angry young man with the troubles of the world on my shoulders. The supposedly straight world had wrecked my life. I was staring at ten years in jail for protecting a kid I hardly knew.

I'd spent six weeks in the hell hole of Armley jail before I was bailed. The joy of being free did not last long. While I was banged up on remand I lost my home because I couldn't pay the rent. I also lost my job as a council painter with the City of London. I wasn't at home to answer their letters ordering me to turn up for work.

My mind was in such turmoil that even today I can't remember where I was going or why I was on

Stratford station that day. I stared down at the underground rails. I was in so much shit. I was free ... but not free. I wanted to explode. What had I done to deserve being homeless and jobless? The landlord had seized my flat when I didn't pay the rent because I was inside. I had no money, reduced to living on handouts and dossing on floors. I paced up and down the empty platform wondering what fate had in store. Just like every other battle in my life, I had to face this one head on. Whose fault was it? Mine, I guess. But all those injustices couldn't be right. Not for one man.

Prowling up and down the concrete platform deep in my thoughts I was oblivious to anything. I was tooled up — my Stanley knife in my pocket. I never went anywhere without 'Uncle Stan'. It was such a small weapon I just popped it in my back pocket and forgot about it.

Suddenly, the hairs on the back of my neck stood on end. I could feel someone was screwing me. I was just minding my own business, looking down at the track covered in weeds and rubbish, my mind a million miles away from violence. But I could feel something boring into the back of my neck. You only get that feeling if you're in a club or in a pub and someone's screwing you; maybe a rival firm having a bog at you. Or you're in some strange pub up north. 'Who's the big black man?' The locals want to test you out and start screwing you.

I know all about that feeling of being stared at. It's Sunday afternoon: I'm not in a club; I'm not with the boys on a Friday night. Am I going mad? What you don't do is turn around and stare at someone.

But hold on, I can feel it. It's like a sixth sense when trouble's on your back, and I'm feeling it right now. But who would bother me in Stratford, my new home town where everyone knows me? I'm not in South London; I've got no enemies here. So I half-turned and out of the corner of me eye, I saw the shadow of a big black man. I thought, Cass, you're goin' mad. So I turned back again.

But I could still feel the hairs on the back of my neck. A black man staring at me. It didn't make sense. This was the time of the National Front and black geezers stuck together. We were all brothers, right?

I racked my brains. Who had I upset? None of my fights were with black guys, well, not recently, anyway. So, I thought, Cass, you're losing it. With everything that has happened, you're going off yer marbles. Snap out of it, another black man wouldn't be eyeballin' ya.

But I could still feel it. Right, it's off. I slid my hand deep in my back pocket and felt the reassuring shape of the Stanley knife. Big black man or not, we'd end up rolling on the lines and I'd cut him to pieces.

I half-turned again. The black man stood ten feet away, his back against the wall. Huge muscles bulged from his knees below the bottom of his lycra cycling shorts. I'm a big bloke but, like most black guys I know, I've got chicken's legs. I lifted my eyes. This geezer was as big as me. The hood of a grey Lonsdale top was pulled tightly over his head, covering most of his face. Jet black eyes gave me an evil stare.

I thought, Jesus, Cass, you've bitten off more than you can chew this time.

I turned fully to my right to face my opponent. As I moved round I saw straight away what all the fuss was about.

Standing right there behind me, with his back to me but below my eye level was the biggest, meanest skinhead I'd ever seen. His pink, shaven head hardly came up to my chest but his shoulders were as wide as the platform. He was a lump of a bastard. I sized up the situation straight away and heaved a sigh of relief.

It ain't me the black guy is eyeballing, thank God. But I'm charged up now and I can't switch off just like that. All the troubles gnawing in my head wanted to explode.

In front of me is my worst enemy — a Nazi skinhead. The most powerful one I'd ever seen. The only people in Stratford on a Sunday afternoon were tooled-up skins coming back from a Paki-bashing

Six

rally in Brick Lane, the heart of East London's teeming Asian community.

The skinhead is eyeball to eyeball with the big guy. Any second they're going to be at each other hammer 'n' tongs. I'm behind the skinhead and he doesn't even know I'm there.

I thought, Why are you holding back, brother? I know he's the biggest skin I've ever seen, but I think I could handle him. You're like Man Mountain; you'll win this one, fella. But when I looked again, focused properly and got my senses back together, I could see why he was holding back.

The skinhead wasn't alone. He had three obbos, dressed in the skinhead's uniform of Ben Sherman shirts, Staypress trousers and Air Wear Doc Marten bovver boots. Two of them were against the brick wall either side of their prey, the old classic hands in back pocket ready to pull a flick knife. The other was moving in on their victim. Four against one and it's just about to go.

This bastard skin and his three mates had blades but I didn't care — I was going to rip them apart with my bare hands. The big man's eyes unlocked from the skinhead's gaze. The brick shithouse of a skinhead turned to see what his quarry was looking at.

He saw me. He had a flag tattooed on his forehead. He looked hard, but his shocked eyes widened the size of flying saucers. I could see him thinking, Fucking hell, two big black cunts. Ooooohhhh, fuck it, I'm off!

The skinheads creeping against the wall with their knives in their hands rammed them back in their pockets and ran like sewer rats down the stairs and into the underpass.

I went for the kill — steaming after them across the platform, my stanley ready to slash and cut these skinheads to shreds. It was just like being back on the terraces.

I shouted at the big fella to come with me. It's two against four but I always went into battle thinking I was worth two of any man, and this big black bloke has to be worth two, if not three. Two of us against four of them — to me that's even.

Spoiling for the fight, I screamed at the black guy, 'Come on! We gotta do 'em, NOW! If we give 'em time to come to their senses they'll realise we're outnumbered. Then, they'll be back. This station's deserted: we'll have one hell of a fight on our hands.'

A raging torrent of adrenalin raced through my veins. 'We've gotta go, NOW!' There was that steely stare again. He didn't move a muscle.

I was up for leaping the flight of stairs they'd scarpered down in one bound. We were going to lose them if he didn't move his arse.

This big, powerful guy said nothing. He just gave me a slight nod of the head and a look that said 'I ain't going nowhere'. It was unbelievable. I thought, Let 'em go? Are you black or what? We could slaughter 'em.'

At that moment a train pulled in. I came to my senses. I was talking to myself, 'Cass, what are you doing standing on the platform with a Stanley knife out? You're in so much shit already. Do you want to go back to prison for somebody else's row.'

The doors swished open and he just stepped on board. I was mad. I climbed on well away from him. I could see him sat in the next carriage.

I didn't think any more about it. I never said a word to anyone. It was just another day in Cass Pennant's troubled life. I'd been there before so many times. When I think back, half the time I've been in trouble it had started because I'd helped someone else out.

I had enough worries of my own, so I thought no more about it.

I'd become interested in boxing — it took me away from the terraces while I was out on bail. The first boxing match I ever watched was a welterweight bout at the Elephant and Castle between my old mate from way back, Gunter Roomes, and Manchester's Bobby Rimmer. Roomes won on points.

I got my tickets for the fight from Neil Bowers, who was to become one of my closest pals. Now, Neil is like a godson to Terry Lawless, one of Britain's top boxing trainers. In the sixties Neil's dad, 'Happy' Jack Bowers, had been the first-ever boxer Terry Lawless took under his wing.

Football violence had become a drug. I started to see boxing as a release from my football fix. I got the same buzz going to boxing that I got from soccer, though I was never involved in any trouble at a boxing match. I became such a regular I started earning extra money by selling fight tickets. The percentage was really low, but I knew lots of people so I did quite well. And to encourage me to sell more, Terry even upped my commission. It became like a full-time hobby.

Late in 1984 — more than two years after the ruck at Stratford — Neil took me to Terry Lawless's house in Hornchurch, Essex. We were there to pick up a batch of tickets to sell for Tony Sibson's fight against Mark Kaylor for the British Middleweight title.

Terry was Kaylor's manager and while we were at the house, the great man sat down with us and poured out his private hopes. He was training a big black boxer who he believed would one day become the heavyweight champion of the world — and the world knew nothing about this young boxer at that time.

Six

This big black fella was going to live like a son with Terry and his wife, Sylvie. I got the impression Terry was telling me all this because he realised his young hope was going to be a black guy living in a white area and him and his lovely missus had me in mind as a friend for their man.

Not long afterwards, Neil and I were in Terry's world-famous gym above the Royal Oak pub in Canning Town. The gym was two floors up, crammed under the roof timbers. Imagine the gym in Sylvester Stallone's film, *Rocky*, and you've got it in one. It was cramped and stank of sweat. The only light came from dirty panes of glass in the roof above the practice ring.

It was here Neil introduced me to Terry's new hope. Frank Bruno was his name. A few minutes later, Frank pulled Neil to one side and whispered: 'I know your mate ... from Stratford.'

When Neil told me, I immediately thought our paths must have crossed on the terraces, but I couldn't place his face. No wonder, I was on completely the wrong track.

Eventually, Terry took the trouble to introduce me to Bruno. By then the press were gathering to see the new black heavyweight, the man with so much muscle and power he already had the hopes of a nation on his enormous shoulders. As Frank sat down after yet another punishing workout, Terry said to the big fella, 'I want to introduce you to a friend of mine.'

He came over from the bench, his huge hands still swathed in tape. Terry, dwarfed by his giant boxer, said to me, 'This is the fella, I told you about, Frank Bruno.'

I put my hand out in friendship. This great big hand, even bigger than mine, came out, hesitated for a moment, and then as he grabbed my outstretched mitt, he turned to Terry and said, 'I don't really need to shake his hand, we've already met.'

With an 'excuse me' he went straight back to his gym work. I was still puzzled.

I used to like going into the gym to collect tickets to sell because I could get all the gossip and see how the fighters were shaping up, so I could have a nice wager at the bookies.

Every time I went into the gym to pick up tickets for this bout or that, Frank was in the ring. He was training non-stop but he would still give me a friendly wave, or his voice would boom out 'Ello!'

One day at last, we sat down on the bench together. I was waiting for Terry to come out of his office and Frank was beside me, sweat pouring out of him and a towel over his head.

I couldn't stay quiet any longer. 'Look, something's bothering me, you know. You said you've already met me, yeah? I've seen you close up now and I don't know how you know me. I'm a well-known name myself because I'm notorious on the terraces at West Ham. There ain't many blacks in football. In fact, I know all the black guys who run with soccer gangs in London. I've got some powerful big black mates who work the club scene and I can't think of anywhere I've seen you. So if it ain't the club scene, it ain't football, where do I know you from? Can't be school 'cos I went to an all-white school and it ain't prison.'

He just said, 'Stratford, mate.'

I didn't want to embarrass the fella, so I said, 'What, pub or a club?'

'No man, Stratford station.'

He could see I couldn't remember, so he said, 'Skinheads, mate, skinheads. Remember the skinheads.'

As soon as he said that everything clicked. There'd only been me there on that deserted station. I'd never told anyone the story, because to me it wasn't a story.

Remember, the guy on the station had a Lonsdale hood pulled over his face. As I sat on that bench in the Royal Oak gym I looked down and saw those knees. Frank was wearing boxing shorts and Lonsdale boots. Bulging muscles popped out all over his legs.

Everything clicked. 'It's you!' Instant bond.

He said, 'I always wanted to thank you for that.'

I got embarrassed. What's he thanking me for? I

wanted to explode at the world and along came this bloke and four skinheads.

So I said, 'You ain't got to thank me. All in a day's work. It's nothing.'

I helped him out for my own reasons, so I could unleash all the fury and shit I'd gone through on those four Nazi skins. That's how I thought about it, but to this day Frank remembers it as the moment I saved his bacon.

On the terraces where I came from you always help people out of a tight corner. In Frank's world, he wasn't used to anyone stepping across the road to sort out his problem.

From that moment in the Royal Oak gym I became Frank's biggest fan. I sold tickets for all his fights. One day I climbed the stairs to the gym and Frank wasn't there. As I came down the first flight, the dressing room door was ajar. As I got to the bottom of the stairs I heard Frank's big booming voice — he tries to whisper but doesn't know how — telling the masseur, 'You see that fella that's just gone by, he saved my life.'

That's when I realised what that day at Stratford meant to him. Frank more than repaid the debt. But more about that later.

After that explosive Sunday at Stratford, things began to look up. I eventually got a roof over my head when Terry and Bombhead invited me to stay permanently. In the end I was there for a couple of years. I was still Bombhead's 'other son' and regarded as part of the family. Any weddings or funerals, I was called straight away.

I went to the council offices to try and get my job back. All I got was, 'Sorry, mate, you're sacked. We didn't hear from you; you didn't send a sick note.' When you're in Armley jail for a stabbing you're adamant you didn't do, the last thing on your mind is sending in a sick note.

A painter mate of mine, Ron Wakefield, got in touch and gave me all the old Citizen Smith stuff. He said, 'I don't approve of football hooligans, but you ain't even been found guilty yet. Those bastards in the office are bang out of order.' He gave me the name of a proper old-fashioned union man who would fight for the little people. Within six weeks I got my old job back, plus all the pay I'd lost when I was in jail.

Bombhead was a French polisher and he often used to work in the same parts of the City as me. Well, I say 'worked'. Most of what he did was a scam. He'd tout for work in a pub — French polishing the bar or tables — the landlord would give him a load of money to buy materials. Bombhead would then spend all day in another pub getting pissed on the up-front money. He'd never go back to finish the job. So when my painting work was finished for the day I'd often meet Bombhead for a drink. He'd be propping up the end of a bar telling amazing stories. One favourite was how he squared up to the Krays and survived. In the sixties Bombhead had been an up-and-coming East End boxer. He also did 'jobs' for Reggie and Ronnie's firm. One time he forgot to do an errand for them, collecting a bit of protection money. People who upset the Krays usually ended up beaten to a pulp ... or worse. Well, Bombhead got fed up waiting for the Twins' heavies to take their retribution. So he tracked Reg and Ron down to a club where they were holding court south of the river. In walked Bombhead: 'I hear you're lookin' for me, so let's get it over with.' Amazingly, he survived. The Twins so much admired Bombhead's bottle in marching straight into the lions' den that they let him away unscathed as long as he paid back the money they'd lost.

Soon after Bombhead told me this story some of the ICF mob were bushwacked on the tube by a gang of Millwall hooligans. During the ambush one of the Millwall mob stabbed a mate of mine, Paul Dorsett, through the heart. I was even more annoyed when I discovered that the Millwall mob had bottled a black kid called Roger, and as they hit him over the head they'd been calling him Cass.

Even though I was still on bail, I was so angry I

wanted to wreak revenge. Bombhead's story gave me
an idea — we would literally go into the Lions' den.
Me and Tel set off on a spying mission to discover
which arseholes were claiming credit for stabbing
Dorsett. I knew a lot of the Millwall mob drank in the
Royal Oak, a disco pub in Tooley Street just behind
London Bridge station. In the evening local lads
slipped into this boozer hoping to pull the office birds
who drank there. A lot of these jack-the-lads were
Millwall boys. We took off for the City dressed in
office worker's whistles so we wouldn't stand out like
spare pricks at a brothel. We were tooled up: I had an
axe, Uncle Stan and some squirt; and Terry took his
trademark cut-throat razor. We were feeling
invincible. On the double-decker crossing London
Bridge, Tel had a row with a City gent in the full-
regal: pinstripe, bowler, brolly and briefcase. The
argument was short-lived. A quick shove and he went
flying from the bus. His angry outburst was lost in the
stiff wind blowing up the Thames. In stitches, we
jumped off and strolled down Tooley Street.

The Royal Oak was a groovy little dive, playing all
the right sounds with plenty of working-class skirt
and only office wankers eyeing them up. Leaning
against the bar we were in a good position to see
everybody in the place. Day became night and we
were still propping up the bar, but neither of us had

any dosh left for the next drink. The crowd had changed. Locals replaced the office wallies but they were just Bermondsey boys, not Millwall mob. Terry said, 'No Millwall and we've no money. We might as well be in Canning Town.' I was certain the Millwall lot would show up, but we just had to stay a bit longer. But how, with no money? I looked at a pint jug on the bar overflowing with crispy notes. We had the bar to ourselves and there was this whip — kitty — in easy reach.

Terry knew what I was thinking. 'Yeah, Cass, no one will notice. They're all on the dance floor, pissed out of their brains.'

We had a dip and got another drink. Then another dip and yet another drink. Definitely no Millwall here tonight. We might as well have a free piss up. Mission now off, we had our backs to the dance floor when I heard, 'Cass!' A shudder went down my spine. 'Cass, we know who you are and what's more you've been seen taking money from our whip.'

Fucking hell, we've been rumbled. Tools ready, mate, it's gonna go big time.

I turned round. There were at least twenty of them, maybe even thirty. A mixture of lads and older blokes. I'm itching to pull out the axe hidden in the back of my belt. We're going to have to fight our way out. I scan for exits. There's only one.

It's far too far and this firm in front of us won't be backing off, no matter how many tools we pull out.

I figured we'd be able to do up to ten of them but we wouldn't make it. We had to get nearer to the exit by fronting it out. I whispered to Terry, 'Make sure you put as many as you can in hospital and make for the exit when I do.' We weren't scared. It was just the shock of being caught out. I look straight at my accuser. 'So you reckon I'm Cass. What makes you so sure?'

'I'm sure because I'm West Ham.'

What the hell is this? This lot have South London stamped all over them. The exit forgotten, I looked my accuser in the eye. I thought I knew everyone at the Hammers.

Then comes the clincher: 'I was at Sheffield when you got nicked for the stabbing you never did. I'm marrying into a top Bermondsey family. This is my stag night. I'm marrying a Millwall bird tomorrow. The guys behind me want to know what you're doing in their pub.'

Just as I was thinking we might not have to pull out the tools, Terry pipes up, 'We're here to find out who stabbed our mate.' I thought, 'Effing hell, Tel, I admire your backing, mate, but you've just blown any chance we might have had of bluffing a way out.

The family this kid's marrying into only happens

to be related to 'Mad' Frankie Fraser. A gangster-looking character pulled the West Ham groom aside. Then, with his eyes almost pleading with me, the young Hammer said, 'Cass, they think you're mad but they admire your front to help a mate. They wouldn't dream of going over to the East End to sort out a stabbing. They say you can have a drink with them but first you've got to sort the whip. If you put back the money you've nicked they won't harm you.'

I'd never trust Millwall, but I pulled a fiver from the pocket nearest my hidden axe and made a big show of putting it back into the whip. A geezer said if we put a bit more cash in the pot we could have a drink. I stuffed more notes into the jar. I told Terry to get dancing to show we were cool but to be ready with the tools in case of a double-cross. It never came. Apparently the older guys were villains and had overruled the younger blokes. Still, we weren't taking any chances and before the lights came I signalled to Terry to slip. We didn't want to leave at the same time as them in case they jumped us.

As we stood on the cobbles outside, breathing in the cool night air, we just looked at each other. We'd made it through the exit and we were still in one piece.

As we jogged up the road to London Bridge station, Terry gasped, 'You silly cunt, why did you put all the money back in the whip? Now we ain't got our cab fare home.'

'I ain't that silly,' I laughed, pulling out another tenner.

'Taxi!...'

I'd done my bit for the honour of West Ham. Now it was up to the lads to help me out. Every week on the terraces they kept commiserating with me over what happened in Sheffield. I told them all, 'Thanks for your sympathy but what I really want are witnesses. Something solid I can take to court.'

By the time the Sheffield case came to trial in April 1982 I had sixteen rock-solid witnesses who would all testify truthfully that I was not involved in stabbing Alan Butler.

The authorities moved the case from up north to the Inner London Crown Court. Butler had survived and I was charged with ABH. The trial was a farce. To start with, the entire jury was female. I've got nothing against women — I love 'em — but the fact is most ladies hate any form of violence and they don't understand what goes on at football matches.

To make matters worse, the prosecution got me rattled over my name. When I was being cross-examined, the brief for the Crown kept accusing me of lying about my name. He kept calling me Caswell and then Carol. I'd long since changed my name by deed poll to Cass and I refused to recognise the name Carol. But he'd found my Achilles heel. I refused to answer to my name. The judge and jury didn't know what the hell was going on. Out came my temper and I shot this brief a look that would melt steel. By now the jury really did think I looked like a leader of the notorious InterCity Firm.

It was then the judge stepped in and said, 'Look, what's the problem. The jury are sending me notes saying they don't understand why you're so upset.' I told him, 'All I'll say to the jury is this, you've heard of the song "A Boy Named Sue" by Johnny Cash. Everyone's heard it. If you listen to the words, that's my story.' The prosecution dropped it after that.

But the case still went from bad to worse. The prosecution tore apart my witnesses one by one. Even though they were telling the truth, they were all discredited because they had convictions for football violence. The prosecutor told the jury, 'You've heard Pennant's evil record; well this lot aren't far away from it either. Criminals sticking together.'

My last hope was a fella called Des. He had a clean record, worked in the City and wore a suit in the witness box. He had the jury spellbound. We broke for lunch and Des took the stand again to carry on with his evidence when the police came in ... and arrested him!

Six

They put him in handcuffs and told the court he was wanted in another court on another matter. He tried to explain there'd been a mix up and he was innocent but nobody was listening. The job was done: they'd nobbled my prime witness.

It turned out there really had been a mix-up with Des but the jury never got to hear about it. By then the judge had summed up. Everybody who's ever been convicted reckons the judge is biased but this guy virtually told the jury if they couldn't see I was guilty then they must be as blind as bats. That summing up destroyed what little was left of my case.

The judge was Keith Bruce Campbell. The next time I heard about him I was sitting in my cell in the Scrubs part-way through the one-year sentence he'd given me. There was his picture on the front of the *Sun*. He'd been nicked for smuggling fags and whisky from France on his yacht.

Most people who appear on an ABH charge end up with a fifty quid fine or six weeks inside at most. My sentence was the maximum Judge Bruce Campbell could throw at me. I lay on my bunk staring at those four walls in Wormwood Scrubs and went over and over every shred of evidence that had convicted me. It didn't take long because the prosecution only had the word of one real witness, Alan Butler the 21-year-old Sheffield Wednesday fan.

Just as they'd promised, the cops said I'd punched this guy Butler in a ruck in the street then somebody else had stabbed him. The police told the court I'd 'volunteered' to go to the hospital in Sheffield. The truth is I was dragged there, against my will, to be identified by a young guy who was still recovering from a life-saving operation. Butler was so doped up with anaesthetic he couldn't have known what day of the week it was — never mind finger anyone for being there when he was stabbed.

Hate? I had so much hatred inside me my body I ached.

My brief appealed immediately, with what he reckoned was the longest letter of appeal he'd ever written. But as we all know, the wheels of justice grind slowly. With time off for good behaviour, the chances were I'd be out before the appeal had even been heard.

Andy Swallow, Terry Sherrin and Scully soon came to visit me. They said how sorry they were and they'd had loads of messages of condolence from the lads at West Ham. I leaned across the tatty pine table so the screws couldn't hear and told them, 'Stop feeling sorry for me. It's *you* I feel sorry for.'

The three of them stared at me as if I was off my rocker. I went on, 'Don't yer see? What they did to me, they're going to do to you next — each and every one of you. If we allow them to get away with it we've all had it. We've stayed ahead of the cops for years. Think about all the cracks we've pulled off. We're Britain's most wanted hooligans. We're too smart for them so they're out to do us all, believe me.'

Andy, Scully and Tel all looked at each other, stunned. As I talked, a plan was forming, 'Listen, they think they've just put another nigger away, just like that. Well, I reckon we're the most organised football gang in Britain. So let's show these fuckers just how organised we are. We've never lost a challenge yet, yeah? This is our biggest challenge ever ... you're gonna get me out of here. Forget Colditz, shinning over the walls, helicopters or any of that stuff. We're going to fight back in a way they don't think we're even capable of ... with a Free Cass Pennant campaign.'

The boys livened up sharpish. 'Yeah, Cass, we can do it. Everybody knows what happened. It's the talk of the East End. Hundreds of fans have been stopping us in the street.'

I interrupted, 'No, listen, calm down, lads. This can't be done as a hooligan thing. We've got to play the authorities at their own game. We've got to do it the smart way, the Joe Public way. We'll involve my solicitors and we'll go political, through MPs. I'll organise everything from my cell. It's got to be done right, every step of the way.' The Free Cass campaign was on. Terry started by writing to his MP, Arthur Lewis in Newham. Meanwhile Lenny heard that the fella who'd actually done the stabbing was still bragging about it. Word soon got out that the Wanstead Firm were after him and he quickly changed his tune. In fact, on one of their visits, Swallow and the team told me he wanted to see me in the Scrubs to say sorry. I'd never forgotten that bragging punk. He'd gone over the top stabbing the lad in the stomach and here I was doing his bird. I never wanted to see his face again.

In the end the bragger even offered to write a confession, thinking that if he coughed I'd get off. But when I heard I got word out that on no account was the lad to sign a confession. I'd been done as an accessory, so the cops would do him for slicing the Sheffield fan and they'd still have me as an accomplice. Next thing the bragger had written an unsigned confession, full of details that only the real knifeman could have known and handed it to my solicitor, James McGoldrick. The bragger said in his typed confession: 'I don't know why they arrested this bloke. There wasn't a black bloke in sight when the stabbing took place ... I feel sick about the bloke doing time for a crime I committed.' The lawyer said it was hearsay and couldn't be used. East End lads aren't interested in legal jargon, so Neil Bowers got hold of a local newspaper reporter who was a pal of his dad, Happy Jack. This scribbler, Peter Faulkner, started running headlines like 'Black Man Doing White Man's Crime: Innocent or Guilty?' 'Amazing Confession after Youth Goes to Prison.'

Within hours of the *Stratford Express* going on sale, a West Ham steward called Robert Hosford came forward. Robert had no connection with hooligans but he revealed he had been on stewarding duty at the Sheffield game and told the paper, 'I know Cass Pennant by sight. The police were herding fans into the station then keeping them there until the train arrived. Cass was definitely one of those inside that police cordon.'

More people stepped up to swear my innocence and folk all over the East End were signing my Free Cass petition. The campaign snowballed. Old-time villains listened to their sons who told them whatever I'd done in the past, I was not guilty of this one. These men with heavy connections also started using their contacts.

I could have been just another nigger banged up, but the East End came to my rescue. They decided to take my fight right to the top — to march to Downing Street.

You have to remember the country was in the

middle of the Falklands war at the time. While the pride of Britain's youth were fighting the Argies, the Government couldn't have a 'rabble of scum' from the football terraces marching on Maggie's Den. So they banned the march.

Banged up in the Scrubs, my heart plummeted when the Government kicked our demo into touch. I'd put all the newspaper cuttings up on the wall in my cell and everyone in the nick was right behind me — even the screws. Jesus, where did we go from here?

For a moment I'd forgotten just how cunning and resourceful hooligans can be — they simply defied the ban and went ahead anyway. More than 150 of them made their way on the tube from Mile End to St James's Park and they marched from there the half mile to Downing Street.

Well, they should have marched straight there but on way they discovered the Ban the Bomb mob were in town to protest against the Falklands war. So the West Ham hooligans diverted — Cass will have to wait a mo — and they steamed into some of the CND supporters! Fists flew as they gave those grungy pacifists a few clumps for pouring piss on our boys fighting in the Falklands. That sorted, they eventually made it to Downing Street. Despite the ban, somehow it was all official. Number 10 knew the boys were going and, in fact, Maggie passed my petition to the Home Secretary, Willie Whitelaw.

After that, MPs asked questions in the House of Commons, letters flew backwards and forwards but the Home Office couldn't intervene because an appeal had been lodged.

When I was taken down those steps from the dock at Inner London Crown court, the police must have thought, That's the last we'll hear from him, another nigger gone down nicely. Instead, people in the highest place in the land — the Houses of Parliament — were asking questions about my case. And we'd done it all ourselves. We weren't rich, there was no money behind us and no political party to push the campaign along. It was true 'people power'. The good hearts of loads of ordinary, hard-working people who couldn't turn a blind eye to injustice made it happen.

My appeal came up fairly quickly after that. I lost. My last chance lay in Europe at the Courts of Justice. My lawyer was right behind me but legal aid wouldn't wear it. That was it — I was out of the game.

The big Victorian jail loomed up and the gates swung open to let the prison transporter in. I was back at the Scrubs. I felt like Steve McQueen in *The Great Escape*.

I shared a cell with Ali Forbes, a black villain who had been an unlicensed boxer. He was only a little fella but he was fit. He moved all the cell furniture around into a mini gym, using the bed, chair and locker for his exercises. Plastic containers full of water were weights. If he needed something heavier, he filled them with sand from the fire bucket. Before long he had me joining in.

I returned from breakfast one morning to find a stranger in our cell. The con had his back to me, having a distinctly unfriendly conversation with Forbsey. This guy had a razor behind his back ready to slash my mate in the face. I'd arrived just as Forbsey was about to be cut to ribbons.

The con turned round. My huge frame filled the doorway. This geezer was looking through me trying to find his obbos who were meant to be keeping an eye out. They'd shot off down the landing when they saw me approaching. The con walked casually past — reckoned he was just 'having a chat'.

I turned to Ali. 'What was all that about?'

'Nothing I can't sort out myself,' he replied convincingly.

He soon sorted it. Ali lay in wait and smashed our visitor's head in with an iron bed leg sending blood spurting all over the recess. On very old, well-worn beds like they had in the Scrubs you could easily detach the leg sections, giving you a heavy iron pipe about eight inches long. That's a serious weapon inside jail.

The con's razor was no match for a bed leg brought down on his skull. In fact, Ali whacked the geezer with such force the con ended up in the hospital wing. By the time the screws searched our cell for a weapon the bed leg had been wiped down and was back in position. You'd never know it had been taken off.

When the injured con returned to the wing he was sporting a huge dent on his forehead. My mate Mad Jaffa started calling him Denthead. Everywhere he went on the landing inmates were shouting, 'Oi, Denthead!'

Eventually, Denthead could take no more and he skulked off to see his buddy 'Ginger' John Bowden. Nearly all the short-termers lived in awe of Ginger John who was doing life for killing a meths-sodden tramp. Ginger chopped up the body to get rid of it but the Old Bill found his victim's head in the fridge. Ginger John swaggered around the nick in his self-tailored prison uniform like he was on the Old Kent Road. He made sure everybody knew he was a killer. He actually plastered his cell walls with photos of his victim hacked to bits that had been used as evidence in his court case. He made me sick.

Before long Ginger John started making noises about avenging his mate, Denthead. It was like lighting a touch paper: very soon the wing was going to explode. Ali Forbes was a hard man and a proud man who didn't worry about anyone — screws or cons — but he was always OK with me and gave me respect. I liked him a lot and I told him if trouble kicked off I'd weigh in on his side. Jaffa joined us. It was just like being on the out. Our group v Ginger's mob. Jaffa made knives for us by sharpening up paint scrapers he'd nicked from the prison decorating kit. We started making moves to arrange a time and place for the tear-up. Wherever a meet was arranged, on the access, landings, exercise yard we always showed up, but Ginger John's team swerved each time.

We weren't scared just because one of them had butchered a helpless tramp. They knew it and kept trying to recruit other cons to their side. Ginger John had one throw of the dice left — the other lifers. There's an unwritten rule inside that lifers stick together. Prison is going to be their 'home' for years so there's no point in fighting each other unless it is unavoidable. But if the lifers did come after you it was like having the Devil himself on your tail. Every one of them was a killer with nothing to lose. Ali, Jaffa and myself would search out Ginger John's mob in the exercise yard and beckon them into the toilets where we could settle the score out of sight of the screws. But they never moved, just stayed put, looked smug and chatted to the other lifers.

Then we heard an amazing piece of news. Ginger
John was so desperate for help in taking us on he'd
even begged the handful of Hell's Angels in the Scrubs
to join his posse. Hell's Angels were usually only ever
inside for murder but the odd thing was they would
never really mix with other lifers. They always stuck
with other Angels, even though they may have been
deadly enemies on the outside. In the Scrubs Angels
from the Windsor and New England chapters mixed
with their hated rivals the Essex Road Rats. Ginger
John was in for a shock. The Hell's Angels told him,
'Bollocks, we ain't going against Jaffa. We deal with
him on the out.'

Now we had Ginger John on the run. In fact, I
was so relaxed that the threat was over and we were
never going to be ambushed that I put in a chit for an
extra shower. There was no way I'd be attacked in the
showers. The whole wing is banged up at the time. A
screw comes to unlock your door and escort you
down to the block. Only one inmate is ever loose at a
time. I was standing under the shower, chuckling to
myself, 'Those mugs thought they had us by running
off to the Angels. How can anybody rate a tramp
basher?'

'Hey, what's happening?'

Someone had whipped the shower curtain open. I
was staring down at two well-known faces. They

certainly weren't a pair of queens. One was a well-known villain from south London. The other was an alleged hitman who was banged up for avoiding helping the police with their enquiries by holding a shoot-out with armed cops at the end of a massive car chase. Talk about caught unawares, with my dick in one hand and bar of soap in the other. I defy anyone to feel up for a fight in that position.

This was it, Ginger John was about to get his revenge and I'm unarmed and stark, bollock naked. My mind raced, trying to anticipate the first blow and try and parry it. My only hope was to shove my fist hard down one of their throat and run for my life.

Instead, they were talking to me. I knew their game, a lecture before they do me. I listened, still waiting for that first punch. It didn't come. Hang on, this lifer was calling *me* dangerous. I couldn't believe my ears. 'If I'm so dangerous, step aside and let me grab a towel and some clothes.' I went to step out of the cubicle but they moved in menacingly. I thought, Fuck me, they're serious all right.

The lecture continued, 'We've been asked to back up a fellow lifer but so far we've stayed out of it because he ain't our cup of tea. But we've been watching and it seems like half the nick is getting involved. Everybody's watching each other and the screws are keeping their beady eyes on us all. We're doing life here and we want to do it as easy as we can. This feud is affecting us as well, so I'm putting paid to it.'

It wasn't even my row but they'd got me down as the ringleader. Why had they singled me out? I was still a bit baffled but aware they hadn't so much as hinted they were going to fill me in.

The other one spoke for the first time, 'We reckon you're a dangerous bastard because of what you are, a football hooligan. Forget what we're in for. We do what we do for money or a reason. It's the only way we'd do stinking bird for it.'

The face who seemed to be some sort of a Godfather butted in again, 'What you and your football mates do is just for kicks. No money, no reason. That's what makes you and your kind dangerous in our book. So it ends now. It's over, OK?'

'OK,' I said. And I meant it.

As they turned and went, I pulled the shower curtain across, peeped out from behind it to make sure they really had gone, and dressed in a flash before any more surprises poked their heads round the corner. I returned to my cell with a lot of food for thought. The guys who visited me were proper guv'nors and they'd admired our front. They had to sort it because a gang war in prison gets in the way of business.

Also, I knew I'd been caught with my pants down.

They could get me any time they wanted and they had nothing to lose by taking me out. The cell doors opened. I met up with Jaffa in the recess and told him, 'It's all off, Jaffa. It's over.'

'Why?' he asked.

'Because Ginger John's mob don't want to know. We've got to tell everyone it's off.'

Jaffa wasn't totally convinced. He said, 'Well, I'm still going around with my sharpened-up putty knife, just in case.'

We stayed tooled up for a couple of weeks and nothing happened, just as I knew it wouldn't. I never told them why I knew it wasn't going to kick off.

Years later I was watching the news when they announced a lifer was holding the Governor of Parkhurst at knifepoint and threatening to kill him. Trained negotiators were talking to the con with a blade whose name was John Bowden — Ginger John.

I thought to myself, They'd better tread carefully if he puts in a request for a fridge.

Chapter Seven

The nightclub door began to buckle. Arms clawed through the gap to burst the door open. Once those creaking aluminium doors gave way a tidal wave of well over a hundred raging rastas would flood through. The screaming hordes were intent on murder. It would be a bloodbath. The rastas would flail defenceless clubgoers with axes, machetes and scaffold poles. The only thing standing between them and unimaginable carnage was me and five bouncers, and we were fighting for our lives. A hand, gripping a huge razor-sharp axe, appeared through the buckled door. With two fingers and a thumb still round the axe, he managed to lock his other two fingers on to the bar holding the door in place and began to pull. Any second the door would spring open and we'd be swamped.

Lives were in danger, here. The rasta was about to lose his arm. I raised the axe in my right hand high above my own head and smashed it down with all the force in my body.

Welcome to the crazy world of Kisses nightclub, where devils danced with angels. I fought a battle here almost every night for six solid months. It was a war zone.

When we left prison, Jaffa and me went into the bouncing business.

After putting the fear of God up the hard men of the Scrubs we reckoned we were pretty invincible. We were desperate for work and took on clubs no one in their right mind would touch with a barge pole.

Kisses nightclub sat above a greengrocer's and a pub in Queen's Road, Peckham. Streets don't come much rougher than this. It backed on to the notorious North Peckham Estate where the council shoved life's losers: boat people; illegal Jamaicans; alcoholic Jocks and skaghead Scousers. Peckham was like Trenchtown, the toughest, roughest ghetto in Jamaica. This was the Yardies' manor — we called them dreads then — and the club was their front room. For years it had been a famous reggae hangout. At one time or another the place had been known as Mr B's or the Bouncing Ball.

It was owned by a black guy, Ken Edwards. In

those days black blokes didn't own clubs. Ken was the first real black club owner. He revamped the club just as the soul explosion was happening. He wanted the soul crowd there — white girls and smart hard-working blacks with money. With the rastas there he couldn't get a trade. The locals were so rough decent people just kept on driving past.

The rastas hung about harassing the white girls. They turned over any white fella and they invaded the club with knives stashed under their tea cosies. They were just too tasty for the local security. Ken needed a team of hard men who were mean enough and tough enough to smash the undesirables. We were up and coming, straight out of prison and ready for action.

Club owners rarely tell you the truth about what's going on, so before we said yes to the job I checked out the real story with the man who was running the door. It was Gary Mason, then an unknown heavyweight who eventually went on to become British champion. Gary was built like a rhino. His briefing was short and sweet: 'Welcome to the madhouse; I wish you all the luck in the world.'

Whenever I met a club owner for the first time, I always took along big Steve Ward. Forget Man Mountain, Steve was a walking Mount Everest. At six feet nine inches he towered over me, and was as wide as a bus — and it was all muscle. Owners were always impressed by Steve, though we often eased him out of the job because he was really a gentle giant and was too likeable.

Many clubs weren't keen on having an all-black team of doormen. Potential white clubbers would look at the bouncers and think it was an all-black club and drive off. So I took Jaffa along. He's only about five feet eight tall, but he ripples with muscles and has a 46-inch chest and a 30-inch waist. He also has nerves of steel, the heart of a lion and piercing grey eyes that can put the fear of God into the hardest thug.

Ken Edwards looked at Jaffa and said, 'I'm not sure about the white man; he ain't big enough. All the other guys are just what we're looking for. I don't want the little fella.'

The geezer was going on size, so I told him, 'I have real dangerous people working for me. I don't employ bodybuilders. Let them do the West End. The first risk of getting a scar and they're off, frightened they'll lose ten points at the body beautiful competition. Jaffa's on the team, no ifs or buts. He's the one who taught me all I know about the door business.' He still couldn't see it until one midweek night when we had just a handful of doormen on duty. Four cars, windows blacked out, pulled up in the street outside. Fifteen mean-looking guys climbed out. They pulled on ski masks, armed themselves with baseball bats and ran towards the club to attack a bunch of guys who were dancing in the disco. My guys slammed the doors shut to protect the club.

A terrified girl stood outside on the pavement. She hammered on the club door for help. As Jaffa shouted through the glass, 'It's all right, love. You'll be safe, this mob aren't after women ...' Whack! A baseball bat cracked across her skull and she slumped to the floor.

Jaffa, who hates bullies of any kind, erupted: 'I'm not having that.' He grabbed two bloody big bayonets from behind the entrance desk. With Little Danny following close behind, he charged out, slashing and cutting at the mob. Jaffa smashed three of them before they turned tail and ran. My guys gently helped the sobbing girl, blood trickling over her face, to the safety of the club. As the girl staggered in, the doors slammed shut — leaving Danny and Jaffa stranded on the pavement. The thugs had run towards their car expecting a whole team of heavily armed bouncers to be on their tail. But when they realised there were only two good guys out on the street, surprise, surprise, they got brave all of a sudden.

Fifteen against two ... Attack! Danny hammered on the doors for a bit of help. Ken the club owner watched from an upstairs window as Jaffa stood his ground, swinging his blade like a one-man

Braveheart. Whack! He smashed the first in the shoulder. Bosh! Another one down. Then another. Blows from baseball bats rained down on his head and body. He still fought on. Suddenly the doors sprung open and Jaffa flew back in. On the Friday night we arrived firm-handed, ready for trouble. The owner pulled me to one side: 'The little white guy can have a job here for life.'

That was the start of our war in Peckham. Every single week for six months — 25 long weeks — we fought all-comers. As soon as we finished one mob off another gang came along. But of all the gangs who hated our guts, the rastas despised us most. It was their club and we'd taken it over. We were a bunch of black blokes who spoke like East Enders, not Jamaicans, and our worst crime of all was to work with a white bouncer. Talk about racism — they hated Jaffa even more than they loathed us.

To make matters worse, I even barred their hero Desmond Dekker. This guy in his fifties turned up at the door. He was too old. Kisses was trendy and young; he was the wrong image so I turned him away.

The rastas outside screamed at me, 'Don't ya know who dis is? Desmond Dekker. Yo turnin' away Desmond Dekker, man.' They just couldn't accept the club had gone up-market.

I knew who he was, all right. I had all his records

at home, but I told him straight, 'You might be Desmond Dekker, but ya ain't coming in. I've got pretty young girls in there; they don't want old blokes like you hanging round.'

One night a dude in a £500 white suit was giving it large and upsetting the nice people. In his Persil-white whistle he looked like Eddie Murphy — he was obviously some kind of gangster. I tried to get him out of the door without smashing him. Every week guys would start trouble by running their mouths up but they'd back off when we stepped in. There was no point in steaming in with a sledgehammer to crack a nut. So now I'm playing community doorman with a conscience, trying to ease him out without throwing a punch, but he dug in his heels. We ended up rolling on the floor and his dazzling white suit split wide open at the seams. He went berserk.

After I slung him out on to the street, he charged next door to the rastas' illegal drinking den in the greengrocer's shop. He must have been some heavy black gangster because the next thing we knew we were under siege from a mob of well over a hundred rastas with murder in their hearts. After riots in Brixton and Bristol the whole country feared the rastas. This lot were going to maim as many club-goers as they could, then burn the place down.

Just six bouncers stood between the mob and a

bloodbath. Our only advantage was the entrance. To get into Kisses from the street you went through a narrow foyer and up a set of stairs to the dance floor.

If this mob got past us in the foyer and through the second set of doors, they'd be in the club and everyone would get done — club-goers and women, they'd stripe the lot. We had to smash them back on to the street.

I stood shoulder to shoulder with Danny Byles, the guy who fought with me on The Shelf at Tottenham, and Kenny Charlery. Danny, as you know, was even taller than me and Kenny was huge — he had a neck like Mike Tyson. Three abreast, we filled the foyer.

Behind us were Jaffa, the West Ham Under Fives' leader Ritchie Wildman and Little Danny. It was like fighting Gengis Khan's Mongol hordes.

The rastas stretched back across the street, all of them screaming, shoving and pushing to get at us. I threw my fists in all directions, clumping as many as I could. As the first row of rastas fell, more would take their place. They were like banshees, fired up and flailing their fists.

As well as the banshees outside, I had another problem ... inside. Tiny and his gang of local faces were upstairs in the disco.

Tiny was the only other black terrace legend we knew of and he led West Ham's most deadly enemies, the Millwall mob. He was older than me and he'd risen to the top of the heap before me. My ICF lads and his Millwall gang were always trying to put us up as Godzilla meets King Kong for the battle of London to see who was the top black over football. We were arch-rivals but we had no malice against each other. This was Tiny's manor and Kisses was their club, too. By now some of my team were doing bits of business outside the club with Tiny's crew. Also, Jaffa had done bird with Tiny's brother. The only real problem came down to me and Tiny being deadly enemies from West Ham and Millwall. In the end we came to an uneasy truce. If we showed them a little respect by not searching them every time they came through the doors, they wouldn't cause us any trouble. The boys seemed content enough about it.

That night, as the rastas laid siege to the front of the club, my biggest fear was that Tiny's mob would get their revenge by attacking us from the rear. Oh shit! There they were. Out of the corner of my eye I clocked some of Tiny's guys stood at the foot of the stairs. They were clutching weapons. We're dead, I thought. But instead of laying into us, they started passing us an armoury that would make a Viking quake.

I grabbed my favourite weapon at times like this: Spear & Jackson's finest axe. The others had knives and baseball bats. Jaffa grabbed his trusty cut-throat razor and a squirt bottle filled with ammonia. Now, at last, we had a fighting chance.

Big Danny, Ritchie and Kenny smashed their baseball bats over the tea-cosy-covered skulls of every rasta who ran into their path. Little Danny used his fists, punching a blur of faces. For an hour and a half we held the line against the onslaught. Battered bodies littered the floor. Some screamed in agony, done up by the ammonia.

One group broke through. For some unknown reason, Tiny blocked their path. Jaffa handed him an axe and they stood, side by side. Jaffa flashed the gleaming blade of his cut-throat razor. Eyes blazing, he growled, 'The worst you can do is kill me. I'm not scared of dying. I'm gonna count to twelve then I'm cutting. You lot at the back might be alright but I'm taking this lot at the front with me!' One ... two ... three ...' The whole lot of them turned and bulked down the stairs.

I slammed the metal doors shut as they fled. We were still gasping for breath when ... clang! ... clang! The whole entrance shook as the baying mob came back, battering the doors with scaffolding poles.

My blood ran cold as the crowd, screaming for blood, chanted, 'Burn 'em! Burn 'em! Burn 'em!' then the street filled with cries of, 'Kill them! Kill them!' Shards of glass showered the foyer as scaffold poles speared through the armoured glass. Covered in glass shrapnel, we held on to those doors for dear life.

Every jarring thud from the makeshift battering ram threatened to buckle the double doors, splitting them wide open. The dam would bust at any second, letting the rastas flood in.

A hand clutching an axe came through a hole they had bust in the door. This geezer almost had the pull bar up to spring the doors open. This was it. Shit or bust. I swung my axe to chop his arm off. He felt the swishhhh as the Sheffield steel head and the wooden shaft hurtled towards his forearm. He panicked and in a split second he'd dropped the axe and snatched his arm out. My axe embedded itself in the door where his arm should have been. That was one lucky geezer.

I grabbed his weapon and held both axes above my head, laughing manically: 'Come on then! Come on!' They must have thought I was mad. They stepped back just far enough for me to make sure the doors were firmly shut.

That was the turning point. They wanted to talk but a meat wagon crammed full of Old Bill pulled up. This was virtually a no-go area and as usual the coppers were far too late. Instead of tearing across the road mob-handed, they sent over the oldest bobby I've ever seen ... on his own! The others stayed in the van and watched him. Rastas milled round outside the entrance. Ken the owner talked to them from behind the shattered glass. They accused him of turning his back on his roots, selling out by denying them entrance to his club. Then the leaders told him, 'These doormen are evil, especially the white devil. He squirted ammonia at us.'

I'd almost taken one of their hands off and they didn't even mention it but they were obviously out to get Jaffa. To ease the tension he walked away to the top of the stairs.

The copper, who looked like he was two days away from retirement, came over and the owner told him, 'This lot have got scaffold poles and axes. They're trying to burn down the club.'

The copper didn't want to know. He said, 'Well, I can't see no problem here,' turned and walked off.

At the end of the night we got the punters safely out but Jaffa's life was still on the line. A pack of rastas hung about waiting to pounce on him as he left the club.

Jaffa made a phone call to Lenny Aylen in Wanstead and half an hour later a Jag screamed round the corner, with Lenny at the wheel and a girl in the front seat. Lenny wasn't bothered about the danger. Another bloke stepped out of the back door of the Jag with a .44 Magnum revolver in his hand. He swept this great Dirty Harry gun, which fired bullets the size of a finger, in an arc daring the Rastas to move as Jaffa leapt into the motor.

The next day Jaffa strolled into the rastas' shabeen — their illegal drinking den in the greengrocer's shop. More than two dozen rastas sat around drinking and playing dominos. Just as they were about to pounce and beat the shit out of him, Jaffa slipped his hand into his pocket and pulled out a rusty old hand grenade. The tea cosy heads went white when he pulled the pin out.

Jaffa told them, 'Listen, man, I'm here for good. Any of you lot object and I'll chuck this on the floor. I'll hit the deck and if I'm unlucky I might blow the cheeks of my arse, but you lot will all be dead.'

Not one of them moved. Jaffa walked out of there unscathed and they never bothered him again. When Jaffa was stood outside the club, kitted out in his dickie bow and bottle-green velvet suit, the rastas wouldn't even dare walk on the same side of the road.

They would see him and cross over. Safe on the other side of the road they'd point at him and screech, 'Him da white man with the Devil in his eyes!'

The whole of the East End heard about the seige at Kisses. We expected the next Friday to be D-Day when the rastas would come at us again — this time with the whole of Brixton. I rounded up two hundred of the West Ham and Wanstead firms' finest. Everyone was primed for a big tear-up. They couldn't wait for a chance to start bashing the rastas. East London was psyched up to take South London once and for all. This battle would make the Brixton riots looks like a street corner skirmish. World War III was about to break out on the streets of Peckham.

By now some of the girls who'd gone out with Tiny's firm started going with my blokes because they were the talk of the club. These girls knew our plans; they'd seen the knives, guns and grenades we had stashed in our flats. Word got back to the South that we had employed a serious team. There was no going back on our part. We were going to sort this big time. Ken the nightclub owner was terrified but he had to go along with it. He knew we were determined to show those rastas we were the guv'nors now and couldn't be beaten.

During the week I got a strange phone call. 'Cass, Ken here. You've got to come down the club, CID want to meet ya.'

'CID? What you doing calling the police in? I told you no police. Play it all down so they think everything's normal and we'll come back with an arsenal and a fucking army next week. We'll sort out all those South London bastards once and for all. Why do the CID want to see me? I don't wanna see them.

What the fuck's going on, Ken?'

He replied, 'No, Cass, it ain't like that. It's alright, they don't wanna nick ya. They want a meeting right now in the club.'

I told him, 'This better not be a set-up.'

He replied: 'On my life. They've assured me they're not gonna arrest you. They just wanna talk.' As head of security for the club I was the man responsible, but I told Ken, 'I ain't telling them nothing. Nothing whatsoever, 'cos as far as I'm concerned there ain't a problem. We'll have it Friday. Everything's set. I can't call it off now. Everyone's geared up and ready.' I went over and the CID were round the table with a bloke who introduced himself as the community leader for North Peckham Estate or something. He looked like Father Ted but he was worse than the Old Bill. He said, 'For the sake of the community, I'm asking you to call it off.' I told them straight, 'Look, we aren't troublemakers; we're just here doing a job. We're under attack; we have to defend ourselves and defend everyone in the club.' I turned to the CID chap and told him, 'The old copper you sent saw with his own eyes what happened last week. They tried to burn down this club. You know what goes on here; you don't need me to tell ya.'

Anyway the community leader went into a huff

and after he left the CID man pulled me aside. He said, 'Look, we *know* what goes on down here. We would love to nick this lot but if we do we're in trouble. You understand what I'm saying; it's political.'

For the first time I really understood what this no-go area was all about.

Then he told me, 'Strictly between you and me, you do what you've got to do but you ain't hearing this from anyone, alright? You do what you've got to do and we'll pick up the rest.'

In other words we'd bash 'em then spit 'em out on the street and the Old Bill would scrape 'em up. They would have loved to be able to deal with all these bad arse rastas but their hands were tied by high-up officials because it was all linked to Brixton. So I winked at him and said, 'Well, nothing's going to happen, officer, is it?'

He looked at the owner. 'We'll just be here doing our job as normal. You just carry on doing your job as usual, too.'

I went straight back and found the boys. 'It's all on. We've got the Old Bill's blessing. We've got to do 'em and they'll pick 'em up.'

Friday night we had everyone in place in pubs close by and in vans and cars all round. Peckham was like a ghost town. There wasn't one rasta in sight. Maybe tomorrow. A few dropped out but we got everyone over again — a huge army tooled up with every weapon you could think of. Again nothing. A handful of local rastas were on the street outside the club but not the ones with the sharp suits, the dreadlocks and all the gold teeth. I thought, Jesus Christ, they're waiting for everything to die down. It'll be next week. We were on tenterhooks for two or three weeks but nothing happened and that's how it stayed for the next three years.

We had tamed Peckham. People from all over London came to the club because it was safe. The owner made a fortune and bought Lacey's club up the West End. Ken wanted us to work up West but we'd have boring nights up there. We didn't want to work with the good life set in the world of the steroid bouncer. We were now the most up-and-coming firm in London. The boys were restless; we needed somewhere lively to work.

Gordon Mac the warm-up DJ at Kisses went on to set up Kiss FM radio station. He and the other DJs, like Steve Walsh and Froggy, used to put up our names when they worked at rough-house clubs that needed sorting out, and soon we had door contracts all over the South-east.

Eventually, Kisses was sold and it became a reggae club again. The Yardies came back. Big Danny was still working there. Two punk Yardies walked up to the door and opened up with a shotgun. They peppered Danny and a giant of a doorman Glenn White, who nearly lost his life when half his belly was blown away.

Tiny, the king of Millwall, pulled me aside one night not long after the battle of Peckham. Until then it had always been stares, eyeballs and animosity but in our first-ever chat he gave me a bit of sound advice. Tiny was almost a double of myself. We were both black terrace warlords in a predominately white sport — but we followed teams from different sides of the river. He told me, 'I can see where you're coming from, Cass. I've been there myself. I don't bother much with football because I'm making money nowadays. That's what you should be doing. You're just used on the terraces and there's no money in it.'

I had chats like this before with other people but they never made any difference. I was addicted to terrace violence and trapped by my reputation as the Hammers' hard man. But when the advice came from Tiny, I respected it. I could see he had money and he still kept his reputation as a hard man.

That's when I decided to make this bouncing thing into something bigger. Instead of having just one club, I'd take on a few. My firm's reputation would grow and I'd still be fighting and in the thick of the action. But it would take me away from the terraces and I'd have a chance to earn some real dough. Thanks to Tiny's advice I started to build an empire of the meanest, toughest, doormen ever seen in London. Not long after, Tiny survived having the side of his head blown off by a gang of dreadlock brothers off the North Peckham Estate in an unrelated incident at a cafe next to Kisses nightclub.

While my security business was growing, I still kept a day job. I'd always been grateful to my foster mum Doll Chambers for making me take up a trade. I was never out of work long. I landed a job as a painter with 'loony left' Islington council. I kept me head down for the first few weeks because the building workers on Islington council supported the Arsenal and Tottenham. I was a well-known face over West Ham and I needed this job desperately after coming out of nick, so I had to stay out of trouble at work. Fighting was for Saturdays at the Hammers and on the doors at night. But I ended up being picked on by the foremen who pulled my work to pieces. I'd gone Tom & Dick a couple of times to watch West Ham play night matches away. I didn't know the rules but, apparently, you're not allowed to go sick in your first six weeks of a new job. Everybody knows when you work for the council you spend half the week on the Tom & Dick and still get paid. It was one of the perks of working for the council. I was a qualified tradesman and there was nothing wrong with my work — they were just digging me out for some reason.

I used to leave the house at seven o'clock in the morning, get into the caff at half seven and on to the job for eight. One morning I left the caff and wandered on to the site at five past eight. The foreman was sat on the wall waiting: 'Gotcha! You're not on the job and you're five minutes late.' It was an injustice; this job was in front of schedule, and five minutes shouldn't have mattered.

No one treats me like that or I respond in kind. Here was some little half pint trying to push me around over some poxy painting job. I wasn't having it. I virtually picked him up off the ground and had a go back, without going far enough for him to give me the sack. He ran away and got higher management to come along and I'd be eyeball-to-eyeball, shouting in his face. The management would back off and then keep trying to dig me out even more. I felt victimised. After my last experience, losing my job when I was on remand, I went to call in the union — but there wasn't one.

The painters at Islington council didn't have a shop steward. According to the convenor, the painters were the biggest whingers in the yard, they had the most problems with the management, but nobody was interested in being their union rep.

The next week I went along to my first-ever union meeting. The leaders on the platform were talking crap and going through the motions. Upwards of three hundred guys sat in the audience, most of them yawning or nodding off. Three-quarters of them were only there because the meeting was in work's time.

I looked at 'em all and thought, If this was my West Ham firm we'd have this sorted. Before the meeting I'd got hold of the personnel book and saw that all the people above us, foremen, management, the lot, were on the same sort of contract we had but they were making up their own rules for the people below them. They'd pull up at a site and send blokes with families home like little boys for daring to come down the ladder and have a cup of tea. They were beaten and downtrodden. They'd go home moaning that they'd lost half a day's pay because the foreman had kicked them off the site for having a tea break. I seized my chance. The union men were going on about the poor bonus scheme which stacked the odds against the painters who could never make a proper living each week because they were being sent home all the time.

Now the council wanted the painters to accept a new bonus scheme that was worse than the pathetic one we were already on. The union didn't know how to fight. They kept saying, 'We gotta compromise. We'll argue this but agree that. At the end of the day we'll accept.' It was all stacked in the managers' favour. Rage boiled inside me. The blokes were like lost sheep. They'd forgotten they held the power. I stood up and told them I'd be the painters' steward. Half the workforce had never even seen me before. I heard them whispering, 'Who's this big black fella?'

'That's the leader of West Ham, that's Cass. He'll give the management a run for their money.'

The old boys were looking at me like I was a future heavyweight champion. All of a sudden they started waking up, and said, 'We're too old; we've got families to look after but this man can fight. He could do our battles for us.' They started nudging each other, then one of the old boys turned round and said, 'Go on, son, stand. We'll back you.'

I looked over to my rivals, the Arsenal mob. They just winked and went, 'You stand; we'll back yer.' I thought, Great I've got some football people. They know what fighting's all about. We'll take 'em on. So I stepped up on to the stage. The hands went up. I was in.

I grabbed a paper off the desk and held it up. I told the blokes, 'This is the council's bonus scheme that your reps have been prodding about with for weeks and have done nothing. It's still the same bonus scheme from four weeks ago. The changes are not what we want. We're working our arses off for the management to sit on their backsides, drive around and send us home. I'll show you what I think of their bonus scheme.'

I'd got 'em captivated now; it was just like being back on the terraces. I was Cass Pennant of West Ham again but this time I'm standing with three hundred workers in front of me and a load of union reps thinking, Jesus, he's just been voted in and he's turned into Citizen Smith.

I ripped it up. I ripped the bonus scheme into a shower of tiny bits: 'Your reps here were gonna sign that on your behalf!'

'No! No!' they chanted and started ripping their papers up too. The convenor leapt to his feet, pushed me off the mike and said, 'This man is prepared to put his 'ead in the oven for you guys. Well, the union's right behind him. Are you behind Cass Pennant, because I've been down this road before with no backup?'

They started chanting, 'Yes! Yes! Yes!' and stamping their feet. I seized the mike back and shouted, 'Follow me! Let's show 'em, lads. Let's take our fight to the Town Hall! Are you with me?'

'Yes! Yes! Yes!' they chanted.

I jumped down from the stage, fought for a

gangway and went out the door. When I looked behind, three hundred workers in donkey jackets and painter's overalls were following me down the Holloway Road, along the Essex Road, into Islington Town Hall. The adrenalin buzz was just like being on the terraces again. The union reps got in front of me as we charged through the Town Hall entrance.

Three hundred angry workers were looking at me. 'What's the next move, Cass?' I didn't know what the next move was. Everyone in the Town Hall was panicking. Someone shouted, 'Get the police!' The union men said, 'Don't worry: they won't get the police, this is Labour. We'll take over now, Cass; you keep the painters 'ere.'

The convenor, who was a real Irish rebel, and his union men raced up the stairs to the council leader's office to put our grievances. The leader was Margaret Hodge who went on to become a Labour MP. The union men didn't really like her. They thought she was a phoney socialist because she was a rich bitch. She had a nanny working for her at home and her kids were in private school. She was one of those rich kids who'd rebelled against her parents' way of life and latched on to socialist causes.

She came storming out like the Queen to see what all the fuss was about. Who were these workers from the back alley banging on her door and interrupting a high-powered meeting? I could hear them telling her, 'The workers aren't going to go. A new union rep's been voted in and they've all got grievances they want you to hear.' She seemed annoyed and said, 'I can't hear them now. I'm in the middle of an important meeting. There's a way to do things.'

Just then the police arrived. We've got problems now, I thought. Here's all these painters on the march with a convicted soccer hooligan as their ringleader. But suddenly, the Old Bill disappeared. Sure enough, the Town Hall officials told them, 'There's no problem.' It would have looked bad on Labour. They didn't want to be seen using the cops against their own workers like the Tories did to the miners. We had seized the Town Hall. No one could stop us. The painters were chanting, 'WE SHALL NOT BE MOVED!'

Eventually the union officials came out and said, 'Cass, we've gotta deal. If we get the blokes out, Margaret Hodge will have a special meeting with you and all the union reps to share every grievance we've had over the last year.' We were going nowhere. We didn't trust her. Was it a stitch-up? But the union blokes were convinced. 'You've won, Cass. We've got our meeting. There's no going back. She will listen to our grievances and we'll fix that lot in the office for good. The workers' grievances have never got out of the yard before. Now they'll hear the workers' voice. You've done it, mate. You're here to stay.'

The blokes marched back out of the Town Hall and that's when we started having fun and games. I had about a year as a union rep and I caused absolute havoc. I terrorised the management, defending every worker. I never lost a case and even got a bloke who'd been off sick for two years without proper certificates his job back. I was living the life of Riley as a kind of Citizen Smith in the yard, determined to give the bosses the same kind of unnecessary hassle they'd used to trample down the workers over the years.

I knew I'd won the day when one of the foremen came to me and said the main man, a bloke called Parker, was walking around the office muttering my name. He couldn't get my name out of his head.

Then I gave them another taste of their own medicine for being tyrants. I walked into the office one day and said, 'I've just been reading in the *Evening Standard* that Islington's black population is now ten per cent. Well, I've noticed in the yard we've got six hundred men and just three of them are black.'

Now Islington council had been boasting how it was into equal opportunities. So I asked, 'Six hundred men — three of them black. Where's the equal opportunities in that? I'm putting it to the next union meeting that I sit in on your interviews in line with the council's equal opportunities. You got anything to say about that?'

Within weeks I was sitting in on job interviews with top management. In walked a rasta. He had no shoes or socks on and he was deaf. Now I was thinking, I wouldn't give him a job on safety grounds alone. How could he hear if a paint kettle was falling off a ladder on to his head? Also, I'd been brought up to go to an interview in your best shirt and tie and this guy turned up like he was going to the beach. I thought the brother ain't doing his job prospects any good in that casual gear. You couldn't have him working in people's houses; he'd scare the old ladies. After the fella left the room, the manager turned to me and said, 'Well, Cass, I think we can find him a job here.' I was speechless. It was political correctness gone mad. And these were the people who wanted to send me home because I was five minutes late at the job! They seemed to have forgotten the fact the guy was deaf. They just said, 'There's ways round it. We'll give him certain jobs and we can write things down on paper.'

I laughed. 'But it ain't going to stop something falling on his head.' And the boss just said, 'Cass, it's what you wanted, ain't it?' That's how a stone-deaf rasta ended up working for the council when you can bet your life he'd have been shown the door any other time.

They tried to come back at me again. This time my crime was going on too many courses. Anything to get out of work. I'd get full pay and expenses for what was no more than a glorified piss-up. I went on six courses in one year. The most any union rep in the yard had been on before was three, and the average was just one.

The boss told me, 'According to the council's rules, the maximum number of courses a union rep can attend is five. You've been on six. We've got you, Pennant, you're finished.'

I hit back, 'Don't tell me how many courses I can go on. Your bullying days in this yard are over.'

Next day I banged on the boss's door and said, 'Put me down for another course.' He looked stunned and stammered with anger. The council would veto my request. But he'd forgotten the council had just made a big political statement in the papers claiming Islington was an equal opportunities borough. So I said, 'I'm the only black shop steward here and I haven't been on a Black Awareness course yet, so you go and tell that to the council.'

I was playing them at their own game. You've got to remember I'd been brought up by white parents with a totally English view of life. As a child I played happily with golliwogs and my sister had white dolls. So I was anti all this political correctness.

Seven

After a year they admitted they couldn't beat me. That Black Awareness course was the final straw. Then they put a proposal to me. I don't know how official it was, but this is the truth. I was too powerful in the yard and they wanted me to chuck in me union thing. I thought, They must be mad; that's my protection. If I wasn't in the union they'd sling me out.

But no, they were offering me another job, as apprentice training officer. The council only had six apprentices and the job didn't exist, but they would create it for me with a management contract. I wasn't selling out by becoming management and, besides, the money wasn't as good as I was earning as a painter. 'Alright,' they said, 'you can keep your painters and decorators contract but don't pick up a paintbrush.' In return all I had to do was keep an eye on the apprentices ... and quit the union. This was bribery, and as it happens I was about to sign up for their bribe when another offer came along. The owners of the Breeze Inn at Sydenham in South-east London wanted me to manage the nightclub and a gym they were opening. I could also run my growing door security business from there. In the end I ran the security on the doors of nightclubs from King's Cross to Bromley. At that time the authorities were closing down clubs where trouble flared up regularly. I'm proud to say none of my clients were on their hit list.

I sorted out a door problem for an ex-copper called Fred who had a big club and restaurant on the A20. He used to play golf with Alan Jones who had a pub in Redhill, Surrey. One day Alan asked me if I'd send some of my boys down there. I checked the place out myself and had a great time. It was one of the friendliest places I've ever been in. The whole community of Redhill seemed to revolve around Alan's pub, the Red Lion. Some heavy South London faces who'd moved out of the smoke to the green fields of Surrey used it as their local and a lot of students got in there as well. Alan could see a scenario where a drunk kid might upset an ex-armed robber who'd want to take his revenge by grabbing a lemon knife off the bar. So he decided he needed proper security as a buffer.

When I turned up in the bar Alan marked my card, 'There's Johnny Wraith. He's involved in everything round here. If he kicks anything off, they'll all follow him.'

I actually knew Wraithy because he supported QPR. He never gave me a moment's trouble and in fact we got on like a house on fire. He was a laugh a minute. My favourite story about him is typical Wraithy and I'm gutted I only heard it: I'd have paid good money to have been there. Now, Wraithy could pull a bird. He'd long ago lost count of the notches on his bed post. There was a really friendly girl, dressed a bit posh, who pulled pints behind the bar at the Red Lion. Anyway, Wraithy had been seeing her but the relationship came to an abrupt end because of a dare Wraithy had taken. He'd been in a pub in Reigate one Monday lunchtime when someone bet him a fiver to strip off stark naked and crawl along the long bar, take a daffodil out of a vase at the other end, stick it up his arse and crawl back again. Wraithy won the fiver to the applause of all his mates. Unfortunately he hadn't noticed his girlfriend sat at a corner table with her mother who enquired, 'Isn't that the nice young man you brought home last week?'

One night when I wasn't working Wraithy and me went drinking in the neighbouring town of Horley. We went to the Game Bird, one of the first-ever fun pubs, and it was packed. I came out all ready to go home and thought I'd get a burger. Johnny was still inside the pub. A large crowd had gathered around the burger van in the car park and I tried to weave my way through.

Screams came from two girls in the middle of the semi-circle of blokes crowding the van. Over the years as a bouncer I'd seen the old 'kiss me quick' hat scene loads of times. But these weren't the screams of a thrill. They were screams of terror, and they were getting louder. One girl was fighting to get out of there. The crowd was shielding a small group of blokes who were trying to rip the girl's clothes off. She was desperately fighting for her dignity. Hands were touching her everywhere — it was a sexual assault. At first I thought it was horseplay that had gone a bit too far. I told one of them, 'Getting out of hand, ain't it? It's gone too far for those girls.'

The guy, who looked like he was on steroids, spat back, 'What's it got to do with you?'

I reared up to him and the next thing he had me pinned up against the hotdog stand, with my arms trapped by my side. I had a CS canister in my pocket, but I couldn't get my hand to the leveller. So I brought up my right knee, smashing the knee cap into his chest. He was so pumped up on steroids he didn't budge at all. He was growling like a grizzly bear so I nutted him, sending him staggering back. His mates grabbed me. The girl's screams were getting even louder. As the crowd's attention turned to me she broke free and ran for her life.

Johnny Wraith came out of the pub and saw me struggling with a gang of lumps. He charged over and leapt straight in. They upped him and he crashed on to the deck. I went berserk, kicking, punching, lashing out in all directions. I thought I'd taken on a tight unit of three or four; I didn't realise there was nearly twenty of them. My doorman pal Leon —

who is as big as me — rushed over. As I struggled against the mob I shouted to Leon, 'No! no! Get the van! You've gotta get the tools from the van!'

Once it registered, Leon did a quick U-turn and sprinted across the car park. Leon jammed his huge frame behind the wheel of the tiny Rascal van. With wheels squealing and the engine screaming for mercy, he drove the van straight at the crowd. I punched my way free and leapt in the passenger door. I shouted above the whining, screeching engine, 'Get the tools!' Moments later we leapt out with machetes in our hands. A clutch of bouncers stood frozen in the Game Bird doorway. They should have been involved but they didn't move a muscle.

I thought, Fuck you! and went ballistic. We chased the gang through the car park, hitting 'em, smashing 'em, gassing 'em. There was pandemonium as these great hulks ran this way and that in panic, with two machete-wielding blokes on their tail. As we scattered these puff-pastry bodybuilders I came across Wraithy, up but dazed, punching thin air in a blind fury. As Leon raised an axe covered in silver tinsel, I yelled out, 'Wraithy, get a tool from the van.' I was hunting out the bastard who'd had me pinned against the hotdog stand when I heard manic screaming from behind. I turned, ready with the machete, to see Wraithy steaming up waving a spear … covered in pink fur!

Sirens. Police cars were racing down the road. We scattered and leapt into the van. With its poxy 1,000cc engine we were just half a mile away when Old Bill caught up with us down a country lane. There couldn't have been too many black men in white Vauxhall Rascal vans in the area at that time of night. When they searched the back of the van the cops thought they'd hit the jackpot. Here was a big black geezer with machetes, axes, baseball bats and even a couple of whips. But they couldn't nick us for possessing offensive weapons — the blades were all made out of wood. They were props!

None of that mob of jokers in the car park knew my great mate Tony Bowers, who ran the Peacock gym, had been thinking of starting up a British version of American WWF wrestling. Some of my doormen were going to become major wrestling stars. Floyd would be the Witch Doctor, Bill would be Mr T and Dave Courtney's mate Dave Legeno was the Lone Wolf. These were their props for the show — they were all totally blunt. They could never have cut anybody in a million years. We even had a woman wrestler, Classy Claire, and the whips were hers.

We were charged with affray along with the mob, who turned out to be a coachload of rugby players from up north on a beano. Because we were both black the witnesses couldn't tell us apart and we got off, but it was a close call.

Next day the local paper said we were heroes who'd gone to the rescue of a girl being sexually molested and assaulted. The article pointed out that no one was seriously injured. But it didn't stop them running a huge headline 'MACHETE ATTACK'.

It's a risky old business doing the doors, even when you're off duty, especially when you get involved with young damsels in distress.

Chapter Eight

Only one short message was waiting on the answerphone when I got back to my flat in Hackney. A voice, almost pleading, said simply, 'Cass, I need your help to save boxing. Terry.'

There was no mistaking Terry Lawless's soft voice — he always sounded caring, like your favourite grandad. I'd known Britain's top boxing manager for a handful of years. We had a good relationship and spoke often, but in all that time he had never called me at home. I was a ticket seller, not one of his boxers.

Whatever it was, it had to be serious. As I dialled the number of Terry's ancient gym above the Royal Oak pub in Canning Town I was excited to know what he wanted. When I got through, all he would say was, 'I need to see you, now. Can you come down straight away?' This was *really* serious.

I rushed right round to the gym and parked my battered red Mini Metro in the side street next to the pub. My heart pounded as I raced up the two flights of stairs to the gym crammed under the roof. The deafening boom! boom! of the punch bag shook the rafters; blokes were skipping — everything was normal.

I stopped one of the trainer's assistants, Frank Black, and asked where Terry was. He pointed to the closed office door and said, 'He's in there. He ain't been out all day.' Now *that* was unusual. Normally, Terry was rarely in the office, preferring to be out watching like a hawk as Frankie Black and Jimmy Tibbs put his star fighters through their paces.

It was like standing outside the headmaster's door, not knowing why you had been summoned. It didn't feel right. I knocked, opened the door and climbed down the six, steep steps to Terry's tiny inner sanctum. I stood, all six feet four of me, in front of Terry who sat at his desk.

Pacing the floor behind Terry's chair was a man with silver hair and black-rimmed glasses. He looked a bit like Chelsea's chairman, Ken Bates. It was Mike Barrett, probably the country's top boxing promoter at that time. I'd never seen him at the gym before. Terry came straight to the point: 'Cass, we're in deep

Eight

trouble. I called you here because I need your help, mate.'

'Sure, Tel, any help I can give you, I will. You know that.'

I guessed then it had something to do with the forthcoming fight between Mark Kaylor and Errol Christie. The whole world was talking about this fight after the two boxers came to blows in the street — at the press conference to publicise the bout.

Whoever won this bruising 12-round battle would get the chance to try and take Herol 'Bomber' Graham's British middleweight crown.

Christie was Britain's answer to Sugar Ray Leonard, a mini Muhammad Ali. He had all the skills and all the talent, and at that time was being tipped as a world title challenger. Kaylor wasn't really world-class but he was a great honest British boxer — a battler with guts who was schooled in the Lawless fighters' tradition. Kaylor had another advantage, he came from the East End where local boxers are gods.

Both fighters had been training for weeks and they hated each other's guts. Anyway, Kaylor and Christie ended up rolling around on the cobbles at the press conference. Christie was having his picture taken when Kaylor jumped on his opponent's back. It was a sensation: the boxing world had seen nothing like it. The next day, photographs of a hotel porter watching, his face like stunned mullet, as Christie wrapped his huge left hand round Kaylor's neck and threw a right-hander, were on front pages all over the world. The press went mad — they made it seem like World War III had broken out on the streets of London. And to make matters even worse, they even claimed the hatred between the two boxers was racial — Kaylor the white guy against black geezer Christie.

Kaylor always fought wearing shorts in West Ham colours and a whole army of Hammers fans followed him to fights. Trouble often flared as the ICF turned Kaylor's bouts into riots. Pitched battles — just like on the terraces — kicked off big time at two of Kaylor's fights, against Roy Gumbs and Tony Sibson. Sibbo's followers had a rowdy reputation and the ICF who followed Kaylor couldn't wait to get among them.

So, now the papers were predicting a bloodbath between 'far right, racist' West Ham thugs and Christie's black following inside Wembley Arena. The anti-boxing brigade had gone into overdrive. The Old Bill even stuck their noses in and ordered the fight to be cancelled. A week later the two fighters shook hands in public and the bout was back on.

Terry went on, 'I'm worried. More worried than I've ever been.' I'm thinking, there's more to this than just headlines in the papers. Just carry on listening, Cass. Mike Barrett said nothing. He still paced the room, occasionally looking out of the window. Terry continued, 'The phone's been red-hot. The press never stop ringing, MPs are calling me up and even chat shows want me. Everyone's distracting me from getting on with my job of preparing the fighters. It's not fair to the boxers.'

'I'm listening, Tel, but I don't see where I come in,' I said.

He shook his head. 'We're finished, we are finished.' The sport's governing body, the British Board of Boxing Control had been on the phone. Their warning was stark: if there was any crowd trouble at the Kaylor v Christie fight both boxers would be instantly banned. It wouldn't just end there. The anti-boxing lobby would win the day and the noble sport would be no more.

Tel went on: 'The Boxing Board think it's going to kick right off with the West Ham lot. If there's just one bit of trouble, boxing's finished. They're deadly serious. That's why Mike's down here today.'

I said nothing. I felt slightly sorry for the pair of them but at the same time I was a bit annoyed. I thought, Hold on, here. Right, I may be a soccer thug, but when it comes to boxing, I've done nothing but be respectful. I love the sport. I hope you ain't gonna start suggesting I'm running around causing trouble at boxing matches. Terry must have read my mind. He said, 'We aren't saying you're to blame. If I thought you were, mate, you wouldn't be standing here. Look, Cass, I don't understand this football violence thing. You know 'em all. We're hoping you can call them off.'

I felt like laughing out loud and telling him, 'It ain't that easy. It ain't like cowboys and indians.' The reason West Ham's football hooligans were so powerful, the reason we beat everything that's ever been thrown at us, is because there was no one leader. With other firms if you took out the leader the rest of them caved in. With West Ham you couldn't do that. We had so many strong characters and no one had the divine right to say he was number one. Anyone claiming to be top dog would have been toppled straight away. The press might have been hyping up the fight, but they were right about one thing, the West Ham mob were literally fighting to get their hands on tickets because they expected a full-blown riot.

So, I said, 'I've listened to you, Tel. I understand what you're saying and I'm just as concerned as you. I know from talk on the street, it's gonna kick off big time. I hold me hands up. The West Ham mob are looking for trouble. But I ain't part of it and also I don't control 'em. No man has that kind of power.'

He looked at me, ashen. This was not what he

Eight

wanted to hear. I sensed his disappointment. Mike carried on pacing and shot Terry a look that said 'We need to discuss things'. I knew then it hadn't been Barrett's idea. Terry had made a wild throw of the dice in contacting me. If the police couldn't stop violence at soccer matches, boxing didn't have a hope in hell of preventing trouble kicking off. As I walked down the stairs, I couldn't get Terry's worried face out of my mind. He was gutted.

Back in my flat I played Terry's answerphone message again and again. 'Cass, I need your help to save boxing.' I felt frustrated. Terry had always been good to me. I didn't want boxing to end either. I didn't want Mark Kaylor's career to finish in disgrace. I paced the floor, thinking about Terry's problem. It was an honour to be asked. How far had my reputation with West Ham spread if the likes of Terry and Mike Barrett thought I was the leader of the notorious InterCity Firm?

I started thinking about all the crazy things I'd pulled off in the past. I'm sure the police didn't think when they were fitting me up that there would be an uprising in the East End that would go all the way to Downing Street.

Think about it, Cass. If you pull this one off, it could be good for you. Instead of getting all that bad publicity this might be your chance for a bit of good publicity. Think about your mum, seeing those headlines — 'Football Thug Jailed' — this is your chance to put that right. I liked the sound of that. I played the answerphone back again: 'Cass, I need your help to save boxing.' I'm thinking, I gotta do something, gotta do something. I really want to help. I love the people I met through boxing; it's given me a buzz and has kept me out of trouble at football. I'd be letting down my friendship with Terry.

An idea was forming. My mind flashed to *The Dirty Dozen*, the film where all the convicts, bastards and baddies end up fighting together. An idea was forming, it was crazy. But maybe it was so crazy I could pull it off.

First, I rang Andy Swallow. I put it to him like Terry had put it to me: 'Andy, we need your help to save boxing.' I told him I'd got an idea but I was going to need the backing of him and a few other faces before I'd be able to tell whether my crazy scheme would work.

I was thinking of getting all the baddies together — a super team of thugs, bouncers and minders to take on the baddest firm in the land, West Ham's ICF. Not go against them, but instead step in the middle, to keep the peace and save boxing. Cool it, just for the night. There'd be plenty of other fights they could kick off at.

Eight

I didn't realise Andy had been a boxer. He's a little bloke, but he's got the drive of two men and he's tenacious with it. Boxing is in his heart. He'd been an amateur with West Ham boxing club. When I put the story to him he immediately agreed to help because he felt he owed boxing something. I suddenly realised most of the lads in East London had boxing connections. Next I rang Bill Gardner, the rock on the terraces at West Ham. I knew Bill was another boxing nut. It had given him something in his life and he wanted to save the sport he loved.

Soon I had all the top leaders in London's football gangs, from Tottenham and Arsenal, plus the top West Ham faces on my side. That would take care of the football mob. But there was still one group to be sorted — the underworld. Villains don't respect soccer thugs and they could have us for breakfast. I expected some right bad arses to be there on the night, so I needed some well-known faces from the criminal community.

I rang my mate Tony Bowers. He was a partner in my security firm. Tony ain't got the time of day for football but when I told him he could help save boxing he was in. Although Tony was a young man, he was old school. Years ago he was given a ten stretch for armed robbery and although he's never been in trouble since, he had the respect of serious faces in the

East End. That was the last 'yes' I needed.

Straight away I phoned Terry and told him I'd had a change of heart. He was so relieved. The phones were still going non-stop. The frenzy over the fight was growing with every day that passed. I went back up to the gym and Terry greeted me warmly. This time I was doing the talking: 'There's a way. It's a gamble and there's no guarantee, but I'll give it my best shot.'

Terry replied, 'There's nothing else, mate. I've been racking my brains and I can't think of a way out of this mess. I'm at your mercy.'

So I explained the plan: 'I'll put in a team of peacemakers, a bit like the Angels on the tube. We're not going to be sorting out security. We'll be there to keep the peace. We'll know all the troublemakers because they're in our gangs and we've got their respect. I've already got some right heavy faces and I need to get one ringleader from every single gang in London. I need money to get some of them on board.'

By now Terry was hanging on every word. He offered me as much money as I needed to make it work. To show him I'm a genuine boxing fan, I told him, 'I don't want paying. I just need some cash to put the operation together, to buy uniforms and pay the guys. Otherwise I'm in for nothing. I'm the only man who can organise this. I'll travel all over London seeing the ringleaders. I've got a week to pull it off.'

Terry wanted to talk to Mike Barrett. I stood outside the office door as Barrett and Terry had a debate about whether my crazy idea could come off. The truth is they had no choice. The door opened and Terry called for Jimmy Tibbs who was in the ring training Kaylor. You didn't disturb Jimmy Tibbs during training. Never. Tibbs looked like thunder as he walked past me. Within half a second he was back out of the office again. They called me back in. Barrett was pacing up and down again. He wouldn't look at me.

Terry sat at the desk. 'Cass, we're gonna go with it.' It was obvious they'd asked Tibbs if he thought I could do it. Terry took out his chequebook, but the first thing I asked for was a meeting with the police and Wembley security. I was already running my own security firm. We'd been in some right battles before and I knew what I was talking about when it came to security. Wembley were a bit put out. Their head of security was the type you get nowadays who are only allowed to operate by the book. But I didn't take him for a mug because he had an ex-services, been-there-done-that look about him. His name was John Pearson. Then I was introduced to a police commander. He had more silverware on his shoulder than West Ham had in their trophy cabinet. I listened for a while and it became crystal clear they thought our blokes were going to be there as just a few extra doormen on the night. I stood up and told them we were nobody's lackeys.

I turned to Mr Pips — he was the Superintendent for the whole Wembley area — and told him, 'Forget who I am. You've probably done your homework on me. You know I've got a criminal record but I'm the only person who can make this work. We don't really need the Old Bill here. Police in uniform are like a red rag to a bull to the mob that'll be there on the night.' Then I told John Pearson, 'No disrespect, but this lot will have your security men for breakfast.' Pearson said nothing. He just looked fierce, as if his nose had been put out of joint. Then, I explained the plan. As far as I could see, Christie didn't really have a following. Nearly everybody there on the night would be backing Kaylor and they were the West Ham mob. If trouble flared, the police and security were *not* to go in. Instead, they had to let my team in first to calm things down. My guys were not going to be given orders by Old Bill, or any security firm.

Immediately, the copper got up and stormed out. The meeting was off. The police commander was having nothing to do with a convicted football thug. I was angry. I'd put everything into this. Yes, it was a

Eight

mad, hare-brained idea, but I was convinced Cass Pennant, king of the football thugs, could pull it off.

I called Terry Lawless and told him I had the right hump. I'd been so convinced my 'mission impossible' would work, I'd even sold my ringside tickets. Now I wouldn't even see the fight. Terry told me to leave it to him. A couple of days later he called: 'You're back on.'

'But what about the copper?' I asked

'Don't worry about him. He ain't happy, but he's been told,' Terry explained.

I knew John Pearson wasn't a problem because, as I'd walked out of our meeting, he came after me and told me, 'I've been in some tough situations and I understand exactly what you're trying to do. I trust you.'

Every time I met Terry before the fight, he had his chequebook ready, asking me how he could pay me. I didn't want his money. In the end I said, 'OK, if I pull it off, I want recognition for my security firm.'

I spent the whole week before the fight going round pubs as far away as Tilbury and Hornchurch speaking to all the gangs, telling them I wasn't selling out. I hadn't become a cop or anything like that. I explained this was to save Mark Kaylor's career. If they wanted the fun and cracks to continue, then we had to make sure there was no trouble. Otherwise, we would never see Kaylor fighting for the world title. Even the West Ham men said, 'Yeh, we're in.'

The fight was on Guy Fawkes Night 1985 and I prayed the only fireworks would be in the ring. The atmosphere inside Wembley Arena would have powered an electricity substation. I had T-shirts made — in West Ham colours, of course — with the slogan 'KEEP IT COOL' emblazoned on the chest. I couldn't resist a bit of free advertising, so they had Cass Security on them, too! As I gave my team their final instructions and handed out the T-shirts in the dressing rooms under the Arena, my voice was nearly drowned by deafening chanting — 'KAYLOR! KAYLLOORR! KAYLLLOOOORRRR!' — echoing all around Wembley. The fighters weren't even out yet.

I turned to Big Dan and Kenny, who'd been with me in the teeth of the riot at Kisses in Peckham. 'Listen,' I said, 'it's all West Ham and Kaylor out there; Christie ain't got any support. He'll need our help. Shove the Wembley security off and we'll bring him out to the ring.'

My guys knew Christie from working the clubs. Although he was from Coventry, he actually trained at a gym in London and went out clubbing south of the river. He was often in Kisses. Christie was mighty glad to see my guys. He was actually terrified. The noise

Eight

and the aggression of the crowd intimidated him. So Dan, with Kenny and Noah Charlery, brought Christie in from one side of the arena. Myself, Tony Bowers and a known face called Bugsy from Mile End brought out Kaylor. The seats were up and everyone was on their feet. We fought our way through that tanked-up, baying mob. The noise of 10,000 voices screaming, 'KAYLOR! KAYLOR! KAYLLORRRRR!' pounded our ears.

As the fighters climbed in the ring, I looked round. The arena was charged with pure, raw testosterone. It could have been Lenny McLean and Roy Shaw in the ring.

I couldn't help thinking boxing had brought this on itself. Two years before the promoters had stupidly billed a fight between Kaylor and Commonwealth middleweight Roy Gumbs as a clash between West Ham and Tottenham. Gumbs had nothing to do with Spurs. But to sell a few more tickets and get extra bums on seats the promoters paraded him in a blue and white Spurs' shirt at Tottenham's ground, White Hart Lane, during a London derby with West Ham. That was the day soccer thugs really got into boxing. The fight venue, Ally Pally — Alexandra Palace — became a bloodbath. Now soccer thugs were in danger of bringing boxing to its knees.

'Seconds out! Round one!' Kaylor and Christie

tore into each other from the off. Within a second Kaylor, in his light blue West Ham shorts, sent Christie sprawling on the floor. The Coventry fighter clambered to his feet, shook the sweat from his eyes and came straight back with a right-hander that sent Kaylor flying on to the canvas. The fight went on at a furious pace for seven more rounds. Kaylor even hit the deck again in the third and bounced back. Either man could have won it at any stage. But in the eighth round Kaylor crashed a devastating right hook on Christie's chin. Kaylor watched, exhausted as Christie collapsed face-first on to the deck. Summoning up amazing courage from the depths of his soul, Christie rose to his knees, his arms searching blindly for the ropes to steady himself. The crowd watched in hushed silence as Christie began to crawl towards his corner. He was still on one knee with his back to Kaylor as referee Harry Gibbs reached the count of ten.

I didn't see much of the fight. I was running round like a blue-arsed fly making sure a riot didn't kick off in the screaming crowd. As soon as I got a report from my boys of trouble brewing I'd run round and get in the thick of it. There were problems with the cops wanting to go in all boots and helmets. There were problems with our lot claiming we'd sold out, that we'd turned into coppers. Bangers and firecrackers exploded all over the place. By the time Harry Gibbs counted Christie out I was so exhausted I felt like I'd done eight rounds in the ring myself. My head was all fuzzy; I hadn't eaten anything; I'd been working on pure 100 per cent adrenalin. I was mentally drained.

But we'd won. There had been no trouble. There were no arrests for violence. A handful were locked up for being drunk. Boxing was saved. The night was hailed as a massive success. The next thing, BBC *Sportsnight* stuck their cameras on Cass. They'd heard the rumours about a 'special force' who had pulled this off. I didn't want to blow my own trumpet and tell them about my tasty back-up team, so I just stood there while the cameraman took a picture of me wearing the Keep It Cool shirt.

On the way back to the dressing room I felt a tap on my shoulder. It was the copper with all the silverware on his shoulder. It was the first time I'd seen him all night. I looked at him full of contempt. I still hadn't forgotten that meeting where he walked out.

He smiled and said, 'I had my doubts, but I have to give it to you: you were a great help tonight. I just want to say thanks.'

I was speechless. It must have been really hard for him. They'd put a criminal in charge of the circus. I knew I could pull it off, but this police commander had every reason to doubt it. So it must have taken a lot of effort for him to come looking for me and say 'thanks'. A compliment from the enemy. It was like winning a medal.

I went to the dressing room to congratulate the boys. Everyone wanted to get away. Pubs in the East End were all staying open so we could have a piss-up to celebrate Kaylor's win. I went looking for a couple of missing T-shirts. Wembley Arena was empty apart from the cleaners clearing away a mountain of rubbish. I checked the dressing rooms, thinking that as Terry had paid for all this clobber I'd got to get it back. I pushed the door ajar on what I thought was an empty dressing room and heard a noise like a muffled whimpering.

I peeped through the crack. There was Christie, sat on a bench, hunched up all alone, whimpering. That's the only way to describe it. I was about to try and cheer him up, but stopped dead in my tracks. He was in a trance, unaware I was even there. I've been in boxing dressing rooms many times at fight shows, and seen boxers after they've lost a fight. But I was witnessing something I'd never seen before. I was looking at a totally broken man. The place echoed with emptiness. Errol Christie hadn't just lost the fight that night, he'd lost his spirit. This was such a private, personal moment I couldn't bear to look any more.

But the picture of one of boxing's heroes totally alone, whimpering like a whipped animal, wouldn't leave my mind. Hero to zero. Where's his trainer? He had nobody.

Kaylor, the underdog, destroyed Christie that night. Kaylor looked beaten so many times but he came back and destroyed Christie. Was it because he had a bigger heart? Or was it that terrifying barrage of noise? When I watch videos of the Kaylor v Christie fight today, the hairs still stand up on the back of my neck. I'll never forget leading Kaylor into that army of 10,000 shouting for the gladiator: 'Kaylor! Kaylor! Kaylor!' I can still hear it ringing in my ears. The atmosphere was awesome. What must it have been like for Christie to walk into that solid wall of hatred?

I wanted to find Terry. The little fella had been in a right old sweat in the run-up to the fight. I also wanted to know if Tel had heard of any trouble outside the venue that could spoil our success. When I caught up with him he looked a different man. This was more like the Terry I knew. All the worry lines that furrowed his head when we'd met in the office were gone. But if it had all gone wrong he could have been like poor Christie.

Terry put out his hand. 'I can't thank you enough, big fella. I don't want to go through that experience again. We're gonna learn from this. From now on we're gonna have security at all our shows. Thanks to you we saved boxing.'

Terry Lawless was a man of his word. The following evening the fight was on *Sportsnight*. Immediately after the ref stuck Kaylor's arm in the air Harry Carpenter asked Tel, 'Who were the special forces you called in?' Terry replied, 'Yeh, we did have a special security firm working behind the scenes.'

'Who were they?'

'Well, let's just say they're people that know who the troublemakers were.'

They knew who the troublemakers were all right — all the troublemakers were on my team!

Mark Kaylor was on a high after knocking out Christie but he got an even bigger boost knowing his career had been saved — even if it was by a bunch of thugs. He still had a big sweat hanging over him because of the fight on the cobbles. He could be fined, disciplined or even given a short ban. But at least he would not be barred for life. In the end, the Boxing Board fined him. Mark wanted to thank me personally. Not long after, I became the manager of a new gym in Sydenham, in South London, and I asked Mark if he'd do the honours and open it for me. The picture of us both outside the Breeze Inn gym is one I'll always treasure. Kaylor is still one of my heroes. He was a West Ham man and he fought like a Hammer — to his last breath if he had to.

Christie's camp told him to put Wembley behind

Eight

him. It was just a defeat. He had so much talent and it was just a setback on the road to glory. They hadn't witnessed the broken man I'd seen. I thought to myself, he's never going to be the same fighter again. And sure enough, he wasn't. He changed trainers and handlers but his boxing career went nowhere from that night. The next thing I heard about Christie, the great middleweight was being booed off stage in his debut as a stand-up comedian after going down faster than a lead balloon.

The papers treated it all as a big laugh — Christie's Hitting the Comedy Circuit and rubbish like that. It was no joke. Every time I read about him I still picture that sad, forlorn figure sat alone in a deserted dressing room under Wembley Arena.

Chapter Nine

The Ancient Briton is an old-fashioned boozer tucked down a back street in Limehouse. It was here I met Ricky Davis, son of East End legend George Davis. Unlike George, Ricky was as straight as a die and he actually worked for the Labour Party. One day in 1986 my mate Mickey Bowers rang to say Ricky had a job for me. It wasn't normal door work. It wasn't even a nightclub. It was a minding job for the Labour Party. Now, Limehouse Town Hall had just been turned into a museum to celebrate the Party's history — suffragettes, the battles of the workers, how the health service started, the unions — it was all there. Well, the former Prime Minister Harold Wilson had just published his memoirs and the great leader decided to hold a book signing session at the Labour Party Museum. It was a big day for them, a bit like the

Queen Mother visiting your nursing home. Ricky and his boss Terry wanted everything to go just right. Suddenly, they remembered, 'Oh Jesus, we've no security'. This was in the days of Militant and the loony left. Trots and commies were running riot all over the country. It seemed Harold had a bit of a dark history, which I wasn't aware of. When he was in Number 10, Labour had boosted party funds by doing some snipey deals with rich factory bosses. The Party didn't want extremists mobbing Sir Harold and wrecking the big day. That's where I came in.

They didn't need gorillas who would go over the top and scare the little old ladies among the faithful. This was Labour, not the jackboot Tories. With my history as shop steward at loony Islington council I was the ideal man for the job because I knew all the political troublemakers in the manor. Watching Harold Wilson's back and keeping an eye on the building would take two people, so I called in my mate, Natalie. Two convicted soccer thugs looking after an ex-Prime Minister! Here I was, a notorious football hooligan on the edge of the underworld, and my first minding job is looking after my parents' hero.

I was quite nervous of meeting such a famous politician. As a kid my foster mum and dad, Doll and Cecil Chambers, had drummed into me, 'You're working class; you're a council tenant; you vote Labour.'

Nine

I wondered how Sir Harold would take two hulking great black men hovering over him. As it happened, he was as good as gold. He understood why we were there. He didn't think it was necessary, but he appreciated it. I remembered he was a football fan who followed Huddersfield Town. That broke the ice. It wasn't a gimmick, either; he actually went to the matches and was a proper supporter, so we happily chatted away about football.

Most of the people who came to see him had walking sticks. They were in their eighties, all telling him stories about the war, Nye Bevin, Stanley Baldwin and all that. It turned into a quaint tea and scones afternoon and the great man loved it. Natalie and me even had our picture taken with him. As I towered over the little bloke with the silver hair and dandruff on the collar of his crumpled old suit, I thought, what a working class hero.

Eventually the old Labour members trotted off home. By now it was pitch black outside, so I decided to make sure there were no reds waiting to ambush him as he left the building. Harold Wilson being hit by an egg would make embarrassing headlines.

But Sir Harold made it plain he didn't want us to see him safely off the premises. He was diplomatic about it, but we were definitely being given the brush off. I said to Natalie, 'He can't just walk out in the pitch dark with no backup.' So we let Harold think he'd got his own way but we followed at a discreet distance. He went out of the door and turned left down the side of the Town Hall. Docklands hadn't been built then, and this was still a right rough area. The alley he'd gone into, Newell Street, was a dead end where joyriders dumped their stolen cars. I thought, Hold on, the old boy's lost. I raced to the corner to shout out, 'You've gone the wrong way, Sir Harold,' but the old man had disappeared. The only thing down the narrow dimly lit street was a huge limousine — it looked like a Roller, the sort of motor that should have been parked outside a stately home. I stood shocked as this black beast of a limo, with a uniformed chauffeur at the wheel, drove past me at a furious pace. In the back was the great man of the people with a startled look on his face. He'd just given all those old suffragettes the working class hero bit and here he was being driven home by Jeeves. No wonder he wanted to give us the slip!

Early one morning a few months later I was setting out equipment at the gym and health club I managed in Sydenham ready for the early morning rush. The phone rang. It was Ricky Davis. 'You remember the Harold Wilson job? Can you do some more work?'

'Yeh, sure. When?'

'In about an hour,' came the reply.

Nine

'An hour? There's nobody else here. I'd have to close up and abandon ship. I can't do it, sorry.'

Ricky pleaded, 'It's urgent, Cass. It's a good earner but you can't say anything to anybody. Oh yeah, make sure you come alone. I'll tell ya about the job when you get 'ere.'

'Well, you know it's a bit short notice,' I said.

By now Ricky was desperate: 'Cass, just get 'ere. Whatever money it takes, it's sorted. Come at all costs.'

I liked the sound of 'all costs' so I closed up the club, jumped in the motor and flew round to the Labour Party Museum in Limehouse. When I got there Ricky's boss, Terry said, 'The work's not here. We gotta go to Tower Hamlets Town Hall.'

For the first time in millions of years Labour had lost control of this working class stronghold, letting the Liberals in. Paddy Ashdown's Lib Dems had taken the borough and because they were a new party they didn't want any of the pomp that goes with having a mayor. In their eyes the mayor was there to do a job, not dress like Baron Hardup in a pantomime. They didn't want gold chains and all that stuff.

Also, there'd been a spate of mayor's chains being nicked. One worth a hundred and fifty grand had been nicked from Islington and melted down. So the Liberals decided to make a politicial message out of it and hand the mayor's chain over to the Labour Party Museum. BBC South East local news were going to be filming the Liberals showing how they were a modern new party and not pompous like Labour and the Tories.

I said, 'That's fine, but I don't see where I come in.'

'Simple,' said Terry, 'we need you to mind the gold. The Town Hall security is only an old boy with a peg leg.'

A puzzled look came over my face. 'I've had to shut me club, and rush here just to mind some gold chain that's obviously fully insured.'

It was then Tel came clean. The council had opened the vaults that morning to get the paperwork for the chain and discovered six more mayor's chains that had never seen the light of day for generations.

Apparently, these chains came from the days before Tower Hamlets when the East End had lots of little councils, each one going back to days of the merchants when the Thames was alive with shipping.

Together, these six chains were worth three quarters of a mill. Phew, they wanted me to mind £750,000 worth of gold. And it got worse. There was another problem: because they'd been in the vault for decades and nobody knew they were there — they weren't insured!

Tel said, 'This is really embarrassing and I couldn't

tell you before. The council's insurance cover only goes up to two hundred and fifty grand and it's too short notice to arrange to insure such a huge amount. I don't want you telling any of your friends or anyone about this. The council's paranoid enough about me getting you in. There's a lot of villains in this area. You don't want a thump on the head and the gold to go missing.'

Now I got the picture. We've got gold, which must be worth two million at today's prices, and no insurance. The Liberals have just got in and if the Tories get wind of it they'll have a field day. The Town Hall officials were on cat hooks because of what happened at Islington when the mayor's chain was nicked and melted down into a pile of gold sovs. I was taken downstairs to an office below the Town Hall next to the vaults and had to stand around. Council officials made a big fuss of making sure I didn't see the combination on the vault. Out came seven chains and I stood around like Ned Kelly while the cameras rolled. I had to be seen on telly so it looked like they had proper security. It was over in seconds, then the officials rushed the chains back into the vault and sent me out of the room while they locked up. It was the easiest number I've ever had in my career as a minder.

When it was over the council men brushed me aside. 'You're not needed; go and collect your money.'

As Peg Leg, the old security man, hobbled down the stairs to let me out of the door I thought, Jesus Christ, no wonder they called me in. He should have been the caretaker, not security.

The museum manager apologised later for keeping me in the dark. He explained, 'It's already awkward because I've employed Ricky Davis. People do make noises about George Davis's son working for the Labour Party. Imagine what they'd have done if they discovered I'd sent a football hooligan with criminal convictions, including robbery, to mind three quarters of a million pounds in gold!'

I had another fearless minding job, this time for the *Sun*. Britain's biggest-selling newspaper hired Ronnie Joyce, an associate of my mate Tony Bowers, to drive superstar Michael Jackson around on a rare visit to London. Tony and me ended up as minders. We hit all the hotspots in London. By the time we stopped for a spot of sightseeing at Tower Bridge and the Tower of London the nation's press circus was in tow. We even paid an unannounced flying visit to Browns nightclub where staff fell at our feet, fussing over us: 'Lovely publicity; have a free drink, Cass.' We were eventually rumbled when we took 'Michael Jackson' to Madame Tussaud's. Everything was so damn convincing, the minders, the limo, even Jackson himself. Then the woman who'd made Michael Jackson's waxwork dummy popped by. Something seemed to be troubling her. The head warden came up and asked me which of us was Michael's manager. I pointed out a little thin chap in a suit. The game was up. The modeller informed her boss that Jackson's manager was a huge fat bloke. By now it was late afternoon so we came clean and were quickly dispatched out of a side door — but too late for the rival hacks who took off for their offices with their scoop. Next day all the papers went front page with Michael Jackson in London. All, that is, except for 'The Soaraway Sun', whose front page screamed: 'Don't read all those other mug papers. If you want the truth stick with the *Sun*.' The Michael Jackson who fooled everyone was a fake who'd spent £14,000 on plastic surgery to look like his idol! For a whole week the *Sun* milked a scam they'd set up themselves.

At the same time my door security business was booming. Work was always coming to me. I never put the frighteners on anyone. Work always came through reputation. We were unbeaten. We were professional at our job and I used to pick the right people for the right job. If we had a madhouse in the city, I'd go for nutters. Everyone who worked for me had to be able to handle themselves. If I thought, I wouldn't like to mess with you, they were on the firm. But my skill was in organising and leadership. No one was going to go to a club if they thought some nutter on the door was going to lose it. Most of the blokes were the toughest around. Some of them were 'uncontrollable' but I had a talent for controlling the very fiercest men. I got them to work in the right way for me through respect and trust.

On Friday and Saturday nights I'd travel round checking my empire and paying my bouncers' wages. I drove a beaten-up old Mini Metro because I was often carrying baseball bats and weapons for the doormen. In a flash BMW or a Merc the Old Bill would have stopped me every couple of miles, and with some of the tools I had stashed in the boot I'd have been banged up. One of the clubs on my rounds was Dr Crippens wine bar in Bromley, Kent. You might think Bromley was one of the soft spots, but it could be a rough old town. Time was always short, so I'd bowl into each of my clubs, have a quick word with the door, a natter with the management and be gone as quickly as I came.

Every time I went through the door at Dr Crippens the first person I clapped eyes on was a blonde chick with eyes that twinkled. She had a very natural pretty face and was obviously not impressed by me at all. Wow, I thought, why can I never meet a girl like her? She worked in the cloakroom and I knew she was petite because her head and shoulder only just reached over the counter. I couldn't take my eyes off her. I turned to my doormen John and Noah. 'I sure look after you guys. I give you the clubs with the best birds.' I felt envious, even jealous, of my own doormen. I stayed for a drink and asked about the blonde working in the cloaks. Her name was Elaine and she was best mate with my head doorman Danny's girl, Linzi. Aha, there was a pathway to her. But I started putting myself down. I'd been on a run of too many one-night-stands after my ex took off to work in Tenerife. I kept thinking, She's too good for me. Will my reputation put her off? The image of her pretty face wouldn't go away. I was in torment. As I made some discreet enquiries I found out she came from an honest, hard-working family: she definitely was too good for me. As the weeks went by I was still mad about her and I knew I had to go for it. My timing would have to be spot-on. I asked her out and we fell in love in a short space of time. But time was irrelevant: it was one of those intense relationships where you feel you've known each other for years. But time did become relevant on a cold January morning in 1987.

Two years earlier, like everybody else in Britain I'd watched telly as the horrific events unfolded on that warm May evening when Liverpool and Juventus fans clashed in the Heysel Stadium in Brussels. Thirty-nine fans died that night.

Heysel didn't only shock Joe Public; it shocked hooligans like me, too. To us it was a game — a dangerous game, but a game. It wasn't meant to be like this. No one was meant to get killed. Yeh, we'd done some serious violence to our rivals, but not manslaughter. Heysel was the moment I realised it was time to give up hooliganism for ever. Football violence was a drug and a hard habit to kick but as I watched those fans dying before my eyes I vowed to turn my back on terrace violence for good.

In the wake of the Heysel disaster, English soccer clubs were kicked out of Europe for five long years and Britain's relationships abroad in business, tourism and everything else were wrecked.

Maggie Thatcher went ballistic: she demanded action from the cops to stop the 'scum'. That was when a copper came up with an idea to beat the hooligans by infiltrating their gangs. He sent a bulky dossier to his bosses at Scotland Yard, arguing that by infiltrating soccer gangs the police would be able to hit hooligans with conspiracy charges instead of the usual minor offences. That way you would get hooligans off the street for a long time.

Operation Own Goal was born. Boy, would that name come back to haunt them. For six months undercover cops tried to infiltrate West Ham's

Nine

InterCity Firm in the hope of getting enough evidence to make a conviction stick.

That cold January morning in 1987 I was woken with a start at the sound of my front door in Hackney being battered with a sledgehammer. It was five o'clock and pitch black. Men with muffled voices milled outside. 'Police! Open up!' I thought it was a joke. I hadn't been up to anything for over a year. Quick, think. Nope, there were no weapons in the flat, so I opened the door before they smashed it to smithereens and nine of them charged in. I was being arrested as part of Operation Own Goal. We'd heard whispers, but because I hadn't been involved in any trouble at soccer grounds I thought I was safe. Even so, I knew this was really serious shit. The previous year they'd done Chelsea and the main men in their firm were doing ten years. I was absolutely gutted. I'd just got my life sorted out: I was the manager of a nightclub; the bouncing business was thriving and I'd finally met a girl I wanted to settle down with. The Sheffield nightmare was coming back to haunt me. I was so shocked I sat in the cells struck dumb. I'd never felt so tired and drained. I'd been fighting the system all my life; did I have the energy to take them on all over again?

Eleven others had been rounded up that morning. I recognised Andy Swallow, Bill Gardner, Paul Dorsett and a couple of other faces, but I'd never seen the rest of them in my life. I thought, I'm in the clear here. Whatever they've been up to, I wasn't part of it.

The cops whisked us to a procession of nicks around London. No one knew where we were. This was getting sinister. Poor Elaine came to the flat to find me gone and a bunch of coppers stripping the place bare for evidence. Now, if you come from an East End family someone always knows what to do in these situations. Elaine was from a decent, honest family from respectable Petts Wood. She'd never been through anything like it in her life. Desperately she tried to find me, to bring me clean clothes and sort out a lawyer, but the cops gave her the run around.

It wasn't fair for my lovely Elaine to be involved in all this, but although she knew nothing of the hooligan scene, she realised we were in the middle of something sinister that had nothing to do with a few Saturday afternoon battles. We were both deeply in love and she was determined to help me fight this threat to our blossoming relationship. Elaine's unswerving faith in me made me realise I had to fight these bastards all the way. The trauma and heartache of the whole thing could have pushed us apart but instead it served to cement us together.

Eventually the West Ham Twelve ended up in court where our names were called out. I was charged with conspiracy but I was eleventh on the charge list. The cops always put their number one suspect at the top of the indictment. So I thought, I'm number eleven here — two to three years tops. Bail refused — back to the Scrubs. Most of the others had never been inside before — usually you only got fines for hooliganism — and even though they were tough cookies it was hair-raising for them. I decided we had to organise our defence and to keep everybody's spirits up — otherwise they would split us apart. I gave Andy, Bill and Ted Bugby the job of making sure we all stayed close.

Eventually charges were dropped against Taffy but the big shock came when the eleven of us who were left applied for bail. Andy Swallow was top of the list — his bail was set at £100,000. I rocked back on my feet in the dock with shock. A hundred grand — the lad was an out-of-work market trader for God's sake! Where was he gonna find a hundred grand? The only time I'd ever heard of £100,000 bail was for the Brinks-Mat robbers and they'd nicked seven million quid's worth of gold. I thought, Jesus Christ, we're in the shit. They've put football hooligans in the same bracket as heavy gangsters. Nobody's got that sort of dough. My bail was set at £60,000. Secretly, Swallow was proud that he was top dog and I had the right hump that he was regarded as forty grand better than me.

Eventually, my bail came down to £30,000 but I still had trouble raising it. One day when I appeared again at Newham East Magistrates in Stratford the court was buzzing. A jailer came down, rattled his keys, and asked, 'You're the one, aren't you? Frank Bruno's mate.'

I didn't answer. Then the solicitors came down to the cells under the court room. 'You'll be alright for our bail today. Your friends have arranged for Frank Bruno to stand bail.'

Being banged up in the Scrubs all week, I hadn't a clue what was going on. At one time my mate Danny the doorman had gone out with Frank Bruno's sister, Joan. They'd met at Kisses where Joan worked on the club reception. Danny had mentioned to Joan that I was in big, big trouble and it got back to Frank who'd never forgotten the incident at Stratford tube station when I'd come to his rescue. I couldn't tell anybody about what had gone on that day, but everybody was getting very excited about Frank coming to court.

Amazingly, Frank didn't show. My hopes shot down in flames, I slumped back to the Scrubs. On their next visit the boys told me that when Terry Lawless discovered Frank wanted to put up my bail he called his top fighter in for a chat. Tel said, 'Frank, you can't do this. The press will have a field day. You can see it now — Scandal: Boxing Sensation Stands Bail for Notorious Football Hooligan. Do this and you'll throw away all we've worked for in the last five years.'

Frank looked at him and said, 'Tel, I gotta do it, know what I mean.' But he couldn't tell him why and Lawless tried to explain to Frank in the best way possible that it couldn't happen. Then Terry learned that Frank was planning to go behind his back and turn up at court anyway. Frank's people read him the riot act and that's why he didn't show.

Terry called Frank back into the office and told him, 'We're so close to getting the world title fight. You're throwing away the dream. Why can't I get through to you? Why do you keep saying you've gotta do it? What's going on between you and Cass?'

Then Frank told Lawless the story of Stratford. Terry realised straight away why Frank felt he had to help me. He didn't have a go but just said, 'Look, we need to sit down and think about this. Cass is a friend to me as well. I can see now why you want to help him so much. But look at it this way. You standing bail won't help him. Once you get him off remand he's still in deep water. I'd like to help Cass as well and the only way we can help him is when he really needs it — when he's in court, up against the big guns.'

Terry then explained his plan to Frank, 'You must pull out from standing bail but in return I'll help Cass where he needs it most by standing in court for him as a character witness. I can do that because I genuinely know Cass and what I know of him he's a decent guy.' Nice one, Frank. Even though he never made it to the court, I knew what he'd tried to do. That was enough for me. That evened the score, though in my mind there'd been nothing to square anyway.

The next time I saw Danny he came with a message telling me Terry Lawless would be a witness and to get in touch. It still didn't sort out my immediate problem of bail. After that setback with Frank my good pal Tony Bowers put his dad up to stand bail. Tony's dad stood for me in court. It was a magnificent gesture. The next thing the police arrested him and he ended up in a cell next to me for some domestic with his ex-wife going back donkeys' years. The police did everything they could to stop us getting out so we couldn't put a defence together.

Gradually we pieced together some of the police 'evidence' against us. One day I'd been standing next to Big Danny on the terrace at Upton Park. It was just after he'd been shot at Kisses nightclub in Peckham. When they heard a black doorman had been shot at Kisses, all the West Ham lads thought it had been me. I told them, 'Don't keep coming up and asking me. Danny's the fella you should be talking to. It was him who copped it.'

Nine

So Danny was telling the story of how he was shot by the rasta. Unknown to us the undercover surveillance team from Operation Own Goal were close by. They couldn't properly infiltrate us because we were too tightly knit. So they 'infiltrated' us from a distance. Two plain-clothes cops were standing almost out of earshot picking up the odd word like 'sawn-off shotgun'. The Old Bill turned Danny telling the story of how he was shot into me and an unknown black man boasting about doing a blagging. It was total nonsense. All they'd heard was the word shotgun.

How could I prove my innocence? Banged up inside, I couldn't contact anyone. Gradually the others got out and there were only two of us left. Finally my foster brother Richard, who ran a car spares business, stood bail for me. He wasn't too happy because I guess I'd brought shame to the family, and to be honest I didn't want to feel I owed him anything, but everything else had failed. I needed to be out to put my defence together. Under the conditions of my bail I was banned from every football ground within a five-mile radius of Upton Park and I had to live sixty miles away in Ashford, Kent.

But the girl of my dreams was in South-east London so I was desperate to stay in the area. My West Ham mate Johnny Andrews was buying a house but he still had a council flat on the ninth floor of a tower block in Queen's Road, Plaistow. He didn't want to give the keys back to the council so I persuaded him to let me stay there. From that window on the ninth floor I could actually see Upton Park! I went all over East London trying to sort out witnesses for my defence. On match days I had to stay in because the police passed the bottom of my stairs. My face was so well known I'd have been nicked.

The next shock came at the committal hearing to send the case to a Crown Court where I would be tried by jury. Remember I told you I was eleventh on the charge sheet — well, suddenly I was number one, top of the whole bleedin' list. You're probably wondering how I went from back of the field looking at a two-year stretch to prime suspect, staring at ten years behind bars? I sure as hell was.

It turned out my unlucky break came when the Old Bill charged through the door on their dawn raid. Sure enough, there was none of the normal incriminating evidence there: no weapons, soccer programmes, travel tickets, or even the infamous ICF calling cards. But what the cops did find was a copy of a manuscript, *War on The Terraces* by Cass Pennant. It was a novel — a work of fiction — I'd written to while away the long hours when I was inside after being shafted in Sheffield. I've always had an ability to write and I wanted to tell what it was really like to be a football hooligan. It would be my way to fame and fortune, and keep me on the straight and narrow away from football.

It had taken the cops a while to wade through all 174 pages in a black clip binder. The hooligans in my story supported West Ham, of course, and had names like Andy Swift. Aha! thought the boys in blue, this isn't fiction: it's a diary cunningly disguised as a novel. Instead of just charging me with crimes alleged to have happened in the six months the cops were undercover, they went back *seven* years.

They were jumping for joy by the time they found a copy of the famous ITV documentary, *Hooligan*. I'd worked with top TV producer Ian 'Butch' Stuttard in making the film for Thames TV. By the time the documentary was made I'd eased myself out of the InterCity Firm but Butch wanted to show what the West Ham hooligans were really like. He didn't want to glorify our exploits but he wanted to make the first-ever documentary to show we weren't all mindless, out-of-work thugs in Doc Martens. He was going to show how we had good jobs and how we were ingenious. I agreed to work with him on two conditions — I was paid and he helped me find a publisher for my book.

I told him, 'Put your camera away and come with us for six months. You've got to win our trust. There's no one leader; we're all powerful people and we all share the same interest. Once you're accepted you won't be seen as a threat. Then we can go to work.'

And that's how it was. He come along and realised he was on to something. It was like a secret society. If undercover police couldn't infiltrate us a TV cameraman stood no chance at all. I had to win over the others. I couldn't just go in and say I'd got a cameraman here or they'd have said, 'You're not in charge of us.' It had to be done with respect and intelligence.

Butch ended up making the most revealing hooligan documentary ever, and it sold all over the world. We became firm friends and we're still pals to this day. He had such a laugh he nearly got caught up with it all. We had to take him into battle to show him what it was like so there was plenty of footage of fights at grounds all over the country.

And just in case the book and the documentary weren't enough to nick me, the cops took a meat knife from the kitchen drawer. I was in deep shit.

It's funny how just when life kicks you in the nuts something else happens to give you hope. One night Andy Swallow got a phone call from a man called Eddie Stretch. We didn't know him from Adam, but somehow he knew Paul Dorsett's girlfriend and he contacted us. One afternoon in November 1987 Mr

Nine

Stretch's 24-year-old son Gary — not Gary Stretch the middleweight boxing champ — was in The Limes pub in Hackney Road, East London, after a funeral. A group of local lads were drowning their sorrows after the funeral in one corner of the bar, and in another corner were seven boozing off-duty policeman.

One of the policemen sidled up to one of the young mourners; they'd been at school together. The cozzer said, 'I want a word in your ear, bit of advice. My officers over there don't like one of your pals. Something's gonna go off. I want you to step away from it.'

The kid he was talking to replied, 'Listen, copper, just 'cos I went to school with you, I ain't stepping aside. These are my pals. If you've got a problem with him, you've got a problem with me.'

Just before closing time all hell broke loose as the off duty coppers had a go at the mourners, and then the two groups laid into each other. Gary Stretch came off worse. He looked like he'd been glassed. There was blood everywhere. Forgetting about their own cuts and bruises, the lads carried their badly injured friend outside to a car to get him to hospital. They used bar towels to staunch the flow of blood from Gary's head. But the drunken coppers hadn't finished yet. He was dragged out of the car and as Gary lay bleeding in the gutter the cops kicked him.

When uniformed police from Bethnal Green station arrived the off duty cops ran off, leaving Gary lying unconscious in the road. They didn't come back till later.

When Gary eventually reached the London Hospital, doctors found he had a broken collar bone. Those responsible had also slashed his neck with a bottle and chopped off part of his ear.

Eddie Stretch was horrified when he got to the hospital. He told me: 'My son was in a terrible way. His ear was hanging by a thread and his eye was like red jelly. I couldn't believe the state he was in.'

The seven upholders of law and order who'd beaten his son up were from City Road police station. Gary's mates were arrested and hauled off. The barmaid, who was actually a policeman's daughter, was so horrified at Old Bill's behaviour she lodged a complaint and all seven officers who started the brawl were suspended. The reason Mr Stretch was telling all this? Two of them — PC Peter Clissold and PC Paul Wells — were on Operation Own Goal and they were going to be giving evidence against us in court.

As soon as Andy told me the story I said, 'We've gotta get the pictures. There must be some photos and X-rays from when the lad went to hospital. Keep in touch with his old man and see if he can help us.'

Eventually we got our hands on pictures of Gary

Nine

Stretch with his neck in a brace, bruises all over his face and his ear a mass of stitches. For the time being we kept the Gary Stretch business a closely guarded secret between myself, Andy Swallow and Paul Dorsett. It would be useful ammo for the trial, which was still nearly three months away.

Not long after, we were all sent letters from West Ham, the football club that we had followed for years, telling us we were banned. Banned for life, and we hadn't even been convicted. Some of the lads worried more about that letter from the club than the upcoming trial. Not seeing West Ham again didn't matter — if we went down we were looking at not seeing daylight again for ten years.

Chapter Ten

Snaresbrook Crown Court in East London is said to have the highest rate of 'not guilty' verdicts in the country but even there juries can put a spanner in the works. Barristers, solicitors and court jailers who virtually live in courtrooms and see juries in action every day of the week can't predict jury form. So all eleven of us in the dock had to concentrate on getting the right jury. Each defendant can object to three jurors. Your mind is filled with possibilities. What if the jury's mainly women? They don't like any kind of violence and wouldn't understand the idea of self-defence like a man. Remember, I'd had an all-woman jury once and they hung me out to dry. In that particular case — the Sheffield trial — I thought all the blokes among the waiting faces looked clever dicks and would have none of me, no matter what I said. You don't want the old bastards. They all look at you absolutely horrified and the trial ain't even kicked off. Barristers think the same way and will get rid of the oldies without consulting you. Old folk argue too much and they're usually paid-up members of the 'put 'em in the army and birch 'em' brigade. And where's the black population when it comes to jury selection? It seems to me that, apart from the token black, they're never pulled out of the hat. The system's idea of a cross-section of the community is to give you a hard-working Asian. They're just as likely to hang you as the old bastards. How come you don't get too many council tenants sitting in judgement? Why is it always professional people staring at you from the jury box? What's wrong with shellsuit folk?

So you go out of your mind worrying about getting a fair, open-minded favourable-looking jury. Even after the case, the jury still plays on your mind. Which ones sent you down? You need to know, even if it's just for next time. One day I was standing at the bar in the Alex pub in Hackney when a bloke called my name, came over and asked me how I was doing. He said I wouldn't remember him, but he'd recognised me instantly. He explained he'd been one of the jury members when I was up for malicious wounding at Snaresbrook. I couldn't believe this geezer's front until I remembered I'd got off. There'd been two of us in the dock; the jury cleared me and found my mate guilty. I was annoyed for my pal, but I'd always been curious about why he went down and I'd walked. Here was an unbelievable chance to find out what had happened in the jury room that day.

Apparently, before the case had even begun in earnest the jury decided that as there were two defendants, one of them was probably guilty and the other innocent. They would listen to the case and decide properly. Throughout the trial the jury concentrated on just one defendant. This juror assured me that he and another member of the jury wanted to find us both not guilty, but the rest of them weren't convinced. In the end they decided my pal was the guilty one but they only convicted him on the lesser of the two charges he faced. But it was a close thing. One of the jurors was adamant that he should go down for the more serious charge. No matter how hard the others tried to convince him, he wouldn't budge. This stand-off went on for most of the afternoon. The judge had demanded a unanimous verdict — one on which all 12 jurors agreed — by 4.30.

Suddenly, the juror with the strong difference of opinion said that although he didn't agree with it, he'd go along with the majority. The others asked him why he'd changed his mind. He had a chicken in the oven and if he didn't get home by half past three it would be burnt to a crisp! My co-defendant's fate had been decided on whether a bloke's chicken was going to burn!

Sat side-by-side in the dock, we were a fighting unit again — only this time our battle was getting the right jury. We thought we had a breakthrough when Danny Daly recognised one of the jurors. She was his old next door neighbour from Tower Hamlets. 'We're all right here,' said Danny. 'I think she fancies me.' So having sent word down the line that we wanted no women, we had to give out the order. 'Make sure you get the blonde. No other women, just the blonde one.' Finally we got her on. When she was sitting in the jury box, dopey Danny only went and waved at her from the dock! Then she stood up and told the judge she knew one of the defendants — a good enough reason to pull out. A lot of the jurors tried to get out of it. They didn't mind a couple of days off work, but three months was an ordeal. We were gutted when she stepped out of the jury box. Bang went our chance of having at least one cert. We all turned round and gave Danny the evil eye. At that moment I could have happily lynched him. Later, downstairs in the cells he tried to tell us he was only rubbing his eyes! We were even more fed up when the others recognised a couple of West Ham supporters among the waiting faces for jury service, but their names weren't even called out. There was worse to come in the lunch break when some of the less shrewd among us were seen talking, in all innocence, to some of the jurors. Those jurors were slung off as soon as the court resumed.

Despite our best efforts, we did end up with six women jurors. We christened one of them 'Evil Eyes'. Usually jury members try to avoid eye contact, unless the prosecution makes a point of asking them to look at someone in the dock. This dark-haired woman kept looking at us with a horror-movie stare, the sort that could turn you to stone. In fact, that stare was so hard that your natural reaction was to duck down out of her line of sight. Every one of us commented on it.

'Did you see that bitch kept staring at us as if we were monsters,' said one.

'Yeh, I felt it. Those eyes are evil. She'd hang us now if she could,' came the reply.

It took the court clerk a good half hour to read out the charge sheet: Cass Pennant, nightclub manager; Andrew Swallow, market trader; Edward Bugby, electrical repairman; Harvey Catling, engineer; Danny Daly, unemployed; Peter Dickey, warehouseman; Paul Dorsett, meat wholesaler; Bill Gardner, builder; Derek Legg, floor layer; Kevin Schroder, window cleaner; Martin Sturges, driver. We were all charged with conspiracy to unlawfully fight and cause affray. We all went 'Not guilty'. They also accused Paul of possessing firearms — a .22 rifle the cops found at his home — possession of ammo and handling stolen goods. Andy Swallow was also accused of handling a stolen video.

The case began in earnest on day two. The prosecution told the jury how seven brave young constables had infiltrated the ranks of Britain's most feared gang of soccer hooligans — the notorious West Ham InterCity Firm — which for years had brought terror to football games all over the country. Prosecuting brief Vivien Robinson QC told the wide-eyed jury all about a series of battles claimed to have been witnessed by the undercover cops. In one incident near West Ham's Upton Park ground, shoppers cowered in doorways as Dickey, Pennant, Legg and Shroder marshalled scores of West Ham fans in a clash with their hated Chelsea rivals. Shroder was heard to say, 'We're going to have you, Chelsea — you're all fucking dead!' And Dickey was supposed to have shouted, 'Kill the Old Bill!' At an away game in Liverpool, Ted Bugby was said to have warned gang members, 'Anyone who bottles out better not turn up at West Ham — otherwise they're dead.'

Mr Robinson told the jury how up to sixty officers had raided our homes that January morning and they'd found weapons like knives, coshes and a number of videos. They played one of the videos to the jury. It was an interview we'd given nearly three years earlier to CBS television in America. Butch, who'd made the *Hooligan* documentary, put them on to us. The video the jury saw showed me saying, 'When we go up north each one of us is a Rambo — we hurt the ones that want to hurt us.' I also said, 'If we were doing this in the Falklands they'd love us. The British have always been fighting wars.' Andy Swallow told them, 'Our trade is football violence. You've got to be the best.' The jury members kept switching their eyes from the screen to us in the dock — we looked a gruesome bunch with our scars from Stanley knives and bottles.

Next day the papers were full of headlines like, 'WE'RE ALL RAMBOS BOASTS SOCCER YOB' and 'REIGN OF TERROR BY THE INTERCITY GANG'. But the horrifying evidence the prosecution had promised to serve up to the jury never materialised. They set up video screens around the court and we sat through 120 hours of surveillance footage. There wasn't one punch up, just people walking about at away matches. Because the police had blocked off every avenue, nothing was going on. Out of 120 hours of video — that's 7,200 minutes; played non-stop it would have taken five days to show

— I didn't appear once! An undercover photographer took 300 photos. I wasn't in any of them either. It seemed to me I'd been arrested purely to show they really had nailed the InterCity Firm.

As the trial dragged on endlessly, I amused myself by rewriting bits of the script for a TV drama called *The Firm*, written by Al Hunter. You might remember him from *Crossroads* where he played a slob called Ray Grise. When *Crossroads* was axed Al got out of acting and moved into writing. He's written scripts for *Casualty*, *The Bill* and *EastEnders*. Al's a Brummie and supports Birmingham City so he decided to write a drama about a gang of football thugs. He based *The Firm* on Millwall's Bushwhackers and the West Ham ICF. The Beeb had put up a big enough budget to hire director Alan Clarke, who's probably best known for the movie *Scum*. And they'd got Gary Oldman as the star. It was his last bit of acting in Britain before he cracked America big time with *Dracula*.

Al had seen the *Hooligan* documentary and approached Butch who told him he couldn't have done it without my help. So Al hired me as a paid consultant on his project. With Al being a Brummie, some of the slang in his script wasn't right, so I whiled away the boring hours in the trial making his dialogue more realistic, know wot I mean?

Later, when filming eventually started, I got to

meet Gary Oldman and he asked my advice on whether the clothes the wardrobe department had chosen were accurate. Al even started working me into his scripts as an extra and other times he got me work doing security on locations. Film companies often hire a 'one-man fighting machine', who is a diplomat and who won't lay a hand on the public. Oh, and who's cheap enough to fit in with their budget. Instead of protecting stars, they put their 'fighting machine' to work guarding a piece of bloody equipment that ain't going anywhere. On one shoot Al was actually working as the producer and they had a problem on set that was holding up filming. Could I sort it out? They were in St Martin's Lane near Trafalgar Square filming a drama about the homeless. The trouble was the *real* homeless, the down-and-outs, kept disrupting the shoot because they felt they were being exploited by the TV crew. They had a point; you can't move round London these days without bumping into a celebrity wielding a ladle in a charity soup kitchen!

Al said, 'Listen, Cass, this film will help highlight their plight but we're never going to get it finished if the real homeless keep charging round here hurling abuse and damaging the equipment.' It turned out the homeless mob had a leader who they called The King of the Streets. His name was Soldier. The cameras had just started rolling when I heard a drunken commotion. I looked up the street and there on the corner was a geezer in a ripped–up sheepskin and a couple of pals from 'cardboard city' shouting, 'We won't be exploited! We haven't been paid!' I closed in on them, grabbed the loud bloke in the sheepskin and pulled him into a doorway out of everybody's sight. He stank, but I got in close to his face and growled, 'I know you're the one called Soldier. I'm being paid to sort you out but I'm not gonna. I understand what you're doing and why, but you're not going down that street to fuck up their filming.'

I pointed to the nearest pub. 'Come on, I'll buy you a drink.' He looked too old to bash up. He was probably about my age but he'd lost a lot of years living on the streets. He protested that he wouldn't be allowed in. I told him, 'Nobody'll say shit. I'm buying and you're with me.'

His face lit up. 'Can I have a fag?' I promised to buy him a packet if he came with me. I got a few dodgy looks in the pub but all the time I had him in there he couldn't disrupt filming. If you could ignore the smell he was an interesting character. He really was the King of the Streets. He'd been around the longest and knew everybody in tent city and box alley. He had no time for youngsters who lived with the homeless in the summer but went home in the winter.

Ten

They were giving real down-and-outs a bad name. Soldier was no longer a problem. I'd won his respect. He gave me his word that the film crew would be left in peace and he wandered off up the road taking his hobos with him. It had cost me the price of a packet of cigs and a pint. When I went back to claim my wages the film crew were in awe. 'What did you do, give him a dig?' I didn't reply. They could carry on thinking whatever they wanted.

Al was part of a writing and acting team with Robbie Coltrane and Lenny Henry. The three of them wrote and acted in a drama called *Alive and Kicking* — based on a true story about a junkies' football team. They were filming on a concrete jungle estate in Brentford, out west near the M4. The crew were worried because a local warlord wanted to 'tax' them for stepping on his manor. It was pissing down when I got there and everybody thought I was Lenny Henry's double. All the actors stood around looking glum and then in walked Lenny and Robbie Coltrane. The pair of them had everyone in stitches, cracking jokes non-stop until the rain stopped. When the sun came out they started filming again.

As the cast broke for lunch Al told me Lenny wanted to see me privately in his caravan. He didn't have to ask me twice. Lenny was a big hero of mine. I enjoy all his stuff on telly but more than that we had similar backgrounds. He spent his childhood in a mainly white community in Dudley in the West Midlands. Like me, Lenny is proud to be black and proud to be British.

We were in the caravan, just me and him, and we hit it off really well. We chatted about music and then got round to talking about my life doing the doors. He'd been to the same clubs, followed the same DJs and we liked the same music. We chatted right through lunch about funk, disco and the soul patrol days. Then I said to him, 'Len, my favourite sketches you do on telly are the ones with the nightclub bouncer.'

Lenny had created a geezer with dodgy wet-look hair and a leery jacket whose catchphrase was 'You're not a member, you ain't comin' in!' Every time Lenny appeared on telly doing his bouncer routine, people came up to me and said, 'It's you, innit?'

I'd never met Lenny Henry before in my life but my likeness had appeared in too many sketches not to have me wondering. That's when he cut me short, 'Cass, I've got to confess, some of them are you, mate.'

I blurted out, 'What!'

'Your friend Al's told me a lot about you,' he admitted.

Wow. Then there was a knock at the door and it was time for him to go back on set. We never got to talk again but I did receive two fat cheques from Lenny's company, Crucial Films. He paid me for my memoirs of life as a bouncer and for some storylines for a film he really wanted to make. It would be a straight role with Lenny playing the King of the Bouncers. The idea came to nothing. I was disappointed because it sounded good to me and *Alive and Kicking* showed he'd got what it takes to be a serious actor. Still, I cashed the cheques and I had my letter, there in black and white: 'Thanks for all your help, Lenny.'

After 13 days without any hard evidence against us, the jury in the ICF trial were starting to fall asleep. After being told this was the most violent gang of football hooligans in the country, nothing had happened — no punch-ups, no sticking the boot in, nothing. All of a sudden a big burly copper, who looked a bit like Desperate Dan, got up in the witness box and told how a railing had divided two hundred Arsenal and fifty West Ham fans at Highbury. The Arsenal charged at the railing to get at the enemy. The undercover cop said his hairs stood on end as one of the men in the dock, Peter Dickey, had pulled out a knife. The jurors sat up. At last, some juicy stuff. Dickey was a young fella but he had a huge ginger beard which made him seem older. The Arsenal mob froze as Hagar the Horrible's double charged at them with a huge blade that glinted in the sun. Lucky the railing was there to stop him. The uniform boys charged in, arrested him and confiscated the knife.

Shit. We all ducked our heads down under the dock. I glared at Dickey thinking, We were getting on well 'til you came along, son. You've made us look bad with that one.

Then Dickey's barrister got to his feet and asked the shaven-headed copper to tell the whole bloodthirsty story again. The jury were looking at us again as if we were nutters. Then — just as I was thinking, Christ, Dickey, get your brief to shut up; he's digging a bloody hole and burying us — it got worse.

The barrister asked the copper how big the knife was. 'About four inches,' came the reply. Then Dickey's brief only went and said, 'I'd like the court to see the knife.'

They didn't have it. The court adjourned and when we came back the jury, who'd been yawning and struggling to stay awake for over two weeks, were suddenly lively and filled with expectation. They must have thought, You ICF boys are going down now.

A court officer carried the bag on a tray over to the witness box. Our barrister asked if this was the exhibit from the Arsenal match in November 1986. 'Yes.'

Ten

'Perhaps, the jury would like to see the knife. Would you take it out of the bag officer?' asked the judge. It was as if he was saying, let 'em see what these little angels in the dock are really like.

The judge was keen, the barrister was keen, but all of a sudden the copper was reluctant. He was getting agitated. He couldn't open the bag; it had been sealed with plastic straps.

'Having difficulty, officer?' asked the old barrister.

The judge peered over his desk, expecting to see a huge four-inch blade.

When the copper held up the knife the whole court burst into gales of laughter. It was a tiny keyring penknife with a blade no more than one and a half inches long! It was the sort you buy at Blackpool to pick your nails with.

Our barrister knew the copper was shafted but he kept going: 'Is this the knife that was being waved about, officer? I think the jury ought to see this terrifying weapon.'

The court officer was like a butler as he took the knife on the tray over to the jury box. The first juror seemed to stifle a smirk as he picked up the tiny knife and gingerly passed it to the next one. Just about every member of that jury was trying to keep a straight face.

This was a serious trial and they had to do their

duty. As they passed round the keyring blade they were all trying their best not to laugh. The burly copper in the witness box went bright red. Was that the best they could do? They had eleven of the most notorious blokes in the country and all they could stick on them was possession of a Blackpool keyring knife. They must have been desperate.

On day 16 of the trial — the start of the fourth week — my son was born. I had to ask the court's permission to be at Elaine's side when she went into labour. My son Marcus had come into the world and I had no idea when I might see him again. As I cradled him in my arms, I wondered if he would be a strapping lad of ten when I would be free to hug him again. What future would life hold for him with his dad behind bars? Ask any father to name the most memorable day of their life and they will tell you it was the day their first child came into the world. My elation turned to depression as I left Elaine and Marcus tucked up in bed and returned to court.

Five days later when PC Clissold — one of the off-duty cops who was one of those who'd been in the attack on Gary Stretch — appeared in the witness box, one of the jurors had to step down. He'd been to a couple of parties the copper had been at and his sister knew Clissold's sister. He was discharged.

My brief reckoned the case against me was so weak

Ten

I didn't need the photos of Gary Stretch's horrific injuries for my defence. So I gave them to the barristers representing some of the others. I wanted to see the Old Bill squirm when the tables were turned on them.

Clissold and Wells turned up in court in smartly pressed uniforms with their boots polished. Immediately our barristers leapt on them and asked why suspended officers were wearing uniforms. Apparently, an officer who's suspended can't normally wear his uniform in court until he has been cleared. Very clever; the truth about these two was coming out. Despite being suspended over the attack on Gary Stretch, these two reckoned a Chief Superintendent had given permission for them to wear uniforms instead of civvies. When he was being cross-examined Clissold said the assault on Gary Stretch wasn't serious. It had been blown out of all proportion and all seven cops who were suspended would be denying the allegation. It was then a brief stuck our pictures of Gary Stretch's battered and slashed face into Clissold's hands.

'Don't these pictures, in fact, show a serious case of grievous bodily harm?' asked our brief. The copper disagreed. It didn't matter that the judge wouldn't let the jury see the photos of Gary's injuries — the whole story was now coming out of how these two policemen were part of an attack on a member of the public, leaving him with permanent damage to one eye, plus an ear partly severed. Now who were the thugs in court?

As each undercover cop came into the witness box their stories hardly matched up. Some of them even had times down in their notebooks that were totally contradicted by the timer on the video footage they showed the jury. Like when the timer in the bottom corner of the video screen showed we arrived at a railway station at 11.10 am but the coppers wrote in their notes that we got there at 2 pm. Another copper said he'd heard Paul Dorsett and a group of others planning violence against Chelsea fans at half time in the long tea bar at Upton Park. But photographs showed Dorsett was in his seat at half time. This copper then said he was in the toilet between 8.50 and 9.00 pm writing up his notes about what he'd heard in the tea room — but their own photographs showed him and another undercover policeman sitting together in the ground at 8.55! The cops mixed up loads of their evidence and didn't realise until they got to court that the video mob and photographers had exact timings which made them look bloody stupid. Some said they'd written their notes sat in toilet cubicles on trains travelling to away matches. How did they have such neat writing? Anybody who has tried to do the crossword on a fast-moving InterCity train will tell you it's impossible to write properly. Others said they waited until the end of the day before writing down what had happened hours earlier. How could they remember every detail of what went on in the morning when they were writing their notes at night? The fact is most of the police surveillance notes were a shambles and the Old Bill were being slaughtered by their own evidence.

A young defence barrister called Michael Moore had been on a case prior to ours where a revolutionary new test had been used. It was called ESDA — Electrostatic Document Analysis — and could detect exactly when writing had been put on a page. The invention, developed in a garage by two British scientists, could tell if the police notebooks had been doctored. When you write on a piece of paper the pen leaves indentations on sheets of paper below the one you are writing on. This ESDA technique detects these indentations. You put the paper through what looks like sand and it picks up if any words have been added later or if new sheets have been inserted. It can even tell if pages have been taken out. Anything written on sheet one should come through on sheet two. Then they go to the third page to find the same indentations. They'll be there but very faint. If the indentations from what you have written on page one are there on page three, but not on page two, then you can tell instantly that a new page has been added. Mr Moore wanted to send some of the police evidence away for ESDA testing. The judge didn't want to spend a lot of money because the trial had already cost over two million quid, so he agreed the brief could send away just six logs. We were fighting for our lives and the judge was worrying about pounds and pence. It was a lucky dip — six lots of logs out of the thousands and thousands of pages of notes made by the police undercover team in the six months they had us under surveillance.

That ESDA sand turned out to be gold dust for us — three of the six logs Mr Moore sent away *had* been doctored! An impression from a page for December 13th turned up on a page that was supposed to have been written two months earlier in October. The officer who had written them couldn't explain it. The judge allowed a few more logs to be sent away for testing.

After twelve weeks, sitting through fifty-eight days of evidence, I finally got into the witness box. Here was my chance to tell my story. The jury heard all about me: how I joined the ICF, my bouncing business, making *Hooligan*. You know it all by now, anyway. I had a top brief, the great Robert Durant, who suddenly stopped in the middle of my evidence and commented on the fact that I spoke very fast. Then he turned to the jury and asked how could the covert team be so accurate when they were overhearing my conversations? Though I say it myself, I was great in the box. I kept the jury spellbound.

Cross-examination started on the second day and I was determined to stay in the box and answer their questions in full. I knew that after two and a half months the prosecution had lost the jury. For the last four weeks the jurors had spent too much time sniggering and laughing at everything the police had come out with. I took my time and, despite being provoked by the prosecutor, I answered all his questions in full. They weren't going to make me a look a mug. In the end the prosecution brief wanted me out of the box as quick as he could. 'We're finished with you; no further questions.' But I didn't go. 'You've asked me a question and I'm gonna answer it.' I just kept rabbiting on, telling the jury how I only ever went over to West Ham on Saturdays to play cards in the Prince of Wales pub. I'd only been to three games that season and I was never involved in any trouble.

The next day we learned that the husband of the woman juror we'd christened Mrs Evil Eyes had died. Amazingly she wasn't giving up the jury and she wanted to continue with the trial. Every day of those

12 weeks she'd fixed us with her stare. I'm sure some of the lads even lost sleep over it. I should have been full of sympathy for her, but I just thought, You evil bitch, your husband's body ain't even cold and you can't wait to hang us. What kind of evil woman wants us that bad?

After a few days' break, I presume for the funeral, the case started again. I let the jurors into a secret I'd never told anyone, how Swallow and me had been smuggled into Scotland Yard to help the Popplewell Inquiry into football hooliganism. The judge peered over those glasses again and the prosecution looked at the police officers in amazement as I explained how in the wake of the Heysel disaster, Mr Justice Popplewell had been appointed to look into ways to rid football of its hooliganism problem. To help understand the problem, Popplewell studied Butch's *Hooligan* documentary.

He contacted Butch at Thames Television and asked if he could meet some of us. As he told us about this amazing request Butch was embarrassed because he thought it would be a total non-starter. But Andy and me always look at things in a different way. We knew the implications of the Popplewell Report would be big. The country had a huge problem and no stone would be left unturned as Judge Popplewell investigated not only Heysel but also West Ham's FA

Above: Relaxing in Vegas.

Inset: 'God' – Paolo Di Canio – shakes my hand. I haven't told him I'm a qualified referee!

Top: With Frank Bruno, outside the club in Sydenham. Frank is a man of his word and came to open the gym, even though his manager was none too happy about this bit of 'unofficial business'.

Below: Me, Elaine and Frank after opening my new security and minicab offices in Forest Hill.

Top: A poignant reunion. Frank took me to Jamaica where I was reunited with my dear father, Cecil Powell, who I had never met. This picture was taken high up in the hills of Jamaica.

Below: My older brother, Steve and older sister, Linda and *inset*, my younger sister, Sharron. I did not know that I had three brothers and two sisters until Sharron traced me the same year that I was shot. Suddenly I had a whole new family.

Top: Elaine and my children, Marcus and Georgina, are what I live for. When I married Elaine, I said, 'The Pennant family starts here.'

Below: My boy, Marcus, sporting the West Ham colours like his Dad and my little princess, Georgina: I defy any man not to be wrapped around her little finger!

Inset: The proud father with his babies – the photo shoot seemed to tire Georgie out!

Top: Surrounded by my best mates on my wedding day: my bond with my mates is a lifelong one, built on respect.

Below: With Mad Jaffa and Alan Mortlock.

Inset: Another good mate of mine, Ian 'Butch' Stuttard. Butch produced the *Hooligan* documentary.

Top: The Peacock Posse go to watch Bruno v. Tyson in Vegas in 1996

Below: When Geoffrey Avis, a staunch West Ham supporter, died aged 36, we launched an appeal to buy a memorial stone for his grave.

Top: Me taking on the might of a sofa store. I superglued my arm to their counter in a one-man demonstration. My actions certainly got a lot of attention, even from Capital Radio and *The Big Breakfast*.

Below: T.B.F. Europe 1975/76. (The Teddy Bunter Firm of the mid-Seventies.)

Above: Me and my beautiful wife, Elaine, at Frank Bruno's wedding. Elaine is my soul mate and has been a steadying force in my life.

Inset: Mine and Elaine's honeymoon: our best friends Tony and Mandy Bowers came along with us to Hawaii.

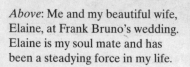

Ten

Cup riot at Birmingham and the deaths of two fans at the same ground when a wall collapsed as Birmingham City and Leeds supporters fought on the terraces. If that wasn't enough, fire had swept through Bradford City's ground, killing 56 fans. In the wake of Heysel, English clubs had been banned from Europe — a ban that would last five years. Soccer was sailing into the abyss. We'd seen Maggie Thatcher on the news telling the world, 'I want these hooligans, now.' We'd all seen the will of the 'Iron Lady' but what would she say when she knew we were sitting round the table with her appointed representatives, discussing where they were going wrong.

Butch was flabbergasted when Swallow and me agreed to go along. We both knew who Thatcher was after so we said, 'We'll pop along and see how long we've got, Butch.' But the truth was that after witnessing those 39 fans die at Heysel it was over for us.

Manslaughter wasn't what having a good crack at football was about. I'd already considered myself retired from football violence when I helped make the *Hooligan* documentary. Andy had semi-retired, too. Unfortunately, he suffered my old problem: reputation doesn't always allow you to walk away just like that.

Also, we mischievously thought it would be a laugh to go along and see what they thought a football hooligan was, and to find out the latest plans to stop us.

When we found out the meeting was taking place at Scotland Yard, the defence barriers went up. What were they planning to do, interrogate us? We didn't need to be apprehensive because there were no uniforms in the room. Lord Justice Popplewell seemed quite a warm, genuine chap who'd had an impossible task bunged on him. He spoke quite openly about what the inquiry had discovered. I asked him about how he thought he would rid football of its hooligans. He admitted he was at a loss because all the favoured ideas had been tried before. In a strange way we felt sorry for him. I felt he was taking such a big gamble meeting us that he was either very smart or very desperate. Outside the window I could see that great big revolving New Scotland Yard sign. By bringing us here, no press or rival politicians were going to get wind of the meeting. Yeah, the man was desperate. I looked at Swallow; OK, we'd give him some pointers. I said: 'Look, you're not that far off. We kept in front by being organised and that's your problem. Your lot have got the tactics right but you're disorganised. Police tactics that work successfully in one town are not tried in another. That's the answer, old boy.'

Lord Popplewell's eyes lit up and a few coffees later we were smuggled out. Outside the huge Scotland

Yard building, Andy piped up, 'Hey, Cass, remember when we had it with Chelsea all around here?' 'Yeah, but that's not what I'm thinking, Andy. That meeting wasn't intended for anybody to know about. What do you think the press would pay us for the story?' We'd done many things for a laugh but tipping off Fleet Street's finest was one I had my doubts about. I never thought that in the years that followed I'd be standing in the dock using it to impress the court as evidence that I was no longer active on the hooligan front. I still chuckle when I think about the begrudging respect they had for us. In order to beat us they had to ask the hoolies themselves.

Reminds me of the night I was asked to save boxing ... Someone call the next witness, Mr Terry Lawless.

The cops claimed that when Mark Kaylor fought Errol 'Bomber' Graham in November 1986, I'd orchestrated a riot at the fight in Wembley Arena. Well, Terry told the court the truth. He'd seen no trouble at that bout and in the five years he'd known me he had never heard me even raise my voice. There, I told you I was a gentle giant at boxing fights.

Butch and Al Hunter also spoke up for me. The jury couldn't believe such respectable people were giving evidence for a 'thug'.

At 12.40 on day 71 of the trial Vivien Robinson,

the prosecution QC, stood up and told the court new evidence had just arrived that would be to the advantage of the defence. By two o'clock he asked for an adjournment until the next morning. As I left the court, my solicitor wouldn't tell me what was happening. He just said, 'I can't tell you too much until the morning, but sleep well tonight. It'll all be over tomorrow.'

Next morning we arrived at ten o'clock as usual and for the first time in 72 days the cell door wasn't locked behind us. Normally, you walk in a free man and the cuffs are clapped on your wrists. You sit in the dungeon below the cell waiting to be called. That morning, May 10th, we could walk in and out. It was the first real sign we were going to walk free.

It was like a party down there in the cells. I took a photo of the eleven of us, but sadly it didn't come out. When Mr Robinson stood up he told the court, 'The Crown considers it proper to offer no further evidence.' It was true: they were throwing in the towel.

He'd spent the night studying the lab reports on the batch of notebooks that had been sent away for ESDA tests. The brief then explained, 'I no longer have confidence in the integrity of the evidence that has been called. New material has been received which bears upon the integrity of the logs. I am instructed to offer no further evidence against these defendants. In due course there will be a full inquiry.'

A cheer went up.

Judge Alan Hitching peered over his desk and said, 'It has been quite clear from the outset that an issue has always been, and remains, the integrity of the officers and their logs. It has been made quite clear by the defence throughout that these documents were not safe.' Then he turned to the jury and ordered them to find us not guilty on all charges. The foreman of the jury, who turned out to be a Spurs supporter, formally cleared us.

I wanted to scream out, 'I AM INNOCENT! I want the world to know I'M INNOCENT.' I punched the air and looked across the court to give it to the coppers who put us there. The enemy weren't there. Those bastards couldn't face us. There was no one to focus our anger on. We'd been staring at ten years behind bars. For three months we'd been handcuffed and locked in cells. For a whole year this case had been hanging over us. Even at the end the bastards had cheated me. I wanted the jury to find me not guilty, not be ordered to do it. I wanted my innocence to come from the people. People who know what really goes on in the world. I got my freedom but not justice. The press flocked round so I gave them some smug comment about having a good old knees-up in the East End.

The trial had cost two and a half million pounds. We were supposed to be poor little pawns in the Government's big game. We were the shifty fellas with the Stanley knife scars, the scum of the earth, and we'd won. We'd beaten 'em all.

I didn't feel real elation until I stood at the top of the steps out of Snaresbrook court. The only person with me was my Elaine. I put my arms around her little waist. She was the only one I wanted to be with. We were back together, two hearts broken by the thought of ten years apart were healed there and then. We were going home to see my son.

Because of the trial I'd lost my job as nightclub manager, so I had to go on the door again. I was working at the Dutch House, next to the A20 near Eltham in South London when a good-looking bird came up and gave me a bottle of champagne. 'What's this for?' I asked. She looked at me and said, 'My dad asked me to do this. You don't know him but he knows who you are. He's been banged up for conspiracy to do an armed robbery. He's expecting his appeal through any day. His solicitors are the ones that worked on your case and they're using the ESDA test to clear his name. Thanks to you an innocent man is going to walk soon. When he heard you were working here he asked me to bring you this champagne.'

Ten

ESDA opened the floodgates and over the next few years I read about case after case where the ESDA test was being used — Birmingham bombers, Broadwater Farm, Carl Bridgewater, the list was endless. In the past, appeals had been booted out because there was no new evidence. With ESDA the old evidence could be re-examined and innocence proved. To mark the end of our ordeal Swallow and me spent a couple of weeks with our girls on the beach in Kavos, on Corfu. From there we sent a piss-taking postcard to Icky, leader of the Chelsea mob, who was still in jail doing ten thanks to Operation Own Goal. Our one-time rival appreciated the joke because he knew that thanks to his West Ham 'enemies' he would soon be joining us on a beach. He actually went to Thailand and, as far as I know, he's still out there. Other hooligan cases the cops had lined up collapsed as well. In all, 123 alleged hooligans walked away.

Four days after the case collapsed we trooped back into court — this time we were in the public gallery — to watch the barristers discussing costs and compensation. Amazingly, the jury turned up as well. My brief asked the court to give me a transcript of the reasons for the acquittal in case the cops harassed me in future. In the end we all got them. The jurors shook our hands, and because they had been ordered to find us not guilty by the judge and not had to reach a decision in the jury room, some of them came for a drink in the pub across the road. Even Mrs Evil Eyes was there, talking to Swallow. I thought he was an arsehole for giving her the time of day, but then came the bombshell — she thought we were all innocent! I nearly dropped my drink when I heard that. We all gathered close to listen as she told us the real reason why she returned to do her duty on the jury. She was obviously a law-abiding citizen and so probably was her husband. It was a long trial and every juror at some time must have ignored the judge's instruction not to discuss the case with anyone. She must have told her husband what was going because his dying words to her were, 'Go back and make sure you get those boys off.' It turned out her husband had once been bashed up in a police station.

So much for Evil Eyes: you've got my respect, lady.

You might be wondering what happened to the cops who attacked Gary Stretch. Well, there wasn't enough evidence to prosecute them, but all seven coppers — including Clissold and Wells — were kicked out of the force.

Chapter Eleven

Welcome to Low Life City — Deptford in South-east London. Look around and all you'll see is grey, grey, grey. There's no colours. The people wear drab clothes. The houses are dirty from dust spewing off the lorries that speed through. The estates are so grim even council houses have barbed wire around them. No one ever stops in Low Life City.

The first thing you used to see as you drove in was a whole street full of meths drinkers, tramps and drop-outs lying in the road. It may look like it belongs in the third world, but Low Life City is first division on the map of villainy. My first-ever bouncing job was in Low Life City, just round the corner from the Mechanics Arms. A well-known firm of protection racketeers frequented the Mechanics Arms and used it as a base to run their business, without the owners' knowledge. Big Nick from Welling had been offered the door of a new club. Nick was even bigger than me and with his huge brown beard he looked like a giant grizzly bear. I was getting known as an up-and-coming fighter and just the kind of bloke he needed on his team.

The club was in one of those buildings where the down-and-outs had hung around. It had been cleaned up and opened as a new type of disco pub called Strawberries, where girls in skimpy mini-skirts danced on the bar. This was the early days of bottled designer lagers. In those days pubs had a public bar and a saloon. If you wanted dancing you went to a nightclub.

The first Strawberries disco pub was somewhere in Swiss Cottage and it became so popular the management opened another one south of the river in Deptford. Wrong move. Methers Alley in Low Life City ain't exactly Swiss Cottage. And to make matters worse they put a northern twat in charge. He'd been running a club in Manchester and had never worked in London before. He wore a white John Travolta suit, had a pencil-thin moustache and a thick northern accent. He looked like he should have been in charge at Butlins.

Unlike him, we knew what to expect in Deptford, so we arrived in two cars with every weapon we could lay our hands on crammed in the motors. As we introduced ourselves to the manager we were stacking a heap of baseball bats at the back of the cloakroom.

A worried look came over the manager's face. 'What are you doing? What's all these things?'

Nick told him, 'We're your doormen and these are to protect your customers.'

By now the manager's face was as white as his suit. He spluttered, 'Doormen don't need this sort of stuff.'

'This ain't Manchester; it's Deptford. Welcome to London, mate,' said Nick as he carried on stacking up the bats.

Billy Butlin started to sweat but he stood his ground. 'I'm paying the wages, you can't bring those things in here.'

Nick winked at me. 'Go and put 'em outside in the motor, Cass. Leave the boot unlocked and we'll just get the tools out of the car when we need them.'

I put the heavy tools in the car and slipped a small Stanley knife in my pocket, just in case. I knew what this place was like. I'd had a hell of a lot of scary battles around here. A lot of the locals were Millwall fans and I knew them from when I used to drink in the Black Boy pub. Inside, the girls were dancing on the bar but there were no customers to watch them. The manager came up to us as we stood at the door and said, 'Hey, lads, can you move inside? You're scaring the customers off. No one's coming in because you lot look so heavy and intimidating.' We politely replied, 'No, don't think so. We make the club look a safe place for punters to come to. This is Deptford, Low Life City. You're a million miles away from the glam of the West End. This ain't their kind of thing.'

Eventually to get us away he said we could have free drinks at the bar. 'Great, free booze and we're still getting paid, but don't say we didn't warn you. There'll be trouble at the door.'

We sat at the corner bar still watching the door for trouble. Half an hour went by ... an hour ... and there were still only two people in the gaff. The manager's red-coat enthusiasm was going down the gurgler fast.

After about four drinks ... crash! bang! wallop! ... the Deptford protection mob from the Mechanics Arms had sent their runners up. We downed beers and rushed straight to the entrance. The manager lay spark out in the doorway like a *Beano* comic character in his white suit and northern 'tache, with his pointy shoes sticking straight up in the air. He was as stiff as a post, lying there like he was dead. The locals, swinging baseball bats and lumps of wood, had come in and he'd just fainted. Nick weighed straight in. The Mechanics Arms mob hit him with lumps of wood but it was like smacking a big bear: they just bounced off. The Mechanics Arms mob might have had weapons, but Nick was fearless and he just smashed into them with his fists.

I stepped over twinkle-toes, who was still lying on the floor, and pulled out Stan. I slashed at the mob. A couple of them started to bleed and the whole lot retreated backwards out of the door. We knew this was only the first round over. This skirmish was just the runners testing out the security. The real villains would come around soon to offer the club protection. As we rushed to the cars to grab our weapons, another little mob was waiting outside. There were about fourteen of them, but when they saw we were quite heavy they decided to wait and return mob-handed. Back inside, twinkle-toes started to come around, moaning that he needed an ambulance.

I was flabbergasted: 'What do you need an ambulance for? Nothing's happened to you! Don't tell me you've had a set-to when you've just fallen on the floor.'

Next thing, an ambulance turned up, our northern friend climbed in the back and left the club. There was nothing wrong with him. We'd got lumps all over us from being hit with chunks of wood but we couldn't see a mark on him. He abandoned us and never came back. At eleven o'clock, when the club was closing, we were expecting the real villains to try and give us a hiding but they never showed up either.

By midnight the club was shut and the geezer in the white suit still hadn't come back. Who was going to pay us? We figured the little coward had done a runner, so we decided to pay ourselves. We took every penny out of the till and ended up with a little bit more than we would have got otherwise.

It was late 1992 and I was back in Low Life City. Britain was in the grip of a recession. After the ICF trial collapsed I'd gone back to running my bouncing empire but things were never the same. Along came the Monopolies and Mergers Commission with their report into Britain's giant pub chains. This high-powered body decided that the brewers owned too many pubs and ordered them to sell off a load of their boozers. It was just the excuse the big boys needed to get rid of their rough-house pubs. Naturally they didn't sell off pubs that were making money but those that caused them headaches were axed. Those were the ones we specialised in, so gradually the pubs and clubs we worked at closed down. At the same time the door security industry was changing. The bouncing game was going legal. Gradually, we all got out of the doors and started running our own businesses. Jaffa joined Alan Mortlock's roofing firm; Danny and Kenny ran a car front; Kenny's brother Noah became a rave promoter and John the Gravedigger became John the Fireman.

Eleven

I went into the minicab game, running a fleet of twenty cars from an office near Forest Hill station in South London. Every day brought a bag-load of headaches but I loved it. I also loved family life. After Marcus came our lovely daughter, Georgina. After a lifetime without relatives of my own, I'd hug them all and say, 'The Pennant family starts from here.' My job was to provide for them. Then came the recession and business was struggling. It was coming up to Christmas and the cars were hardly turning a wheel when the phone rang offering me the chance to take over a door in Low Life City.

Deptford had changed. The Government ploughed inner-city funds into the place to try and raise the gloom. The people got leisure centres and a nice swimming pool. They even built a little theatre — The Albany Centre — a low-slung brick building huddling next to the market. It's now purely a community centre! The organisers thought they would run discos and raves here to give something back to the people and give them a bit more interest in where they were living.

Some hope. They might have tarted the place up a bit, but this was still Low Life City. And the Albany was the roughest gig in town. At first the promoters used Top Guard security, one of the most respected official outfits in the country. They kept the peace at all the top sporting venues around Britain, but they couldn't handle the Albany; there was trouble every night. The bloke who ran the security was desperate. My name was put up: 'You want Cass Pennant; he knows how to sort a door.' That's when I got the call that was nearly to cost me my life.

In the three or four years we'd been away, the customers had changed as well. Rave music was coming along and ecstasy culture was happening. Before, all our troubles had been from hardened beer-gutted fellas who wanted to fight after a few drinks. Now we had weedy-looking blokes drugged out of their heads and wanting to take on the world. They'd cut or shoot you without a second's hesitation.

Things had changed in the bouncer world, too. The Old Bill were nicking doormen for sorting out trouble on the street. Inside the club was private and the cops wouldn't get involved. But if trouble flared outside and a bouncer got in a ruck to stop an innocent bystander getting a beating, the doorman — and not the thugs — could end up with four years for affray. The streets come under police law, OK! That's what they told everybody but whenever there *was* trouble the coppers always turned up too late.

One night in the early days at the Albany a running battle erupted in the marketplace outside. Thirty lads from the rival areas of Walworth, Eltham

Eleven

and Bermondsey were scrapping it out with each other. Girlfriends screaming about the place only stirred it up another gear. It was a noisy pitched battle between tasty youngsters — taking it, giving it, rescuing their mates and fronting their foes. We knew the unwritten rule — this was the Old Bill's problem but, as usual, they were nowhere to be seen. We looked on from inside the glass-fronted foyer, making mental notes for future reference because all of these kids had been in the club that evening. We had searched them all and knew they didn't have tools. They were just youths having a toe-to-toe battle and we knew we could stop it the minute we stepped in. The boys looked at me waiting for the word to go, but I was under instructions from the club not to get involved with any trouble outside.

The battle went back and forth across the market square outside, and girls were running in pleading with us to intervene. We knew we should do something. The six of us were itching to go but the paymaster promoter standing next to us was terrified we'd rip them apart. He didn't want us putting off punters, losing him money.

Above the racket of the row a girl let out a piercing scream: 'Help! Somebody help!' Her boyfriend had been stabbed. Mr T looked at me and said, 'We gotta go now, Cass.' We charged outside, bang in the middle of the two warring factions. I yelled instructions to my bouncers to fan out right across the street, forming a human barricade. Anyone attempting to come through was to be taken out. These youngsters knew we were way above their league but still one gang decided to charge us anyway. A few slaps and they backed off. One spotty kid was still going berserk. I told him, 'Fuck off home: it's over for you guys.' Pointing behind me he shouted, 'It's not over yet. Those lot have stabbed my brother.' As I looked behind, a small group of youths, led by an older geezer of about 26, was charging towards us. Someone from my team shouted, 'They've got a blade!' My hand-picked heavies ran straight at the biggest group and confronted them with, 'If you want it with them you're gonna have to come through us first. And we're going nowhere. If you're smart you'll fuck off now before the Old Bill gets here, 'specially as one of yer has a blade.'

They looked us over all shifty like; one of them said something and they slipped away into the night. It was obvious they didn't fancy their chances with me and my team but we'd given them a way of saving face. As they sidled off I remembered something about this lot that had been nagging away in my mind — that lot had been on the promoter's special guest list and he'd intervened to make sure we didn't search them. That's how they'd got away with carrying a blade. A young guy lay in a pool of blood in the far corner of the market square and a young girl knelt beside him, screaming at us to get an ambulance. Claret trickled through the stabbed kid's fingers as he clutched his stomach.

A group of youths were still hanging around at the end of the street — but they weren't going to cross the no-man's zone we had formed outside the club. 'Where's that ambulance?' shouted Mr T as he gave the injured guy first aid.

One of us asked the promoters to call again for an ambulance. 'It's on its way,' we were told.

The boy in the street's life was ebbing away. I cornered the promoter: why had he overruled my instructions to search everybody going into the club? There was still no sign of the paramedics. Where was that ambulance?

A blank, shifty look on the promoter's face told me this dog hadn't called it. He hadn't got to tell me why. I'd come across clubs before that worried more about keeping their licence than they did about customer safety. They didn't want trouble outside to be connected to their clubs. That kid slumped out there *was* his problem. Mr T exploded with rage and lunged at the promoter. The kid could have died because of those weasels in the office. I stepped in and dragged the lying bastard of a promoter back into his office to call the ambulance. Just then the police turned up and took over giving first aid. The stabbed guy lived — but no thanks to the slags running the club promotion that night who we'd quickly discovered were a bunch of wrong 'uns.

Even the DJ was nuts. When the scrapping was going on outside the club this DJ went out in the middle of them, bouncing up and down and screaming that he wanted to row with the Walworth lot! If we hadn't needed the work we'd have walked out there and then. Now we knew what we were up against we renegotiated our pay — upwards quite a bit. Everyone who worked for me got top dough because we took on the places no one else would touch.

Something strange was going on at the Deptford club. It turned out we weren't just bouncers — we ended up as protection for the promoter. He wasn't a gangster but he had enemies everywhere who were looking for him. Strange faces, gangsters — they all beat a path to his door and we kept them off him. I should have let them get their hands on him.

I had many arguments with this guy. The Albany was like a proper theatre inside with exit doors all round the auditorium. We needed twenty doormen to police the place properly — one man on every door.

Eleven

But the promoter kept cutting the budget and laying off doormen and had the exit doors chained closed to keep out gatecrashers. As his security adviser, I battled with him to keep those men on for the safety of the people inside. A lot of people had forgotten the horrific fire that had swept through a three-storey house in Deptford 12 years earlier where 13 people perished during a party attended by more than 190 revellers.

That terrible incident was like the modern-day case of murdered teenager Stephen Lawrence with accusations flying that the police didn't do enough because the victims were from the black community. I'd never forgotten it and every time the boss cut the number of bouncers I lived in fear of a fire or a terrible accident happening there.

In the end only Mr T and Leon were left working at the Albany. The club was dying on its feet. After that big street row involving the stabbing, punters had switched to Harry Howard's Futures club. Leon and T were experienced, solid, dependable guys. I had my cab office to run so I'd just to go down once a week about midnight to pay them and hang around for an hour making small talk while the club emptied.

For a couple of weeks before that fateful night when I was shot I could feel an evil atmosphere in the club. Mr T had stopped a group of blokes from coming in. He thought they were racists. Again the promoter overruled Mr T. He told my doorman, 'I'm paying your wages, so let 'em in. They're my friends.' This wannabe gangster and his mates were walking around smirking and laughing at Mr T. I told him to stay cool and I'd try and sort it with the promoter.

The next week the racist loud-mouths were in again. One of them called Mr T a black bastard. An argument flared up and I nipped in with Leon to pull T away. The loud-mouth's mate was shouting the odds to attract the others into kicking off a row. I said to their leader, 'You're shouting up a problem that ain't there.'

He replied, 'There ain't no problem, Cass. It's the last thing we want.'

The disco finished, I stood with Mr T and Leon as the clubgoers filed out through the front doors. The lights were low in the lobby. Outside it was pitch black. The characters who'd been blowing hot and cold all night slipped past us without a second glance or a word of animosity. I became suspicious and moved towards the front door. BOOM! Four shadowy figures stood in the hazy darkness. One of them was aiming this big silver gun.

I watched the flame in slow motion, even now I can still smell the smoke and the cordite …

I fell unconscious as the ambulance doors closed

Eleven

and I didn't really know any more until I woke and saw a pretty face staring back at me. She was gorgeous with those Patti Boulaye eyes. I thought I must be dead. Next thing, I saw my wife's best mate, Linzi, hovering over me — no, I must still be alive and wherever Linzi was my Elaine must be somewhere close.

My vision was hazy, like I'd woken from a long sleep. I could make out shapes of people all around me. The only person I wanted to see was Elaine. I wanted her to know I was alive. Nothing else made sense. She came close to me. I tried to move to hold hands, to see if she was real. That's when I became aware of all these pipes in my arms. I could see all the tubes and drips. I thought, Jesus, I'm in a bad way. I must be dying. You may only have a few words left. Think about what you want to say, Cass. You've only a few minutes to thank all the people who meant anything to you before you die.

I tried to talk but nothing happened. Why weren't the words coming out? The pretty girl with the lovely eyes turned out to be a nurse. She shoved a pen and a pad of paper in my hand. All round me friends were looking down at me and smiling. I couldn't understand why they were so pleased about it. So I wrote 'AM I ALIVE?' The nurse showed it to everyone around my bed and they all laughed. Tears ran down Elaine's face. Am I alive? What a stupid question. I figured all the tubes around me meant I was alive but they were battling to save me. I was already out of danger but I didn't know that, so the second thing I wrote was: 'Will I live?' When they read that the people around my bed cried some more. I started to relax when the nurse said I would live and everything was OK.

God knows what I was thinking about in my subconscious, but I didn't know what day it was. How long had I been there in that hospital bed? Had I been there weeks? When did these shots in the dark happen? The only thing I could remember in terms of dates was the West Ham match. The shooting was on a Friday night. The next day West Ham were playing Sheffield Wednesday. So I asked, 'Who won West Ham v Sheffield?'

It turned out it was still Saturday morning and the game hadn't kicked off.

A procession of relatives and friends came to visit me in that intensive care room at Shooter's Hill Hospital. Some of them were heavy, heavy, heavy people. Old Bill were hovering around as well but they seemed more interested in the people who were visiting me. A lot of the faces the cops were keen on kept telling me, 'We'll sort this for you. We'll fix it.' But all I was concerned about was my family. Without a father they had no one; they needed me.

The scum who did this weren't fit to lace my boots, and the only way they could deal with me was with the ultimate force. I'd fought all those battles and never had to use a gun. One-to-one or outnumbered it didn't matter: I'd always take 'em on and always come out on top. This was a different league. It wasn't my world; I'm not a gangster. I've always been what they call a pound note man, always on the edge. Like I said, I ain't no gangster but I am a street fighter. I had a decision to make — take revenge or bury it and live my life.

No one could defeat Cass Pennant. I was stronger than my enemies. I was still here. Twice I'd felt that spiritual lifting sensation of leaving my body. Nothing anyone could ever do to me would scare me because I've seen death. I've experienced it. It holds no fear for me. I couldn't understand when I used to read in those *Readers Digest*-type things about people stranded at the North Pole or left for weeks at sea waiting for rescue. All the time they kept on about how the will to live saved them. Now I knew exactly what they were talking about.

You also have to have a big slice of luck. On the night I was shot the surgeon who saved my life was a heart specialist who should have been at home enjoying his weekend off. But he just happened still to be at the hospital when I was wheeled in with three bullets inside me. This wonderful man did open-heart surgery there and then and I woke up in the hospital ward full of open-heart patients.

I was the youngest guy in there but I had the same scar as the rest of them. I'd been opened up from my belly to my neck. The old geezers wanted to know how somebody so young had suffered a heart attack. I couldn't tell 'em I'd been in gangster land eating bullets, so I just went along with it.

One day the pretty nurse told me the fella that saved my life was coming to see me. His name was Steven Griffin and as he stood there beside my bed he said, 'I didn't think you'd be here. Look, old chap, it isn't my business to ask what went on, maybe other people will be asking that, but you are lucky to be here. The only reason you're still alive is your will to live, the size of you and your fitness. If you'd been an average person I wouldn't even have been operating on you.'

I told him, 'Thank you for saving my life.'

'Don't thank me,' he replied, 'thank yourself for giving me something to operate on.'

I should have been dead but I'd survived with the will to live. Where did my inner strength come from? Was it from Doll Chambers who'd survived Jerry and the Blitz telling me, 'Remember, sticks and stones may break your bones but names will never hurt you,' as she dragged me along, head proud, with people shouting out all sorts of terrible names? Was it that tough upbringing that gave me the will to take on everything? I don't know but something somewhere had given me the power to stay alive.

After just four days in hospital I discharged myself, even though I still had one bullet lodged in my shoulder. I thought I was a hard bastard and didn't need no quack. I kept thinking, I'm OK. I'll show those bastards they ain't got rid of Cass Pennant.

Elaine took me to see Mrs Chambers. My foster dad Cecil came on the bus every day to sit with me in hospital but Doll had been too ill to travel so I went straight round to the house in Slade Green, so she could see I was OK. She was glad I was back on my feet but I could sense something wasn't quite right. She kept exchanging glances with Cecil and then just as we were leaving I saw him nod to her. She said, 'There's a letter for you, son.' Doll picked up a white envelope from the sideboard and placed it in my hand. She didn't say a word about it but I could see from the sad look in her eyes she'd gone through agonies about this letter. I turned it over, Barnardo's was written in green letters on the front of the envelope. When I opened it later I realised what all the funny looks had been about.

The letter explained that someone was looking for me. Apparently things had changed in Dr Barnardo's and they now had an aftercare unit to help re-unite Barnardo's kids with their families. Normally it was the Barnardo's children who wanted to find their parents. But this was rare: my family were trying to find me. The letter didn't say who. It just said someone had recently been in contact. All I could think of was my mother. I couldn't deal with it. Here I was, 35 years old, and I'd been an orphan all that time. She hadn't wanted me when I was a baby and now she seemed to be trying to waltz back into my life.

I thought, Well mother, you ain't got no son.

This letter was dated January and by the time Dr Barnardo's had given it to me it was April and I'd been shot. I couldn't deal with it. Why now? I should have been dead. I started to take my frustration out on the people I love, the very people I tried to call out to when I thought I was dying. Among men I can be an evil bastard but at home I'm mild mannered, the old gentle giant. But suddenly I started turning into the green hulk; I wanted to explode at the wrong people. I couldn't control it.

Sitting there in the house all day, the nurse would come and treat the bullet wounds, patch me up. The police came but I wouldn't tell 'em anything. My wife would come over: 'How are you?'

I'd growl, 'Well, how do you think I am?'

The kids would come in and ... bang! Another big explosion of anger.

Afterwards I always felt guilty. As I was struggling to come to terms with what had happened, Elaine put herself into overdrive. Until then, I'd always run the business and Elaine had looked after the kids. Now I was watching her dress the kids, get Marcus off to school and Georgina to nursery. She'd dress my wounds then go off to run the minicab office. Anyone in the trade will tell you cabs are a grief business. As soon as the boss is away things start going wrong and before you know it you've lost your own business. I could only stand back and admire how, without any previous experience, Elaine sorted out those drivers. She ran the whole place so well that when I'd recovered enough to poke my nose in the door the staff told me to rest up a little longer because business was better under the new boss!

I saw in Elaine a strength of character I never thought a woman was capable of. Support, love, commitment, yes. They're things you can expect from a woman who loves you. But I'd always believed blokes are stronger than women mentally as well as physically. But when Elaine grabbed hold of that business as well as running the house and looking after me and the kids I knew my wife was extra special. Even as my temper raged out of control she never cried or let me see the real effect that shooting really had on her. She knew that while a low life's bullets couldn't break me, the tears of someone I loved so much would.

In the end Elaine persuaded me I'd got to see a doctor. I'd tell her there was nothing wrong, but I knew she was right. I didn't know what I was going through but the doctor knew instantly. He made me an appointment with 'someone to talk to'. It was a woman and straight away I told her, 'I know something ain't right, so that's why I've come here. But don't give me all these going back to my childhood questions. I know what you people are about. I met you lot when I was in prison. They put you in front of the quacks and reckon you're a nutter ...'

She cut me short: 'Don't worry, I'm not going to ask you those questions. I've met tougher guys than you. How about people from the Falklands and the Gulf war? How about people from the King's Cross disaster? What do you think of them? Tough people?'

I had a lot of respect for the people who'd been involved in those situations, the firemen dealing with the charred bodies of children and all that. They're real warriors, the toughest of the tough.

'Well,' she said, 'I see all those people, the real

tough people of this world.'

I couldn't believe it. She sees all them? I thought, What are they doing here? Have they all gone soft?

She said, 'You're tough to survive but I really have seen tougher guys than you. They come to me because they're all suffering what you're suffering.'

'All right.' I asked, 'What am I suffering from, then?'

'Post traumatic stress disorder,' she said. She explained it wasn't a cissy thing and that it had been around a long time, but people have only just become aware of it in the last decade. I'd never heard of it before. Nowadays everyone understands what it means because after tragedies like train disasters the first thing they do is treat the survivors for post traumatic stress.

I thought, 'This'll be a nice little earner; I'll be able to make a claim.' So I started suing the people at the Albany for post traumatic stress.

Some right tough characters I'd met around the East End helped me cope better with this PTSD illness — by showing me their own bullet holes! They'd shove a jacket over their other clothes so you never knew what they'd been through. I'd see these guys at boxing dos and they'd ask me how I was doing. They'd say, 'You're looking well,' and they'd show me their battle scars and we'd talk about it.

Being shot is an experience very few people share. Often they don't even tell their families, but they'll tell me. Half of them have never been treated for post traumatic stress and are still suffering, so we share private things.

I still go over and over it and keep coming up with different answers. I didn't know where the bullet was coming from and why it was coming. To this day I don't know why. It wasn't even my argument. It did prove to me how much the world had changed. Until then I'd prided myself on the way I could anticipate trouble. I'd never lost a battle. But this was a different enemy. In my day the good guys never met the bad guys. Now old ladies are being mullahed in the street. Blokes who'd never earn respect are walking the streets with guns. I'd been away too long. Drug culture had changed the world for ever.

I was still alive. I'd survived Low Life City. I was haunted by the thought that I'd never seen it coming. I decided it was time to get out of the club business for a while and rethink some things.

Chapter Twelve

After all that drama and emotion, I'll tell you a story that'll make you laugh. It was the days of 'loadsamoney'. I'd made a pile of dosh ducking, diving and grafting; in fact I earned £40,000 in one year, the same wage as the Prime Minister, Maggie Thatcher. But while she got her dough from running the country I made mine playing cards in Vic King's Clydesdale pub in Loughton. I splashed out four grand of my winnings on a really expensive three-piece suite. It was all oak and leather and so big we had a right battle to get it up three flights of stairs into our two-bedroom council flat.

After six months the stitching came apart and the sofa looked ropey. A four grand suite shouldn't be like this. My missus kept nagging me about getting it sorted. In the end we rang them up and they sent their 'experts' out from the shop. They ummed and aahhed and talked about fixing it. I left it to Elaine to sort it out. I was busy putting bread on the table over at the cab office. The superstore gave us a crap black settee as a temporary replacement while our top-of-the-range lah-di-dah sofa was being fixed.

Weeks went by, it was getting near Christmas and still we had no proper settee. The phone went in the cab office. It was Elaine. She was no nearer getting the replacement suite we wanted and was sick to death of being fobbed off. I was annoyed with her but in the end I called the shop myself. I got the same jip Elaine had suffered. Now I understood what she'd been going through all these weeks. I got the impression they were talking down to us because we were council tenants. They seemed to expect to put a top-quality suite into some private gaff on a stockbroker estate, not a two-bed council flat in Penge. That really pissed me off.

I don't like being talked down to and I certainly won't be mugged off because I'm a council tenant. I thought to myself, That's it. I'll show 'em. I'll go down there. I won't be fobbed off with no lowly assistants, either. I'll get hold of the top man.

So, I left the cab office. I had the same head on as I did the day I marched on Islington Town Hall. The injustice of it. My wife had done her best and now she was upset. I was fuming. No one treats my princess like that and gets away with it. On the way to the shopping centre, I pulled the Merc over and put in a call to the local newspaper in Essex. I told them what I was going to do but they didn't seem interested. By now there was no way I'd back off. I'd promised my wife that I'd sort this mess out so she could have her settee in time for Christmas.

I marched up to the counter. 'I'm Mr Pennant and I want to know what's happening with my suite. I don't want it back; I want a replacement. Right, who's in charge here? I want the manager.'

They sent the assistant manager. They were fobbing me off again. The assistants just carried on serving other people, trying to make more money with their dodgy settees.

So I stood at the counter and shouted at the top of my voice, 'Don't buy your settees from here!'

A woman came up to me. She looked a right proper bitch. She told me, 'I'm not the manager; I'm a director of the company.' To make matters worse, she was French and I hate the French. She was talking to me as if I was a little boy, but I got her drift. She thought she was too high and mighty to be dealing with somebody's domestic shopping problem. Well, I got the right hump. If she'd been a geezer I'd have knocked her out. But I've never laid a finger on a woman in my entire life, and I wasn't about to break my code, even for this French cow. Suddenly, Madam Important stormed off.

I told her, 'Don't walk away, love. I've promised my wife I won't come home until all this is sorted.' She just laughed in my face, turned and carried on walking. So, now I had no one to argue with. There was nothing else for it. I pulled a tube of superglue from my jacket pocket, rolled up my sleeve and glued my arm to the only counter in the shop. I was well and truly stuck. If I'd lifted my arm the superglue would have ripped my skin off.

The women started screaming. Just at that moment, with perfect timing, the local press walked though the door and started taking pictures. Next, two policemen arrived … 'ello, 'ello, 'ello. 'If you lay one finger on this arm and my skin comes off, are you insured?' They backed off sharpish.

The phone rang on the counter. It was for me. It was some posh geezer in Birmingham who said he was repairing my suite. I told him, 'I don't want some two-bob repairer fobbing me off with a bodged-up job. I want a new suite.'

He was most indignant, 'Sir, I can assure you we are the Queen's personal restorers. We repaired all Her Majesty's leatherwork after the Windsor Castle fire.' So now I had some posh fart telling me I should be honoured he was repairing my suite. But I wasn't grateful. I wanted a new settee. The phone went dead. Two fire engines pulled up outside. And the coppers were still there, too. By now shoppers from other stores had heard the news that a loony bloke was on a quest of honour and they all came to gawp.

Seven firemen, two policemen, the French cow and the Queen's restorer couldn't resolve it. The only person who could fix this mess was my wife, Elaine. One of the women assistants phoned her. She told Elaine, 'Can't you have a word with your husband? None of us can go home and we're worried about his health.'

The assistant passed over the phone. Elaine told me, 'Come home. Your tea's waiting for you.' That was it — protest over. The firemen had superglue neutraliser with them. They gave me the tube and I gently pulled my arm off the counter as all the assistants went 'Ooohhh' and 'Aaghhhhh'.

Next morning I was in the cab office and Chris Tarrant announced on Capital radio that a 6'6" tall man went berserk in a sofa store because he didn't like the colour of his suite — they always get the facts wrong, don't they?

By the weekend a women's magazine wanted to tell my story — according to them, Cass Pennant had become the consumers' champion. Apparently I'd done what every housewife dreams of doing — taken a fight with a big store all the way to the top.

By the way, we got our old suite back from the Queen's restorers. It looked like new.

Now, while I was recovering from being shot a fella called Bob Smith from Dr Barnardo's came to see me. He said the person who'd been trying to contact me was not my mother ... but my sister. I thanked him for coming and when I closed the door I realised I was in shock. A sister! I'd spent all my life thinking I was alone. For some reason I knew my mother was a nurse — perhaps Mrs Chambers told me — and I had this picture of her coming over from the Caribbean on a boat. She'd met a doctor on the ship and they'd fallen in love. But when they arrived on these shores, he had to go his way and she went hers. Later she discovered she was pregnant. All alone and terrified, she handed me over to Dr Barnardo's to find me a loving family.

A sister! For 35 years that's how it had been — a mother who couldn't keep me and an unknown father. I'd been abandoned so they couldn't have wanted children. It never occurred to me for one moment that I might have brothers or sisters. Something else was doing my head in. This woman who reckoned she was my sister had tried to contact me in January and, if luck hadn't been with me, Barnardo's would now be telling her I was dead.

Twelve

I was still messed up. This should have been the best news of my life, but I just couldn't deal with it. By the following March — almost a year after the shooting — I was feeling better and started to come to terms with the fact that I had a sister, but somehow I was still wary. There were things I wanted to know about my family, but I didn't want anyone intruding on my life. Bob from Barnardo's was brilliant and he acted as the middleman. Soon afterwards Bob passed on a letter from the lady, whose name was Sharon. Placing the photograph of the sister I never knew I had on the table in front of me, I tried to write a letter. How do you write a letter to a family you never knew you had? She looked so beautiful, all clean and posh. I thought they were obviously better than me. The words I wanted to put down on paper wouldn't come out. Everything I wrote turned nasty and vindictive. I screwed up sheet after sheet and threw them in the bin. In the end I thought, I'm grown up, I've got my own life: it's too late. I know I'm basically a good person, so fuck 'em. So I told her all about my life, warts and all. The words came tumbling out over 15 pages. In the end it was more like a small book than a letter. My whole life was in there: football violence, prison — the lot. As I read back my letter, I thought she wouldn't want to know this person. She'd wanted to find me, not the other way round, so now she knew everything about me. As I handed the letter to the bloke from Barnardo's I felt a bit guilty. I told him, 'Look, Sharon might find this letter a bit deep and heavy. There's something I haven't told them. I've been shot and suffering from post traumatic stress; that's the real reason I've been a bit off and not appeared to be interested in my sister.'

He understood and passed on the letter anyway. I didn't expect to hear any more but, amazingly, Sharon sent another letter. My life with all its extraordinary highs and lows hadn't put her off at all. There was another bombshell: Sharon wasn't my only sister; I have another sister and three brothers. And they all understood my life completely because one of my brothers had been in trouble, too. In fact, he'd lived a life that was like a mirror of mine — if we'd lived together we'd have been two of the baddest people around!

My wife and the kids and even Elaine's family were all excited for me, urging me to get in touch. You know what women are like — they love all this kind of stuff. I just felt pressurised again. It was such a monster to deal with and I wasn't yet ready to meet anybody. I can't always talk about my feelings but I can write them down, so I thought I'd start off as a pen pal to Sharon. Each letter was like a flower blooming as our relationship gradually opened up. It

Twelve

turned out Sharon lived in Milton Keynes and had two children. She'd had a troubled childhood, too, and had left the family home in Doncaster when she was seventeen to live in Birmingham. That's when she first found out about me. The suitcases were kept in the loft and among them was a battered old case full of birth certificates and photographs. As this case was being moved a faded black and white photo of a baby fell out. Sharon didn't recognise the child and asked who it was. My mother, Celeste, started crying. 'It's your brother,' she sobbed. As tears rolled down her cheeks, she explained how she had been going through troubled times and had handed me over to Dr Barnardo's.

A couple of years later Sharon had phoned her mum and told her, 'I'm troubled. I feel like part of me is missing. That baby in the picture, my brother, I need to find him.' I think that as the years went by the mother had given up all hope of ever finding me, but she gave her blessing to Sharon. And that's how she came to contact Barnardo's.

I didn't have a problem about Sharon nor my other brothers and sisters. I could never forgive my mother for abandoning me, but I figured the children were as innocent as me. I sent more letters — each one was like a book — I sent photos, even the one with Harold Wilson. I didn't realise it, but Sharon was photocopying these letters and sending them round the family. They were all dying to meet me.

Eventually, in the summer of '94 I was ready to meet Sharon — but I had to do it on my own. Elaine and the kids went with my in-laws to a caravan on the coast while I psyched myself up. I got on the train to Milton Keynes. The moment we met all my worries disappeared. Because we'd built up this pen pal relationship, it was like we'd known each other all our lives. Sharon was almost six feet tall and more beautiful than in her picture. She could have been a model in her time. She was quite shy, not pushy at all, and her kids were lovely. I learned all about my brothers and sisters but wisely she didn't mention my mother because she knew I was touchy about her. There was another shock — one brother, Steve, was living in Thornton Heath, just two miles from my home! That started me thinking: my foster sister Beverley had always sworn blind her sister Lilly had followed me at Crystal Place. I couldn't understand it because I was nowhere near at the time. She must have been following my brother.

I stayed the night at Sharon's and went home the next day. It had all been so easy — and now the whole family couldn't wait to meet me. Back home everybody was excited and in the end I gave in. Mentally and physically I was feeling much better,

Twelve

although I had a bullet left inside me. It was still summer, so we had a barbecue and all my brothers and sisters came to us. Friends and neighbours joined in and the atmosphere was unbelievable. It was like a wedding where, although everybody knows each other, because they don't often meet up they're chatting away like good 'uns.

I got on like a house on fire with my new-found brothers and sisters. My half-brother, Steve, is three years older than me. He was born in Jamaica and stayed there with grandparents until he was 12 when he came to live with my mother in Doncaster. His wife, Diana, works as a teacher at a college. She said she knew me, and it turned out that she taught English to builders from abroad. At the start of each term she puts on a video to get the class settled down — because all builders are into football she'd showed them Butch's video, *Hooligan*!

Then there's Linda. She's two years younger than me and lives in London, but she speaks proper Coronation Street. Linda told me of a day 25 years before, when I'd have been about ten years old, that a white woman visited their house in Doncaster. No white person had ever been to the house. She remembers my mother and this white woman having a furious argument on the doorstep. Linda thought they were going to come to blows. The row went on and on and in the end my mother slammed the door, sat down in a corner and cried all night. The white woman must have been Mrs Chambers — remember I told you she'd only been away for one night when I was a child. The day she left she'd made a big fuss of me and my foster sister, Beverley. It felt strange because she'd never left us before. Now all those years later it all made sense. My mother had obviously contacted Barnardo's asking for me to go back. But Doll Chambers was Blitz stock and she'd gone up to Doncaster and fought like a lioness to keep me.

She shouted at my mother, 'You'll get him back over my dead body. He's better off with me. You'll destroy him.'

I can clearly remember Mrs C coming back that day, her eyes all red. She hugged us and bought us presents. It was like Christmas and birthday all rolled into one.

Then there's Robert — he's a year younger than me — and Colin, who's three years younger. They both still live in the Doncaster area. The two of them, along with Linda and Sharon, had the same father, while Steve and myself had different dads. My mother had left Doncaster seven years before and spends most of her time in either Jamaica or New York. I still could never forgive her. How could she have called me Carol and abandoned me?

Twelve

Because Steve lives just down the road in London we've become very close. He looks a lot like me and he's the one who was a tearaway as a young man back in Doncaster. It turns out he'd known about me for years. He was 12 when our mother told him he had a brother. One day Steve told me, 'Knowing you were somewhere out there has always haunted me. It was like part of me was missing. But at the same time I was hurt that you'd never come to see us.' Steve and the rest of the family hadn't realised I never even knew they existed.

Meeting five brothers and sisters you never knew you had meant there was a lot of catching up and talking to do. When I'd finally met them all, the one thing that struck me was how they were all scarred by childhood memories. Each one of them shared painful family memories that it wouldn't be fair for me to go into. But it really did hit home that I should be grateful for being fortunate enough to find foster parents like Doll and Cecil Chambers. They weren't childless and they new nothing about black culture. The only issue to them was that they had the love and care to give to a child that really needed them. For years it has made my blood boil when I hear about potential foster parents being turned away by organisations with children looking for a real home, simply because they are the wrong colour. Nowadays we must take in the child's cultural needs. Cultural needs! What cultural needs when he's too young to know any culture? For that they are prepared to deny a child a loving home. My own children are mixed race and they go to school knowing they have a mum and a dad to come home to. How many of their school mates are fortunate enough to say that today?

Eventually, Steve took me up to the family's home town of Doncaster where another surprise was waiting. When I came out of prison after the three-year sentence, I'd decided to try and find my family. All I'd had to go on was my birth certificate and it gave an address in Doncaster. After all those horrible things I'd said about northerners ... I was a 'flat cap' myself!

I'd quickly given up the search and didn't even bother going to the address on that dog-eared birth certificate. By then it was the early eighties. My mother had been living there in 1958 and surely nobody would have stayed in the same house that long? You could have knocked me down with a feather when Steve took me to the family home — that little terrace house was the address on my birth certificate! If only I'd gone to Doncaster then I'd have been re-united with my family. Maybe something had stopped me. Even now, more than a decade later, I still wasn't ready to meet my mother and forgive her.

Twelve

In Doncaster we met loads of Pennants. One night we were in an ex-miner's club and in a quiet moment when everybody else was away from the table my mother's brother Uncle Slim took me by the arm. He whispered, 'Don't take it out on your mother, son.'

I'm thinking, Hang on here, I ain't said a thing about her. All I'm doing is listening. I hadn't shared my feelings about her with anybody. He carried on, 'You've got to understand what it was like in those days to be pregnant with nowhere to live but one room, sharing with your brother.'

Slim said no more. He carried on drinking and introducing me to other people, like nothing had happened. My mind was miles away, remembering the few documentaries I'd watched on Beeb Two and Channel Four about how life was for the people who came over from the Caribbean in the 50s. I'd heard stories from Elaine's mum and dad about the humiliation and scandal heaped on women — black or white — who had a child out of wedlock. But I still couldn't make my peace with her. I have to admit I was curious and part of me wanted to meet her. But I'm a loyal person and deep down I felt I'd be betraying my foster parents by seeing her. I had real guilt over it.

In 1994 Cecil Chambers died. Him and Doll had been together for over sixty years. It was as if Doll couldn't face life without him and within a few months she was dead, too. She died in hospital. I often dodged going up there, making up silly excuses and when eventually I did go to see her in hospital she wasn't the mother I remembered. I felt I was a coward; there were so many things I'd meant to say to her but I couldn't. I'd always been too manly to tell her I loved her. I wanted her to know I'd always be grateful for the love she'd showered on her Barnardo's boy.

I knew she was happy that at last, after the fights, the gangs and prison, she could be proud of me and my family. Elaine had given me a purpose in life. We had beautiful kids, a nice house and our own business — all the things any mum wants for her children. I should have thanked her. Not saying those things to her in hospital affected me badly. So I waited for the funeral to say a last goodbye.

For a popular lady who'd lived in the same town all her life and had always gone down the bingo, I was surprised that there was hardly anybody at the crematorium. Her own son and daughter, Richard and Pat, were there. The vicar asked if anyone from the family wanted to speak, to say a few words of tribute for Mrs Chambers' life. They were silent. Nobody would speak for her. Some people are shy and can't get up and read. If no one would speak up, then I had something to say. I sat at the back of the church and quickly wrote down everything I should have said in the hospital. The words to my mum, Doll Chambers, came from the heart.

I got up, approached the vicar and said, 'Look, I've got something I want to say. I want to read this out for my mum.'

I tried to give him the paper with the little speech I'd written but the vicar just said, 'I'll have to ask her daughter's permission for you to speak.'

It hit me like a sledgehammer right between the eyes. I'm her son and he's got to seek authority for her son to read out a letter about his mum at her funeral. I didn't know what to say. I was embarrassed. I was upset. I was angry. I walked back to the pew and sat with my wife and foster sister Beverley, who was disgusted. The vicar looked awkward and said he'd spoken to Pat and it was fine.

It might have been innocence — how was he to know that although I was black I was family? But I didn't take it that way. The damage had been done. I was Doll's favourite; I was her son and yet I needed permission to read out a letter for her. Even at the family funeral, it proved I'd never been family. At the end of the day I didn't belong.

I faced the sparse gathering sat on those crematorium pews and read my speech out with all the strength and feeling I had inside me, 'Along with everyone gathered here today I would like to remember my Mum. I'm sure she is at peace now, God bless her. She said to me in her dying days how she had been married to Dad for sixty years and how much she missed him. Now she can be with him. Although she met death bravely, I'm convinced by the things she said that she readily met death. I'm sure there's many more tears shed than just the ones here today. Although not my mum by blood she is the only mum I knew. I will always remember her for being the mother who raised me in the way that was always right. I've had my scraps in life, too many to be proud of, and I've had my regrets. One such regret is I've never thanked her for raising me from a baby. Never, ever, did I tell her what she meant to me. One thing I can remember and thank her for most is that she told me continuously that I should learn a trade so that I always had something to fall back on. I did so reluctantly and this has been my rescue so many times. I can say proudly this, Mum: you always were right. God bless, Cass.'

Tears streaming down her face, Beverley came and stood beside me. Afterwards we went out and as we looked at the sparse flowers I swore I'd never return to Slade Green. I'd turned my back on that place years ago, erased it from my memory. I only went there to

Twelve

see Mr and Mrs Chambers. Now there was nothing to go back to that town for. It appeared to me I'd never been a real member of that family. Because of that last rebuff, the insult of having to seek permission to speak at my mother's funeral, I've never spoken or had contact with any of the family members since. The guilt and sense of betrayal I felt at contacting my real family had been lifted. Now I was free to contact my real mother, Celeste Pennant, the woman who'd abandoned me all those years ago.

Chapter Thirteen

Nineteen ninety five was a great year for Frank Bruno. I was ringside when he beat Oliver McCall to take the WBC World Heavyweight title. And when he fought Iron Mike Tyson in Las Vegas the following year, I knew I had to be there, too. Ginger Del Thomas's mate Graham came recommended. He could organise anything. So he fixed up the Official Frank Bruno Supporters' tour to Vegas. For £2,500 a man we'd fly first class and stay at the fabulous Luxor Pyramid Hotel. I took out a three-year loan and handed over the dough. The trip was the brainchild of the Bowers brothers, so naturally the meet was at their world-famous Peacock gym in East London.

It was four o'clock in the morning and the Sky TV cameras were there as big hands Tony Bowers greeted us all: The Duke, Lou Nichols, Martin Bowers and his dad Wally, Roy Hilder, Mick McGrath, Stevie Clark, Dave Kent, Square, Tony Burns, Danny Tobin, Johnny Eames, South London Lee Smith and me. Everybody was buzzing. We were all travelling a long way to support a British boxing hero but for me it was a personal mission. I'd lost contact with Frank after he split up with Lawless, and he was now managing himself. I needed to let Frank know that I knew just what he'd tried to do for me when he'd offered to stand my bail. I wanted to thank him personally for his loyalty in risking his career for me. We'd booked public ringside seats for the Bruno v Tyson fight but my best chance to speak to Frank would be at the weigh-in. Sky had fixed up passes to get us into the weighing room, and they'd even arranged limos to collect us at the airport.

But our adventure started going wrong from the off. Checking in at Heathrow it didn't go unnoticed that a large lump of my two and a half grand was going on a ticket to fly with the German airline Lufthansa.

One wag piped up, 'I didn't know the Luftwaffe were allowed to fly planes any more!'

It got worse. Breakfast became lunch as our plane sat on the runway awaiting a spare part. The excitement and anticipation of the early hours had turned to worry. Some of the boys started demanding

Thirteen

answers from the Lufthansa desk staff who weren't forthcoming with answers. Sensing a change of mood, the airline people started talking to each other in German. This only antagonised Roy Hilder's little crowd and the old jokes about the war started flying about. Someone was goose-stepping around the desk. It was a laugh, nothing serious. But the Germans weren't laughing. Looking back, we're not sure they stitched us up but one thing's for certain — we were fixed good and proper.

'We can't get the plane fixed in time so we will have to change your plane and routes,' explained the miserable-looking geezer behind the desk.

So at last, the merry crew of the Peacock Posse were on their way to Vegas ... or were we? We flew to Munich but we were too late for the connecting plane to the States. But there was a flight from Frankfurt. So we flew from there and although we'd paid to travel first class, the only seats available were economy. I crammed my 17-stone frame into the tiny seat and looked up at the map on the screen. Five hours after we'd left we were flying back to England. I woke up over Greenland ... 14 hours ... 16 hours ... 17 hours. Time was the only topic of conversation. I was desperate to make that weigh-in to let Frank know I'd be there for him, just like he'd been for me. We landed at Chicago and some of the luggage was already missing. Next stop Los Angeles and a new problem. The shuttle flight to Las Vegas was first-come, first-served and the airport was teeming with people trying to get to the big fight. The last two planes couldn't take everybody so some would have to wait until the next day. If we didn't get on we'd miss the Sky crew taking us to the weigh-in. And I wouldn't be able to greet Frank before the fight.

We ignored the trailing queue. Hilder was at the desk, waving his first-class tickets and complaining that he'd lost his expensive Lady Di Louis Vuitton luggage when a big Yank in a denim jacket and ten-gallon hat yelled out in a Texan drawl, 'I might a known it'd be a fuckin' Limey who thinks he's got God's right to push in.'

I was just about to explain we weren't pushing in, but just having a word about missing luggage, when the Yank turned around to the rest of the queue and said at the top of his voice, 'Those fuckin' Limeys are all over the joint. I just hate fuckin' Limeys ... Yeh, bud, I'm talking to you!'

At that, all thoughts of being reasonable went out of our heads. Lee, a powerful bloke who likes to wear a bit of chunky jewellery, was nearest to the big Texan. Crunch! Lee's shaven head went straight into the Yank's teeth, knocking the big Texan out cold. Now the American bloke was with a bunch of eight or ten oddly dressed blokes. These oddballs, who were Hispanics, Vietnamese and Mexicans, steamed in doing Kung Fu. We responded as only Londoners can with fists and boots. Half our party were already down the tunnel on their way to the flight, but when they heard the screams and shouts of a ruck they came racing back and weighed in. All hell broke loose in the main hall at Los Angeles Airport. Someone must have called security but the first I knew about them was when a geezer jumped on my back. I put my arm round and flung him off. As he crashed to the ground I went to follow with the boot. I stopped dead in my tracks. He was a small Vietnamese-looking bloke wearing a uniform with sergeant's badges. When I looked up we were surrounded by guns. Suddenly a Mexican guy, sporting a ponytail and wearing a lime-green suit, ran through the cordon of guns waving a business card and shouting, 'Lawyer, I'm your lawyer!' In all the rows I've been in, I've never been in the middle of a ruck with a brief running around in the middle of it. It could only happen in America.

Next thing, the real LA cops arrived, carrying submachine guns and immediately sealed the whole airport. Nobody was going anywhere. The Kung Fu guys were stood over the Texan, trying to pull him to his feet. Rubbing his mouth, he cursed, 'Get the Limey who did this to my face.' Lee was sat among the passengers wearing a clean shirt one of the guys had slipped him. He was still nabbed because the cops spotted blood dripping down his forehead and teeth marks on the top of his skull — a bit of a giveaway, that. As Lee was whizzed away we enlisted the crazy lawyer's help. He explained that because of the way the law works over there we had to grass up the other side for starting it. We all just walked away from him.

Eventually the LA police chief came over. He was a huge black guy so I said to him, 'Can I talk to you as a brother?'

'Listening, dude,' he replied.

'Things have got a little out of hand here. We've only come here to watch a fight, not start one. But nobody's listening to our side because we're English.'

I'd won this cop round and in the end he said, 'You can come and pick your buddy up from the station after we've taken a few details. Providing you leave town and don't come back to this airport, we'll let you all move on.'

We had a deal. The guns stopped pointing at us; we gathered our bags and trudged out of the airport, all making a sign with the finger across the throat to the sulking Yank.

Tony and Martin hailed a couple of minibus taxis. Hilder wanted to haggle over the price but the drivers were Chinese and didn't speak a word of English.

Thirteen

Steve Clark pulled out a wad of notes and they understood that. We collected Lee from the police precinct and hit the road on the five-hundred-mile drive across the desert to Vegas.

The journey was a mare as the taxi couldn't go much more than 30 miles an hour. Thirty-five hours after we left London we arrived — so much for first-class tickets all the way! The hotel was unreal — a huge pyramid with a blue crystal light on top that astronauts can see from outer space. Our problems should have been over when we got to Vegas but no chance. No rooms had been booked for us. Another rumpus. We kept putting up the name of this Graham, the geezer who was supposed to have been able to fix up anything. It got sorted. Too tired for anything, I hit the sack and went to sleep knowing I'd missed the weigh-in. I woke up. This was it, fight day. More drama. The $1,200 ringside tickets Graham was supposed to have left for us at the hotel weren't there, either. Mind you there was no sign of him either. The hotel reckoned he'd checked out. He obviously knew half of Canning Town was after him. Somehow the tickets arrived and we were sat in what they called ringside — two miles from the ring, or at least it felt that far away. The buzz was great. Seven thousand Brits all singing and chanting, 'Bruno! Bruno!' Sky cameras zoomed in on Tony Bowers and The Duke who was wearing a dazzling, sequinned union jack top hat and tails, specially made by my bouncer mate Leon.

'BRUNO! ... BRUNO! ... BRUNO!' The noise was deafening. Stars and celebrities sat all around us on freebie seats arranged by the gambling hotels for all the high rollers. This was it, baby! I didn't want to be anywhere else in the world at that moment.

Images of both fighters outside their dressing rooms waiting to enter the ring flashed up on big screens. Frank looked deep in thought. The Stars and Stripes played to a chorus of boos from a load of northerners waving football flags. Until that moment the celebs around us had wanted Tyson, who they regarded as a dirty rapist, to be thrashed by our thoroughly nice chap. They were shocked that anyone would boo through their national anthem. I tried to explain to the film actress sat beside me that there was no malice behind it; it was just a drunken football thing. She didn't buy it. 'We would never boo your national anthem. It's an insult.'

After the booing, instead of being luke-warm to Tyson, the crowd really got behind their man: 'Tyson!' ... 'Tyson!' ... 'Tyson!'

Poor Frank never got the chance to demonstrate the heart and determination he'd shown when he won the title from Oliver McCall at Wembley. I really felt

Thirteen

for him. When Frank came on TV after the fight he was more concerned about letting down his supporters than the state of his own health after being in the ring with Tyson.

For the Brits the party was over, but for Frank maybe his career was over. There was so much I wanted to say to him. On the flight home I decided I would get in touch with him as soon as we landed.

A couple of days later, when my brain had got over the jet lag, I sat down and poured out my thoughts in a letter:

> Dear Frank,
>
> I hope you read this letter as I've been trying to get in touch with you for some time, mainly to say I've never forgotten how you tried to help — when you didn't need to get involved — back in 1987 when I had trouble getting bail. Eventually I got bail and when the case came to trial the judge and prosecution acknowledged we were fitted up and I was officially a free man. The damages awarded much later gave me the chance to give my family a real home. The neighbours from our old flat have passed on the Christmas cards you've sent. I

don't have an address for you, but your cards still take pride of place on the mantle.

Like you, I pride myself as a family man. My son Marcus is eight and daughter Georgina is five. My wife Elaine, who you met at your wedding, like Laura is white. As a Dr Barnardo's kid I was brought up by white foster parents. I lived in towns where I was the only black kid in school. I always kept my identity and I'm respected for what and who I am. I know more about racism than anyone, so when McCall cut it, calling you Uncle Tom and a choc ice, I really felt for you, man. I was so angry ...

To reach a success level for yourself and your family as you have done is an achievement that all British black people can be proud of. You don't know how much it spurs on ordinary black people from the streets. The likes of Linford Christie, Ian Wright, Nigel Benn, Devon Malcolm and Kriss Akabusi give you a goal. They drive you on to succeed at your own work or business.

As you know, I've followed your 14-

year pro career throughout and been to most of your fights. The McCall fight was *the* night, though; that amazing entrance, the atmosphere, the crowd, the performance, to become the first British WBC world heavyweight champion for 99 years. You had to come out of retirement against many people's better judgement, maybe even that of your own family. But that night you achieved your career goal and much, much more. You confounded your critics and lifted up a nation. I believe you won more than a boxing title when you lifted the WBC belt from McCall. You proved an awful lot to yourself that night. You were a master of your chosen career and, whenever that career ends, you will be able to take your seat at any boxing function as a champion. Nobody can take that away from you because you've achieved it and made boxing history. The reaction of the black community after the McCall fight was not unlike how the American negroes responded when Sonny Liston made everyone black proud wherever he boxed.

So where do you go from here? I was
out in Las Vegas, Frank. It took a three-
year loan to do it and like at least 7,000
others I went hoping, if not expecting.
We never had a victory party this time
and, like you, we were disappointed, I
can't deny that. Still, everyone had a
great time because Vegas is such an
amazing place. The other thing that was
amazing was the travelling support you
had. I can't see any other boxer in the
world having a following like that. Many
of your knockers were over there, too.
You know the type, old pros and fight
people who criticised your style because
you don't fight like a featherweight or
they've knocked your opponents. But
could I get a bet on with them? Not on
your life; they were seriously backing
you with their own cash. Some said they
were letting their heart rule their head,
but all the same, when we landed you
were 25–1 and on fight night you were
9–2. That money wasn't coming from
housewives, this was boxing support.

At the end of the day you are a
champion who went to the top and will

remain a champion to various people and groups long into retirement. Your charity work and the hope you inspire in black people who want to succeed in life means you can always be champ.

It was you who had to meet Tyson in Vegas, not any of us, but don't let it dominate your entire pro career, if it is holding you back from retiring at all. Deep inside, Frank, I know your pride is hurt. The frustration of not getting out of first gear is probably giving you your hardest decision to make about retirement. Well, I'll tell you something about hurt pride. It's something I've still got and the truth is you never get over it, but you have to live with it. I was shot several times point-blank by some low-life wannabe who could never be my equal and like you I can't even the score. I've got my family to think of. They need me and they nearly lost me, so I won't sacrifice myself to restore my pride. That forever hurts 'cause this punk took a liberty while I was doing the job I'm paid to do. In the security business I'm a professional and I can still do the job today. But for the sake of my family's peace of mind, I've retired from that line of work. I don't get over that hurt pride; I just live with it. Eventually with work and all the good memories you've had you put it behind you. It never goes away completely, it just sort of rests in the corner, but I know that's where I have to keep it in order to carry on with life.

If you ever wondered what happened to that guy at Stratford station, I'm still around and OK. I respect your privacy and wish you and your family well but I just had to drop you a line.

Yours sincerely,

Cass Pennant.

Not long after I'd posted the letter, Frank was on the phone. He and Laura had been so moved by my words that as they'd sat on the stairs reading it, tears rolled down their cheeks. From that day we've always stayed in touch. We had so much in common: we were both tall and big; we were black British and proud of it; we'd both been in trouble as young men; we'd mixed in very white communities; and we'd both married white girls. As well as all that we also knew the same people in the boxing world.

Thirteen

We met up at the opening of the Bowers brothers' Peacock pub on the opposite side of the road from their famous Peacock gym. I went along with Elaine, my foster sister Beverley and new brother Steve, with his wife Diane. At a Peacock gathering everybody's there — old school, new school, boxers and street fighters, and a smattering of actors and footballers. Frank was now as good as retired and he really enjoyed himself among some very old friends from his boxing career. Our bond of friendship, forged that day in Stratford, was still as strong as ever. That night Elaine asked him if he'd open our new cab office outside Forest Hill station. On November 6, 1996, Frank did the honours in front of the local business community. Frank noticed he was actually opening two offices in one. As well as the cabs, I was getting back into security and I needed a proper office as it involved big companies like the BBC, Railtrack and shopping centres. It was just a mate's interest in a pal's business, nothing more. Why would the one-time heavyweight champion of the world need the sort of security I dealt with.

Ten months later, his boxing career by then definitely over, he called on my services. He wanted me to arrange the security for the christening of his son, Franklin Robert Bruno Junior. 'Wow, count me in,' I said. But I was puzzled. Elaine and me had already received our invitations, so why did he need security for a baptism? It turned out the christening was going to be a much bigger event than he'd originally planned. Now he was free from boxing he wanted to do the things he'd never had time to do before. He fancied having the best party ever. As well as celebrating Franklin Junior, it would also be a hello and thank you to everyone who'd been around him throughout his boxing career. He was inviting five hundred so two bodies would be enough. I'd just the chaps for the job, Mr T and Felix, who's a karate champion. I said, 'Fine, Frank, I won't let you down.'

I went over to his house for the first time in my life. As the automatic gates opened to let my car in, Frank was standing down the driveway waiting for me, with two great rottweilers standing next to him and two others in a big cage at the side of the garage. I got out of the car and the dogs got a touch too excited until Frank's booming voice said, 'Behave, Bomber!'

'Alright, Cass, come in and meet the family … You remember Laura from our wedding; where's the girls?' said Frank as he ushered me into the house. He called out, 'Girls, come here, I want you to meet the man who once saved my life.' The girls were bouncy but polite and they had really grown since the wedding more than six years before, when they'd been bridesmaids. With Franklin on his broad shoulders, Frank and I walked the garden and grounds to make the security arrangements. It was then Frank told me another reason for all the security. The film he'd been doing with the Spice Girls had gone pear-shaped.

The fall-out had been front-page news all week. It was more to do with the security employed on the location than a bust-up with the band but the press had gone OTT. Frank didn't want a media circus invading what was to be a private occasion.

Frank said, 'They could hide up that tree with their telescopic lenses.'

'What tree?' I asked. He pointed to yet another field.

'Blimey, Frank, you own all the land up to those woods?' Sheepishly, he pointed out that the woods were his as well. Well good luck to him. Too many boxers have had long fight careers with nothing to show for it. I later learned Frank had ninety acres and the christening was to have its own fairground and helicopter rides for the guests. By the time we got back to the house I discovered we were now up to 1,500 guests! Frank and Laura wanted seven doormen on duty. They were so stressed from all the planning and upheaval that I didn't trouble them with my fears that they were asking a tall order. Ninety acres, keep the press and gatecrashers out and make sure 1,500 guest were happy ... all with just seven security men. I'd just have to meet the challenge.

I needed a team of supermen, handpicked and recommended. And that's what I got. Adam Waldron was a man with a huge natural strength and winner of the Docklands strongest man competition. He was the son of Johnny Waldron, the true unbeaten prize fighter who defeated Lenny McLean not once, but twice. Adam's pal and sparring partner was Shaun Fray who even I had to look up at. Felix Ntumazah was British karate kyokoshikai champion for four consecutive years. Ex-wrestler Chris 'Demolition' Powell was a 25-stone wrecking machine. Fitness fanatic and fireman Paul Green was a little lion. Mr T couldn't make it in the end because of a commitment but I would have loved to have seen his replacement Max Burrell working with us in the Kisses days. And finally there was David Jones, a big, fit, likeable man who had his own gym.

With that team I wouldn't have to worry about patrolling the 90 acres — this lot could swallow the ground. I think even Frank felt undersized beside them. More important though than size, these guys were natural-born leaders, and they had big hearts and brains to match. I felt pleased as punch I was back doing the job I know best.

Demo and Paul were at the entrance gate as all

Thirteen

1,500 guests were arriving. Every time I bumped into Frank he kept asking if the boxer Chris Eubank was there yet. Now I wouldn't have figured on Frank and him being such good pals. But boxers do strike up friendships between bouts and it seemed that with Chris Eubank here the party would be complete. So I radioed through to the gate and asked Paul and Demo to stop Eubank at the gate, so I could let Frank know he'd arrived. Demo's droning voice came back, 'What's he want him here for?' Demo obviously wasn't a fan and I expressed the same sentiment when I replied, 'Don't ask me. I suppose Frank needs him to start the party fireworks.' It was a sad joke about Eubank's infamous firework incident on Brighton beach where a woman was injured, but I'd forgotten I'd given Frank a radio and he was listening in. Frank's voice boomed over the airwaves, 'Hee, hee, hee. Keep the jokes coming, Cass!'

The guests all went home with memories of a well-planned do with lots of music and great food. We hadn't done so bad ourselves with plenty of enquiries about our services. Probably the most noted one was Kenny Lynch who was opening a sports bar in London.

Seeing how well I'd organised security at the christening, Frank offered me work as his part-time minder. Not that the heavyweight champion of the world couldn't take care of himself, but it's just part of being a celebrity nowadays. I don't think Frank ever forgot an unsavoury incident with a drunken football lout at a Wembley FA Cup final, so I'd be added insurance at public engagements. Frank loves meeting the public and I've never seen him disappoint anyone, but a bodyguard can act as a buffer to deal with any unwanted attention. I worked with him mainly at events like nightclub openings or clubs where he was the celebrity DJ. They were amazing times. In the flesh Frank is twice as funny as on TV and he is always genuine. Above all, he treats everyone he meets with the utmost respect — man, woman, child and even the ignorant.

A lot of people, and I include myself, *demand* respect. This fella *gives* respect to everyone. I don't know about you, but I have no time for some people. Not Frank, he treats everybody the same.

That summer a group of kids from a special school visited Frank's house with their head teacher. After showing them round his magnificent home, set in ninety acres, Frank went with them into Brentwood to the annual fun day. Quick as a razor and totally unprompted, Frank tossed me a camera and got the stewards to bring over a table and a bucket. The teacher looked on bemused. Frank told her, 'Don't worry, we'll soon have the money you're trying to raise for the school.' Then I twigged the golden opportunity. Wherever Frank goes in public he's mobbed but he always tries to please everyone with autographs. Roll up! Roll up! Have your photograph taken with Frank Bruno; all donations gratefully received. Within an hour the school funds had been boosted by more than two hundred quid. That was the day I saw Frank's computer-like memory in action. An autograph hunter wanted to thank him personally for cheering up her daughter who'd been seriously ill in Great Ormond Street Hospital. She started out telling him, 'With all the charity work you do, Frank, you must visit loads of hospitals, so you won't remember but you once met me and my daughter ...'

Frank cut her short: 'I do remember you and you had your sister with you.'

He even described the daughter's illness and then he asked how she was. The woman was overcome. He'd remembered every detail of an incident that had happened five years previously!

Frank always loved mixing music to help him relax after a day training in the gym and when he retired he started dabbling as a celebrity DJ. One or two people in the public eye had taken to spinning the turntables. Footballer Trevor Sinclair was one and Nigel Benn was the first boxer to try his hand as a DJ, and he was damn good at it. It was inevitable some promoter would put together both boxers on the same nightclub gig. Both take their music seriously and Benn was picking up serious money for playing top clubs at holiday spots abroad. While Frank was working the club circuit his nephews often stayed at the house. They were teenagers and loved working in the sound studio above Frank's garage. Frank clocked these lads were hot and would have a chance to make their mark, if only they had the opportunity. Both Frank and I knew from our young days that these lads could go either way — straight or into a world of crime. Frank gave them their chance at a nightclub in Birmingham where he was DJing against Nigel Benn. Frank and his young team rocked the house, much to the surprise of Benn and his hardcore supporters. That's Frank, always looking out for others and giving friend or foe respect.

Frank's not daft. He knows that, popular as he is, he still has his critics like everybody else. I've often asked him why he never seemed to reply to his baiters but he simply says that life is too short. But don't for a moment make the mistake of thinking Frank's a soft touch. When someone oversteps the mark, I've seen him cut them dead. Just a few words in that deep, booming voice is all it takes.

Frank is a keen follower of football. I wouldn't say

he strongly supports any particular club, but living in Essex he regards West Ham as his local team and we often watch Hammers games together.

You're probably thinking, hang on, I thought Cass was banned from West Ham. And you'd be right. When I was arrested in Operation Own Goal the club banned me for life. Typical West Ham — pre-judge the fans before the trial has even been heard. Some of the lads, like Bill Gardner, were really hurt by the ban, but I just concentrated on getting my compo and I'd worry about the ban later.

By the time the police coughed up, things on the football scene had changed so much, what with all-seater stadiums and the new Baddiel & Skinner-type supporters, I wasn't sure I really wanted to go back to the game. I'd even heard horror stories that Upton Park had such a carnival atmosphere away supporters were virtually doing the conga down Green Street, once a no-go area for away fans on match days.

Still, once you support West Ham it's in your blood. Like any parent, you start off buying your kids babywear in club colours, then as they grow older you re-mortgage to buy the new away kit. My lad Marcus grew up to support West Ham like his dad. Where we live in South-east London it's a Crystal Palace and Millwall area. If you only go with teams that win trophies, then you support Arsenal or Man U. The playground can be a cruel place if you're the only Hammer and your team does bugger all.

One evening when I got home from the minicab business Marcus was waiting for me.

'How was school, son?' I asked.

Angrily he replied, 'Dad, why do you make me support West Ham?' Blimey! He's having a go at his dad and he means it. I saw his eyes well up, so something was really getting to him. Thinking of all the club merchandise I'd bought him, I asked, 'Don't you want to support West Ham?'

'No I don't. I wanna support Man United like my friends in class. Dad, why do you make me support West Ham when every Monday everybody's waiting to take the mickey out of me because their results are so bad. They all laugh and tell me West Ham are rubbish. Is that right, Dad? Are they rubbish? Why do they keep losing? Tell me the truth.'

For once I was speechless. I really felt for my boy. His outburst was from the heart and he'd obviously been through the mill at school. How could I forget what it was like to be a Hammer and have to go into work Monday mornings after those weekend results. What could I say?

Well, he was going to get the truth. I sat him down, put my arm round him and spoke softly, 'You're right, son, the team's crap. We lose more than we win but supporting a football team isn't all about winning. It's loyalty to a team, to its area and its people. It's about faith, hope and having a dream ... the warmth of your fellow supporters all sharing that dream.'

Now my wife thinks football's pathetic and when she heard my little man-to-man chat she butted in, 'He's seven years old. How's he going to understand all that people and the community stuff unless you take him over there?'

I turned and looked at her over my shoulder. You mischievous cow, I thought, you know I'm banned. My eyes pleaded with her not to start her little wind-up.

But she didn't shut up: 'I'm right,' she said. 'If you want him to understand, you'll have to take him.'

Now Marcus was at it. 'Please, Dad, can you take me to a real football match?'

They'd got me good and proper. I rang Bill Gardner because he'd got his ban lifted. He fixed up a meeting for me with the club's Stadium, Security and Safety Officer, John Bull. I thought, that's the geezer responsible for nicking me in the first place. John Bull had been in charge of K Division Old Bill at East Ham at the time of Operation Own Goal. I'd heard on the grapevine he'd done a Stalker and moved into football. John Stalker, the former Deputy Chief

Constable of Greater Manchester, had started it by taking up an advisory job at Millwall. Now they were all at it, though I can't see those coppers who fucked up at Hillsborough ever getting jobs at Liverpool FC.

I've now got to meet one of the men responsible for me looking at ten years to get my life ban lifted at West Ham. I love my son and he comes before me, so it's gonna have to be face-to-face with the old enemy. So there we were, greeting each other — him in his new position and me a free man and a responsible father. I looked at him and could only see the copper. I'm sure when he looks at me he still sees InterCity Firm. But all credit to him, he listened to what I had to say. None of it was grovel; I just stated the facts. I told him I was there for my seven-year-old son. John Bull agreed to lift the ban but I'm sure when I left the room he was thinking to himself, What have I done? But the reality is this: he's got a good number at West Ham which he loves and if me and my mates hadn't wrecked his trial he might still be sitting at his desk in East Ham nick. How do I feel about meeting one of the men who tried to get me ten years? I just shrug my shoulders and think I'd still have been in my council flat if it hadn't happened, so let bygones be bygones. We both had to move on.

The truth is I'm grateful to him. I go to football in a different way now. I still see all the old firm in the boozer — it's a different one now — and most of the blokes are proud fathers. When you're working and paying the mortgage, a day away from it all with your son is quality time. I get a real buzz from that. Me and Marcus travel together; we eat slop in the cafe together, have a beer and coke and slag off the same players.

One day walking down Green Street and towards the Upton Park entrance, Marcus — his mouth full of hotdog — said, 'Dad?'

At that age the world is a really big place to kids and there's a lot of asking to be done. I know another question's coming so I say, 'What, son?'

'Don't matter, Dad.'

We walked on, got a programme and after a while he came back again. I'm thinking, this must be a big question.

'You must have went to a lot of schools, Dad.'

'Yeah, yeah, son,' I said praying he wouldn't start asking about my school days. I'd blocked that part of my life out; even Elaine couldn't get anything from me on that one.

Luckily the programme shut him up. But, blow me, he's got me wondering why he'd asked that question out of the blue. What do children think of in their little world? I was curious, so I asked.

Marcus looked up and said, 'Well, whenever we

come to West Ham everybody comes up to you and says, "Alright, Cass. How yer going, Cass? Nice to see ye, Cass." How come you have so many mates and we don't live over here? I thought you must have been to more schools than me 'cos I know all my friends from school. That was all, Dad.'

I laughed to myself. 'Yeah son, I must've been to a lot of schools.' How could I tell a seven-year-old the real reason I'm so well-known over the Hammers?

For a start, if I mentioned the ICF, he'd probably ask, 'What's ICF, Dad — Ian, Chris and Fred?'

Chapter Fourteen

Mother ... stranger ... mother ... stranger. A wrestling match was going on inside my head the day I met my real mother.

Don't imagine we ran into each other's arms in slow motion and cried floods of tears for the lost years. It wasn't like that. My head was telling me, 'This is your mother, Cass,' but my heart was saying, 'No it ain't; this woman's a stranger.'

We met at Sharon's house and to be honest I didn't say a lot. I just kept looking at her. She was tallish, well dressed and looked a lot younger than her years. She must have been stunning in her day. For somebody who'd lived in Doncaster for more than a quarter of a century, she didn't speak like a Yorkshire woman. Her accent was a cross between New York and Jamaica.

The minute I saw her my anger fell away. From the little I'd come to know about Celeste's life, I could no longer hate her. But love her like my 'mum', Mrs Chambers? That was something else. I was desperate for our meeting to go well, but I was so nervous I didn't know whether to call her Mum or Celeste. I didn't want to offend her so I called her 'Mum' but it just didn't feel right. My heart was telling me, 'Why are you calling her Mum? She's not your mum: she's a stranger.' But whenever I called her Celeste, my brain would be saying, 'You should have called her Mum there.'

I'd taken Elaine, Marcus and Georgina with me. Elaine and Celeste were talking away ten to the dozen. There were so many things I wanted to ask my mother, but I couldn't bring myself to. I was terrified the day would go wrong and we'd never see each other again.

As we were leaving, I wanted to show her that I'd like to keep seeing her. It would take time but gradually we'd be able to open up our real feelings, so I put my arms around her and gave her a big hug, but there was no emotion to it. I was hugging a stranger.

When we got home I realised although I'd spent hours with my mother I didn't know anything at all about her, so I had to ask Elaine!

One night, months later, she called out of the blue

Fourteen

from New York. She started off with the usual how's everybody, then without warning she started rolling straight into the story of her life and how she had to have me adopted.

The story was pouring out. I scrambled for a pen, worried that with my memory I might forget. This must have been hard for her because the only thing I knew about it had come from her brother, Uncle Slim in Doncaster, and that wasn't a lot. My pen rushed the details down as she talked of her forbidden love affair with my real father. How he had beautiful teeth and a smile that melted women's hearts. He was a great dancer, a real ladies' man and half the women in Jamaica were after him. His name was Cecil Powell. My mother was so young and pretty and my father's pet name for her was God's Sister. Celeste's family didn't like Cecil, for some reason, and he didn't get on with her mother and her aunt, so the affair was doomed.

Celeste had a brother, Astley — that's Uncle Slim's brother — who'd settled in the UK in 1956. With her parents dead set against her love affair with Cecil, she decided there was no prospect of a decent future in Jamaica. At the time her mother earned just ten and a half old pence for every 30 yards of straw she plaited to make straw hats. Not realising she was pregnant, Celeste borrowed money to make a new life for herself by joining her brother in England.

She lived in one room in Doncaster with Uncle Slim and found a job in Bradford — and she also discovered she was pregnant. She got word back to my father in Jamaica, but he never came for her. She was now in a mess. Aged eighteen, with a six-month-old baby, she desperately needed a job and with no job she couldn't pay the rent and would have nowhere to live.

She was living in one room with her brother. To avoid being thrown out they passed themselves off as man and wife. The landlady was kind and may have guessed Celeste's plight. While still needing the rent, this woman helped Celeste by putting her in touch with a social worker who offered me a place with Dr Barnado's at Barkingside.

Celeste met a man called Charlie and soon after disaster struck again. The next time she heard about me was when Barnado's contacted her to give permission for me to have an operation after a lump of coal became embedded in my head. I must only have been a baby, because I knew nothing about it. The next serious contact came when I was about five when Mr and Mrs Chambers tried to adopt me. My mother refused the adoption.

Celeste had always planned to get me back. But it takes a long time to get a man to take on another's child. It wasn't until I was nine that Charlie agreed for Steve, the child Celeste left in Jamaica to be brought up by grandparents, to come over. Steve was such a tearaway my grandparents were struggling with him. Once Charlie had agreed to Steve moving in, Celeste wanted all her children back under one roof — but she hadn't reckoned with Doll Chambers. The story Linda told me about Doll going up to Doncaster to fight for me was all true.

Her marriage to Charlie ended and in 1987, the year I walked free from Snaresbrook Crown Court, she went back to Jamaica and some years later she looked up Cecil. The flames of love hadn't died long ago. Cecil could have married her no problem, but he didn't fancy marrying the whole Pennant family, particularly her mother and aunt, and eventually they ended their doomed affair. All my life I'd been 'father: unknown'. The clue had been there all the time — Carol Lindo Powell Pennant — Cecil Powell was my dad but the chances of me ever seeing him were slim to say the least.

Any lingering blackness in my heart towards Celeste melted when I heard I was a memento of a great but doomed love affair. I guess it must have been very painful for her to tell me all this.

Now I knew why she'd been forced to abandon me and how she'd tried to get me back I could accept at last she was my mum. But I still couldn't forgive her for my name — the thing that had caused me more pain than anything else.

So I asked her, 'Why did you have to call me Carol?'

She sounded surprised I'd had a problem with that name. She told me there was nothing bad in it. Her best friend at school had a brother called Carol and she just liked the name. Besides, back in the fifties lots of Jamaican men had names like Shirley and Tracy.

After all those years of hating the woman for calling me Carol, there'd never been any malice intended.

As we ended the call, I said, 'Night, Mum.' This time the words felt right. Just right.

It was the day before Christmas Eve 1997. I'd been running my minicab business for ten years and once again I found myself fighting the authorities. I ran a taxi rank at the station at Forest Hill. The locals loved it because we gave them a bloody good service. But, apparently, you couldn't have a minicab firm operating a taxi rank, so the black cabs were taking me to court. They weren't really interested in a small-time firm in Forest Hill. But they were worried a bigger firm with far more money might do the same thing at big mainline stations like Euston or King's Cross. Then all their members would lose a lot of trade and be in big

Fourteen

trouble. So they started taking me to court, using a law from the 17th century! The stress of it all was doing my head in. Here I was running a straight business and being hauled into court for the crime of offering a good service to the public.

When you're self-employed you can't just switch off at the end of the day. As I walked home from the cab office my mind whirred with all my problems. The mobile rang. Frank Bruno's big booming voice was on the other end. I knew he was out of town doing panto in Birmingham. Totally out of the blue, Frank asked, 'You've not been to Jamaica before, have you? You've got a father out there you'd like to see, haven't ya?'

Father? No one was supposed to know about all that. How I'd found my family was private, personal. So I replied, 'Yeh, Frank, I've got a father out there.'

Suddenly Frank said, 'I gotta go 'cos I'm due on stage, but when I finish the panto run, would you like to come to Jamaica with me? We'll go on holiday and relax and I thought I'd take you with me, if it's all right with you.'

'Alright, Frank. Yeah.'

'Got to go, Cass, 'cos I'm on stage, you know wot I mean?'

'OK, Frank, speak to you later.'

As I got through the door of the house it was

obvious he'd phoned home first. Elaine was waiting in the kitchen. Frank had told her he had a surprise for me.

My mind still on the cabs, I said, 'It was nothing really, just something about going to Jamaica when he's finished his panto.'

She looked stunned. 'What? Going to Jamaica.'

Until I discovered I had a father out there, Jamaica had never really appealed. I'm English and I don't really like too much sun. When I go on holiday I like my chips in Spain. I'd heard some real horror stories about Jamaica.

Elaine smiled and said, 'I'm really pleased for you.'

I was a struggling small businessman and I didn't have the fare to fly seven thousand miles to Jamaica. I hadn't had a holiday in years, so I'd given up all thought of ever meeting my real dad. I'm good at sorting other people's problems but I don't share my own problems with many. Somewhere in the back of a limo on a minding job I must have talked to Frank about my father. Frank's computer-like memory must have stored the information away.

Then it hit me. Jesus, what Frank had just said to me on the phone finally sunk in. He was offering me the final missing piece in the jigsaw puzzle of my life. It was an offer not from Frank Bruno the celebrity, but Frank my friend. He'd helped me out before, so I

Fourteen

knew he meant it.

What an amazing Christmas present. I was in shock. There was Frank working away in panto and instead of worrying about himself he was thinking about his friend on the streets. No one had ever done anything like that for me before. It dawned on me I hadn't even said thankyou. I must have sounded arrogant and ungrateful.

Jesus, I've got to phone him. I've got to say thanks, I thought.

I couldn't ring him straight away because he was on stage in Goldilocks. I rang him after the final curtain and thanked him for his fantastic offer. He even wanted to pay my air fare.

Frank said, 'No, no, I don't want you thanking me. I should be thanking you; you've really helped me out over the past year.'

I knew what he meant. When you are in the public eye, sooner or later your private life comes under a microscope. Frank and Laura's marriage had really come under the spotlight that year. He'd even been let down by people on his own house staff who had dished the dirt on him. I'd been there for him as a friend and a shoulder to cry on. With all the problems he had I was touched that he'd had time to think of me. As we ended the call he said, 'Have a happy Christmas, Cass.'

'I will, champ, I will.'

Surrounded by my new sisters and brothers, it was a fantastic Christmas.

Ever since I'd learned my real father was alive and living in Jamaica, I'd been trying to write a letter to him. For ten months I'd started writing, stopped, thrown it away, started again. I couldn't find the right words. My half-sister Linda and her daughter Vicky had gone with my mother Celeste to Jamaica to find my father and tell him he had a son. A while later my older half-brother, Steve, went out there, too. My old man sat for ages leafing through a huge pile photographs of myself and my family, tears welling in his eyes as he looked over them again and again.

It took me until February to write a letter telling my father I'd be visiting him sometime soon. I had my fortieth birthday party in Greek George's restaurant in Bexley village. With twenty of my best friends sat round two tables, Frank and Laura announced to everybody that we were going to Jamaica. We'd never discussed exactly when we were going, so in front of all my mates, Frank said, 'How about next week?'

I'd been sweating with worry since that phone call before Christmas. I kept thinking, Jesus, I'm going to Jamaica with a superstar. How can I keep up the money front with a superstar who has a big house and 90 acres? I'm not on that level; I'm just a working lad.

Fourteen

It's alright having a free trip out there, but how do I live with someone whose buying two hundred quid bottles of wine? They were stupid worries because Frank ain't even like that.

I was also worried about how my father would respond. We'd had no contact. Would he like me? Would he think I was a son to be ashamed of? How would I deal with rejection? I knew I'd be angry.

I started thinking maybe it wasn't such a good idea. I looked for ways of backing out, moaning about silly little things. Would I understand him? I knew he lived in the country, where they speak that really thick Jamaican patois. Most Jamaicans born and brought up in Britain don't understand it when their own fathers break into patois. I've been caught out so many times nodding the head for 'yes', when it should be 'no'.

But when Frank told me we were going the next week, I thought, Cass, you've faced all your problems head-on, you're not bottling this one. I told him, 'Yep, I'm there.' A week later Laura got the Shogun out and took us to the airport. She'd arranged the tickets, the hotel booking, everything. Laura knew the whole story from the beginning at Stratford. She also knew I'd always had Frank's interests at heart, and how much Frank thought of me. She loved the whole idea of putting this together to re-unite me and my father.

On the plane Frank was laughing and joking with

the passengers and the stewardesses. He was always so quick-witted and had everybody in stitches. Whenever anybody asked what he was doing in Jamaica, he'd reply, 'I'm with a friend; we're on a mission.' I was dead quiet, gripped by nerves. Worry lines appeared all over my head. Frank had never seen that side of me before. I'd always been a strong person around him. Cass, the hard man of the Hammers, was a nervous wreck.

Meeting my father for the first time should have been exciting. It wasn't — it was as scary as hell. I kept thinking, I don't need this shit. I've come this far in life on my own; let's just call the whole thing off. Am I doing the right thing? Some people don't like you just turning up on the doorstep. At long last I posted my letter but I never got a reply. I didn't even know if he'd received it. Maybe he didn't want to see me. Perhaps he didn't even know I was coming.

Frank sensed the torment I was going through. He'd experienced the same doubts ten years before when he'd discovered part of his family in Jamaica he knew nothing about. He kept telling me, 'It's your holiday, Cass, not mine. Just relax, we'll go to see your dad when you're ready. I ain't up to anything special.'

Coming into land we flew over Montego Bay. I looked out of the window: the sun was blazing in a clear blue sky, but instead of a tropical paradise below

I saw sheds, shacks and ghettos.

I thought, Jesus, I'd better not slag the place off too much; I don't know what my father's place is like.

Frank saw the look on my face and said, 'I know, bad innit? My family live in a place no bigger than my garage. In fact my garage is probably better. Ignore that, Cass, they've got quality in other things, the land and the sun. They're quite happy. I keep asking my folks if I can buy them somewhere better but they won't take it because they're happy, telling me it's a better way of life, so don't judge things by what you see.'

Sweat poured off me like a tourist when we checked into Breezes Hotel in Montego Bay. It was the biggest, swankiest gaff I'd ever been in. I had my own suite with an ocean view. There was polished marble and gold everywhere. I looked at my shiny new credit card thinking, Jesus, how long's my money going to last in this place? It's like the Dorchester.

I needn't have worried. Laura had made sure the place was all-in: drinks, meals, everything was included.

We were relaxing by the pool and Frank was all excited like a kid. He asked if I wanted to see my father the next day. But I pulled out again. So for two days we just hung out like two lads. I'm sure some people thought we were gay!

A sports TV station tried to gatecrash the hotel and Frank got very cross. He was always polite but put 'em down straight away. He said, 'Listen; I'm not here on business, I'm here for a friend. I'll give you a short interview and then leave me alone.' And they did. He made it clear we'd come to Jamaica looking for a special person. I was honoured.

After a couple of days relaxing, I was ready to meet my real dad. He lived in a remote part of the May Day Mountains and he wasn't on the phone. All we had to find him with was a rough address and a photo of his house my sister had taken. It was on the other side of the island so we set off in an old Jap people carrier taxi.

I was seeing the real Jamaica for the first time now: kids on the road in bare feet and people up in trees cutting down bananas. The roads were pure madness, with wrecks of old cars broken down everywhere, just left where they conked out. We quickly sussed our madman of a taxi driver didn't have a clue where he was going. We kept getting lost and every time we stopped, the locals mobbed Frank. The rough mountain tracks we encountered near Alligator Pond would have been tough going for Indiana Jones. Eventually, somewhere near the town of Manchester, we spotted a police station. It was a like a sheriff's post in a cowboy film. A big Jamaican woman in a uniform came out and looked suspiciously at Frank. When she finally recognised him, Frank slipped the well-thumbed photo of my dad's white-painted house under her nose and asked if she knew where it was.

Then the Sheriff — the handle of his gun gleaming in the bright sunshine — wandered slowly over and looked at the picture. He knew straight away but he was stalling: it wasn't every day the ex-Heavyweight Champion of the world came through his one-horse town. He kept playing up, saying he might know. We went in for tea and a chat and after Frank signed a few autographs he showed our driver the way. Ten miles down the road he turned off up a dusty, red dirt track. Suddenly, the house I'd been dreaming about for the best part of a year appeared in front of us. The picture I clutched in my hand had come to life. It wasn't a shack, but a smart, brick-built five-bedroom bungalow that wouldn't have looked out of place in Marbella.

When I was a kid people used to ask me where I'd been born. I just used to say Kingston, the capital, because it was the only place I knew in Jamaica. All of a sudden now I could answer those questions; now I knew where my folks came from. My heritage was here in these mountains. Being Jamaican, the driver just pushed the gate open and drove in. My stomach was in a knot the size of the *QE2*'s anchor rope. There was no sign of life, so we walked round the back. An old woman wearing a big parrot-pattern T-shirt under a loose frock, with trainers on her feet, was pottering around. She knew instantly who we were. Yes, they'd received my letter. She went off to find him, leaving us surrounded by a small herd of goats and a great big buffalo. I was such a townie I felt threatened. Sweat poured off my brow.

A scruffy man appeared. He was quite a bit smaller and frailer than me. His soiled jeans and old boots looked like they'd seen better days.

Cecil Powell, the man I'd flown across the Atlantic to see, ignored me and whispered something to her. He just kept on sorting out feed for the dogs and changing the water in the pail for the pigs. He came up and looked at me. He mumbled more than spoke and I couldn't make out a word he said.

Frank looked at the pair of us and laughed. 'I can see you two are getting on fine. I'll leave you and come back in four or five days.'

I ran to the front of the house and collared Frank as he brought my holdall from the taxi. I pleaded with him to come back tomorrow. The truth is I felt threatened by the place; the great big buffalo and this bloke I presumed was my father who seemed more interested in his animals than me.

Women are always good in these situations: they

do all the talking. The lady was my father's companion Eunice and she broke the ice by asking questions. How was my trip? How were the family?

A neighbour came over and said, have you heard the news Frank Bruno's on the island. Eunice laughed and told her, 'He's just gone.' She looked at me and then at my father and said, 'It's you they've come to see, isn't it, Cecil?'

Finally, he spoke to me: 'I didn't know you were coming. Excuse me, I'm going to get changed.' So he brushed past me again and disappeared into the bathroom.

I was alone with Eunice, surrounded by cats and dogs. She explained my letter had only arrived the day before and it had come as a shock to my father. He'd been waiting 40 years for this moment too, but I had to understand he was a very shy man. Seems he'd been worrying himself sick over it as well.

Their kitchen was filled with amazing-coloured vegetables, some of which were huge. I'd never seen anything like it before in my life. The food Eunice brought out for tea was totally alien to me. I'd never had proper Jamaican food before. The most I'd had was curried goat at a party. Now I was faced with eggs with black bits in like they'd gone a bit mad with the pepper. I had to eat something to be polite. It was awful. When he came down, my father didn't say a lot. He just asked me to go down to the pub. To keep the conversation going as we walked down a little dirt track I asked him about the buffalo.

He laughed. 'That's not a buffalo. It's a cow.'

The pub was a shed in the middle of nowhere. When Cecil walked in everyone stopped playing dominos and gave my old man respect. They ignored me for a while and then started buying us drinks. A group of Yardie-looking ruffians pulled up on their scooters and wandered into bar. Being a doorman, straight away I was on the alert — we've got a problem here, get ready for a tear-up. But they all politely said, 'Hello, Mr Powell.'

Once the old Red Stripe started going round my father opened up and we talked. He'd always had a twinkle in his eye for my mum; she was quite beautiful; his nickname for her was Angel; it had been a forbidden romance. He blamed Celeste's interfering family for making her go to England. When her parents discovered she was expecting, they packed her off to London.

Eventually Cecil received a short three-word note: 'I'M PREGNANT, ANGEL'.

By then she had moved north to Doncaster so my dad sent someone he could trust to track her down. The friend reported she was living with another man and there were children in the house. After hearing that, he never followed it up. Cecil never forgot her but he got on with his own life. As the Red Stripe took effect I began to feel like his son.

When we set off for the bar my bag had still been in the hallway. But when we returned the holdall had gone. The moment I opened the spare room door and saw my bag laid neatly on the bed I knew everything was going to be all right. It was their way of telling me I would always be welcome.

Crowing cockerels woke me at six o'clock. My father had already been up for an hour working with the animals. It was so peaceful. I found him feeding the horses. We walked and talked over hills and fields. He pointed out anything that was growing; he even had lemon tea bushes. There were no boundaries, no hedges or fences. Everyone just knew where their land ended and someone else's started. We stopped on the crest of a scrub-covered hill. The earth was almost ginger. This was Pennant Hill.

With a huge sweep of his arm, my father said, 'This land is where your mother's family came from. Your great-grandfather lived here. Your uncles had their houses over there.'

All my ancestors had been buried on the land they'd worked. The houses had long gone, but here was my heritage — this was where the Pennants belonged. Dad had named it Pennant Hill.

A wizened old woman seemed to appear from nowhere. She must have been about a hundred, and looked like a washer woman. I could imagine her with bananas in baskets perched on top of her head.

She called to him in her sing-song voice, 'Cecil, Cecil. I haven't seen you for so long. Me legs is gettin' the better of me, so I don't go down the hill no more.' We had a little chat and all of a sudden a look of astonishment came over her face. She stared hard at me as if something had just clicked and said, 'This is your son.'

I was amazed. How did she know? I didn't think we even looked alike. How could an old woman see a likeness in me?

She stepped forward: 'This *is* your son.'

She cupped my face in her old gnarled hands and, like a blind woman, she traced the outline of my eyes, my nose, my lips with her fingers. 'Ohhh, you're fine, you're strong. We're both Pennants, you know.' She couldn't contain her excitement. 'Praise the Lord!'

She touched me again, looked up to the heavens and said, 'God bless you; God bless you both.'

As I watched, the decades seemed to drop off her. Her face lit up, she flapped her arms and skipped for joy, shouting, 'Hallelujah! Hallelujah! It's a miracle. Forty years ago you left these shores and now you've come home.' Then she tripped off into the distance, singing as she went.

I stood there speechless, thinking, Cass, what is this? I mean, here's this woman she's off the hills, come out of nowhere, and she knew who I was. It was like witchery.

We decided to visit my mum's sister who lived close by and he carried on talking. Here we were on top of the mountains, deep in the Jamaican countryside, and he was speaking so softly in beautiful English.

It seemed a stupid question, but I had to ask it. How did he speak such lovely English?

He replied, 'Easy, son, I lived in England for thirty years.'

'Where in England?' I asked.

'Plaistow.'

I thought I hadn't heard him right.

He added, 'I left there in '87.'

'Where in Plaistow?' I asked.

'Pelly Road.'

I freaked. I flipped. Pelly Road! Pelly Road!

I'd lived around Plaistow and Stratford in the East End for more than ten years. And when I was supposed to have been staying in Ashford, Kent, as part of the bail conditions during the ICF trial, I'd actually been living on the ninth floor of Scott House tower block in Queen's Road — it backed on to Pelly

Road.

All that time I'd been thinking about my real father, searching for my identity, he'd been at the bottom of the stairs! I could have seen his house from my window. The questions were coming thick and fast: 'Where did you work?'

'Dagenham, Fords,' he replied. It was amazing. Many of my West Ham mates worked at the Ford car factory in Dagenham; some of them may even have known him.

He said, 'Don't look so surprised. It was the best-paid factory job in England. I worked there when it first opened up and I never left. I saved my money and built my house here in Jamaica on the back of it.'

Dad had come to England to find my mum but when he discovered she was living with another bloke he never got in touch. Instead, he met another woman. They married and had children. It was when they split up after 30 years together and she took their children to Canada that he decided there was nothing left for him in England. He was an old man so he went back to build his house and live off the land that could provide him with everything he needed. Every fruit and vegetable imaginable grew there in that fertile red land. He felt at peace with the world sitting on top of that hill.

My aunt wasn't at home. She was away at the

Fourteen

market, so we walked back up the hill in silence. Everything felt natural and right. It was something spiritual, a feeling of peace I'd never experienced before. Suddenly, I knew who I was. I remembered back to what Elaine had said before we flew out here, how when she'd first met me I was an orphan. I'd traced my lost family, and my father was the last piece in the jigsaw of my life. Now, here under the blazing sun of Jamaica, I at last realised where I truly belonged. The journey was over, now I knew where I wanted to go in life ... home to raise my family, home to the grey streets of London, the streets that had made me the person I am today — black ... British ... and proud.

Epilogue

Fifteen years ago Ian 'Butch' Stuttard who made the famous *Hooligan* documentary for ITV predicted that, far from being mindless morons, the leaders of the InterCity Firm had the brains and the determination to go to the top in whatever fields they chose.

Well, Butch was proved right. We were a gang with exceptional talent. One, along with other members of the ICF, set up a well-known pirate radio station at the height of the rave scene. It became so big the organisers were arrested. One of them started a rave band, married a band member, and set up his own totally legal independent record label. He is now well respected in the business and last year had his first national chart number one.

Others toured the world with indie bands like

Primal Scream. One of them became a professional music photographer and now works for *Loaded* magazine.

One, who I remember moaning like hell after he was stabbed in the leg when West Ham were rucking in Europe following the FA Cup win in '76, now sits in the directors' stand at West Ham with his £50,000 Merc parked outside.

Another built up his dad's building business with ICF lads working for him. He then made a million selling the company. And a brickie who sits with me at Upton Park on a Saturday has just bought a £750,000 house in Wanstead. Neither of these guys, like most of the ex-ICF, have anything to do with drugs. They earned their money through enterprise and hard graft.

Some of the Under Fives used the knowledge they gained as football hoolies – like dodging customs officials as they travelled to matches all over Europe – to go into the counterfeiting industry, and import and export trading. The leader of West Ham's Hornchurch firm was a counterfeit king, and designer clothing company Lacoste were so upset by his activities they put undercover teams on him. He was nabbed driving a Lacoste limited-edition Peugeot 205 which he bought from the proceeds of ripping off the company. After similar run-ins with customs, a couple

Epilogue

of the Under Fives went legit and opened designer clothes shops in Essex.

Another of the Under Fives was once the owner of a large chain of bookmakers. Others own bars and clubs in Tenerife. After following England in the World Cup to places like Mexico, some got the bug for globetrotting. Quite a few now live in Thailand where they own bars and export a bit of cheap designer gear.

The buzz of fighting was like no other drug. Some missed the sense of adventure so much they tried to substitute the adrenalin rush with hard drugs, completely lost the plot and sadly are no longer with us. They include Taffy, the twelfth man to be arrested in Operation Own Goal, who died in the most unfortunate circumstances. Other tragic losses include Little Danny Tiderman, Steve Morgan, Avis and the Pearman brothers. Even the real perpetrator of the Sheffield stabbing, the kid who wrote his confession to help clear my name, is no longer with us. Their memories will always linger on with us all.

To the rest of us, the football scene gave us a laugh and filled a missing void. Maybe we stayed on top so long not because we were more organised but because we had an unusually high number of natural-born leaders among us. Now with football aggro no longer our main pastime, the people who read the headlines and condemned us could very well be working for us.

Also by Cass Pennant:

Congratulations:
You Have Just Met the ICF

For the first time ever, all the faces of the West Ham firm reveal their memories and thoughts about the violence, the battles, the campaigns, the run-ins with the authorities and all that came with it...

Price £15.99

To order your copy of *Congratulations: You Have Just Met the ICF*, send off this coupon with cheque or credit card details to: Blake Publishing Ltd, 3 Bramber Court, 2 Bramber Road, London, W14 9PB

.....copies of *Congratulations*, in paperback, priced £15.99

Either
A.debit my Visa/Access/Mastercard
(delete as appropriate)
Card Number....../....../....../......
Expiry Date.../...

Or
B. I enclose a cheque for .... made payable to John Blake Publishing ltd

Name ....
Address ....
....
....
....
....

Daytime telephone————————————

Signature————————————

(Please allow 28 days for delivery)